Applied Theatre: Ethics

The **Applied Theatre** series is a major innovation in applied theatre scholarship, bringing together leading international scholars that engage with and advance the field of applied theatre. Each book presents new ways of seeing and critically reflecting on this dynamic and vibrant field. Volumes offer a theoretical framework and introductory survey of the field addressed, combined with a range of case studies illustrating and critically engaging with practice.

https://www.bloomsbury.com/uk/series/applied-theatre/

Series Editor
Michael Balfour (University of New South Wales, Australia)

Selected Titles

Applied Theatre: Economies
Molly Mullen
ISBN 978-1-3500-0170-1

Applied Practice: Evidence and Impact in Theatre, Music and Art
Matthew Reason and Nick Rowe
ISBN 978-1-4742-8383-0

Applied Theatre: Performing Health and Wellbeing
Veronica Baxter and Katharine E. Low
ISBN 978-1-4725-8457-1

Applied Theatre: Research Radical Departures
Peter O'Connor and Michael Anderson
ISBN 978-1-4725-0961-1

Applied Theatre: Women and the Criminal Justice System
Caoimhe McAvinchey
ISBN 978-1-4742-6255-2

Applied Theatre: Ethics

Edited by Kirsten Sadeghi-Yekta and
Monica Prendergast

Series Editor
Michael Balfour

methuen | drama
LONDON · NEW YORK · OXFORD · NEW DELHI · SYDNEY

METHUEN DRAMA
Bloomsbury Publishing Plc
50 Bedford Square, London, WC1B 3DP, UK
1385 Broadway, New York, NY 10018, USA
29 Earlsfort Terrace, Dublin 2, Ireland

BLOOMSBURY, METHUEN DRAMA and the Methuen Drama logo are trademarks of
Bloomsbury Publishing Plc

First published in Great Britain 2022
This paperback edition published 2023

Series design by Louise Dugdale
Cover image: Seamless spider web (© ihor_seamless / Shutterstock)

A catalogue record for this book is available from the British Library.

Library of Congress Cataloging-in-Publication Data
Names: Sadeghi-Yekta, Kirsten, editor. | Prendergast, Monica,
editor. | Balfour, Michael, 1966- other.
Title: Ethics / edited by Kirsten Sadeghi-Yekta and
Monica Prendergast, Michael Balfour.
Description: London; New York: Methuen Drama 2022. | Series: Applied theatre |
Includes bibliographical references and index. |
Identifiers: LCCN 2021033861 (print) | LCCN 2021033862 (ebook) | ISBN
9781350161320 (hardback) | ISBN 9781350288706 (paperback) |
ISBN 9781350161337 (epub) | ISBN 9781350161344 (ebook)
Subjects: LCSH: Theater–Philosophy. | Theater and society. | Community theater.
Classification: LCC PN2039 .E878 2022 (print) | LCC PN2039 (ebook) | DDC 792.01–dc23
LC record available at https://lccn.loc.gov/2021033861
LC ebook record available at https://lccn.loc.gov/2021033862

ISBN: HB: 978-1-3501-6132-0
         PB: 978-1-3502-8870-6
         ePDF: 978-1-3501-6134-4
         ePUB: 978-1-3501-6133-7

Series: Applied Theatre

Typeset by Integra Software Services Pvt. Ltd.

In memory of Dr. Ruby Peter, Sti'tum'at, (1932–2021), with gratitude.

To our sons Jacob, Max, Oliver and Otis.

Contents

Figures

Contributors

Taiwo Afolabi is an Assistant Professor, Theatre Department, and a representative for the ITI/UNESCO Network for Higher Education in the Performing Arts, University of Regina, Canada. His research interests are varied and include research ethics, applied theatre in a community context, theatre and policing, and art leadership. He founded Theatre Emissary International (Nigeria), served as the West Africa editor for *The Routledge Companion to Applied Performance*, and is currently a research associate at the University of Johannesburg (South Africa). Dr. Afolabi's books include *Committed Theatre in Nigeria* (2020, with Segun Oyewo and Stephen Okpadah) and *The Cinema of Tunde Kelani* (2021, with Tunde Onikoyi).

Syed Jamil Ahmed is the founder-chair of the Department of Theatre and Performance Studies, University of Dhaka, Bangladesh, and a theatre director and scenographer based in Bangladesh, with numerous production credits at home as well as in India, Pakistan, and the United States. He trained at the National School of Drama (India), obtained his MA in Theatre Studies from the University of Warwick (UK), and a PhD on the Indigenous theatre of Bangladesh from the University of Dhaka. He has authored six book-length publications and numerous academic articles on theatre, applied theatre, folkloristics, and cultural studies, published in Bengali, English, French, Norwegian, Russian, Chinese, Korean, and Hindi.

Jill Carter (Anishinaabe/Ashkenazi) is a researcher and theatre worker who works in Tkaron:to with many Indigenous artists to support the development of new works and to disseminate artistic objectives, process, and outcomes through community-driven research projects. Her scholarly research, creative projects, and activism are built upon ongoing relationships with Indigenous Elders, scholars, youth, artists, and activists, positioning her as witness to, participant in, and disseminator of oral histories that speak to the application of Indigenous aesthetic principles and traditional knowledge systems to contemporary performance.

Ruwanthie de Chickera is a playwright, screenwriter, and theatre director. She has a strong belief in the practice, politics, and philosophy of "devising"—a theatre approach of collective creativity and leadership that challenges existing structures of authorship and power. Ruwanthie is artistic director of Stages Theatre Group, set up in 2000 to produce socially and politically conscious original Sri Lankan theatre. She works with students and teachers to help strengthen creative processes within formal and informal learning. Ruwanthie is an Eisenhower Fellow. Her award-winning film *Machan* has been screened in over fifty countries. She lives in Sri Lanka with her two daughters.

Sheila Christie is a Social Sciences and Humanities Research Council (SSHRC) Exchange University Research Chair at Cape Breton University, Canada, where she also teaches stage management and runs the Applied Theatre program. She studies how people and communities shape their identities through creative practices. As an applied theatre practitioner, Sheila helps people use theatre to tell their stories and foster connections within their communities. Women's experiences, queer perspectives, decolonization, and climate change are priorities in her current work. Along with directing and stage managing for local theatres in Cape Breton, Sheila leads applied theatre workshops and develops original productions to promote social change.

Dennis Gupa is an Assistant Professor at the University of Winnipeg, Canada. His academic/artistic research explores the intersections of Philippine Indigenous ecological knowledge, climate change, and applied theatre by examining sea rituals and fishing traditions in island communities affected by the onslaught of climate crises. He received his MA in Theatre Arts from the University of the Philippines, an MFA in Directing (Theatre) from the University of British Columbia, and a PhD in Applied Theatre from the University of Victoria. He studied mask dance at Sekolah Tinggi Seni Indonesia. He serves as an artistic associate of the Southeast Asian Cultural Heritage Society. Dennis was a Vanier scholar.

Anita Hallewas has taught and facilitated theatre programming for more than fifteen years in Australia, New Zealand, the UK, Turkey, and Canada, both in schools and within the community. She is now working on her PhD at the University of New South Wales in Sydney, Australia, with a research area of Refugee Theatre, to explore how theatre might improve the quality of life for people living in refugee camps in the same way as theatre has increased the happiness of people in her own community. She is an applied theatre practitioner and the founding artistic director of Flying Arrow Productions.

Thomas Jones is hereditary Chief Kweyulutstun; Thomas Jones is his English name. He is from Gabriola Island, which is a part of the Snuneymuxw First Nation. He has been an artist for most of his life, first drawing local art then later learning to carve wood. He started as a Kwakiutl artist following in the footsteps of his father, who is from Alert Bay, BC, later learning the Coast Salish art form following his late mother's history. This grew from carving to speaking language, acting, and theatre. He is grateful to be involved in all this work as it's a part of our culture, preservation, and revitalization, working towards a healthy and bright future for our children.

Yasmine Kandil is Assistant Professor at the Department of Theatre, University of Victoria, Canada. Her research has mainly focused on creating applied theatre initiatives with disenfranchised communities (youth at risk; immigrants and refugees in Canada; and communities in the trash trade of Cairo). She has recently taken an interest in Celebratory Theatre with immigrant and refugee communities, scenario training and Forum Theatre in police training contexts, and tracing the applied theatre movement in post-revolution Egypt. She has published in a variety of international peer-reviewed journals and edited texts. She is presently working on a number of federally funded community-based projects.

Trudy Pauluth-Penner is an Assistant Adjunct Professor in Applied Theatre, instructor, and research scientist at the Institute on Aging and Lifelong Health at the University of Victoria, Canada. Research interests include social dimensions of health and interdisciplinary community-based arts for health across diverse contexts. She is the recipient of the Society for the Arts in Healthcare Blair Sadler International Healing Arts award. Trudy is the artistic/executive director of the Intergenerational Applied Theatre Arts consultancy. Recent publications include book chapters in *Web of Performance: An Ensemble Workbook* (Monica Prendergast and Will Weigler, 2018) and *Research-Based Theatre: An Artistic Methodology* (George Belliveau and Graham Lea, 2016).

Monica Prendergast is Professor of Drama/Theatre Education in the Department of Curriculum and Instruction, University of Victoria, Canada. Her research interests are varied and include drama-based curriculum and pedagogy, drama/theatre in community contexts, and arts-based qualitative research methods. Dr. Prendergast's theatre and drama books include *Applied Theatre* (2009/2016) and *Applied Drama* (2013, both with Juliana Saxton), *Teaching Spectatorship* (2008), *Staging the Not-yet* (2016), *Drama, Theatre and Performance Education in Canada* (2015), and *Web of Performance* (2018, with Will Weigler). Monica's most recent book is *Teachers and Teaching on Stage and on Screen: Dramatic Depictions* (2019, with Diane Conrad). Her forthcoming book is *Applied Theatre* (3rd edition, with Juliana Saxton and Yasmine Kandil).

Kirsten Sadeghi-Yekta (PhD, University of Manchester) is Associate Professor at the University of Victoria, Canada. She is currently working on her research project on Coast Salish language reawakening through theatre. This community-based theatre project is developing strategies and arts programs for Indigenous language revitalization. Her practice is published in a variety of international journals. Her theatre facilitation includes working with children in Vancouver's Downtown Eastside, young people in Brazilian favelas, and adolescents in Nicaragua.

Kim Senklip Harvey is a proud Nation member of the Syilx, and Tsilhqot'in Nations with Ancestral ties to the Dakelh, Secwepemc, and Ktunaxa communities. She is an Indigenous Theorist and Cultural Evolutionist who uses a variety of modalities including playwrighting, TV writing, blogging, and podcasting to promote the equitable treatment of her peoples. Kim is an advocate for individuals' equity and works towards having the voices of the historically oppressed and disenfranchised heard. Her passion for storytelling lives within its transformational nature and she believes that it will move us to a place where every community member is provided the opportunity to live peacefully.

Dani Snyder-Young is a scholar/artist whose work focuses on theatre and social change, applied theatre, and contemporary US activist performance. Her artistic work as a director and dramaturg addresses on political theatre, community-based performance, new play development, and adaptations of classical texts for diverse audiences. Her most recent book, *Privileged Spectatorship: Theatrical Interventions in White Supremacy* (2020), examines white spectatorship of mainstream antiracist theatrical events. Dani is Assistant Professor of Theatre at Northeastern University, United States; she received a BA from Wesleyan University, Connecticut, and an MA and PhD from New York University.

Deneh'Cho Thompson is Assistant Professor in the Department of Drama at the University of Saskatchewan, Canada, and coordinator of the wîcêhtowin Theatre Program. As a scholar/practitioner, Deneh'Cho maintains a professional acting practice and his current research considers Indigenous pedagogy for theatre training and Indigenous storytelling in digital worlds. Both Deneh'Cho's scholarship and artistic practices are collaborative in nature and center values of reciprocal relationship-building and relational responsibility.

James Thompson is Professor of Applied Theatre at the University of Manchester, UK. He was the founding director of In Place of War (www.inplaceofwar.net), researching and developing arts programs in conflict zones. He has had senior university roles, most recently as Vice President for Social Responsibility at the University of Manchester. He has run theatre projects internationally and written widely on applied theatre and socially engaged arts. His most recent books include *Performance Affects* (2009), *Humanitarian Performance* (2014), and *Performing Care* (2020, edited with Amanda Stuart Fisher). He is currently writing a new book titled *Care Aesthetics*, to be published in 2022.

Zoe Zontou is a Senior Lecturer in Drama and Theatre Studies at Liverpool Hope University, UK. Her principal research interests lie in the field of applied theatre with people in recovery from substance misuse. Zontou's research covers a wide range of topics, including autobiography in performance, addiction studies, and cultural theory, which are examined through their relationship with applied theatre. Her publications include the edited volume *Addiction and Performance* (2014), which she co-authored with James Reynolds, "Upon awakening: addiction performance and aesthetics of authenticity," in *Risky Aesthetics: Performance, Participation and Critical Vulnerabilities* (2017, edited by Alice O'Grady), and "Under the Influence of … Affective Performance" in the journal *Performance Research* 22. (6). She has also published articles in *RiDE: The Journal of Applied Theatre and Performance* and *The Journal of Applied Arts and Health*.

Part 1

How We Can Be Together

Introduction: Being Together

Kirsten Sadeghi-Yekta and Monica Prendergast

Kirsten: My last name is Sadeghi-Yekta. A married name—freely translated as "honestly unique"—from a part of the world I have never witnessed, nonetheless the wisdom of poems, smell of dill, mint, and Esfand are continuously present in our home. My maiden name, with a lesser brave meaning, is rooted in the Netherlands, where my parents and grandparents were born and raised. Growing up, it was through their eyes that I learned how storytelling reverses isolation and creates conditions for awareness and kindness. My mother took me to my first theatre performance when I was a toddler.

I am a recent white immigrant to the land that is known as Canada. Most importantly, I am a mother of two young children. I am also a theatre educator and applied theatre practitioner, and an advocate for work that welcomes the arts as an immigrant to their field. The lens that I carry in the world is clearly made up of "between-ness" and "beside-ness" (Taylor 2020: 6): parent, partner, daughter, academic, artist, immigrant, settler, multilingual, and many more.

My values and beliefs are predominantly formed by invaluable encounters with kind people and communities in unknown cultural territory, the majority of those facing hardship and conflict. Their teachings on humbleness (what truly matters), social justice (what is at stake), urgency of presence (how to be), transparency (when to enter and when to exit), generosity (how to give and receive), collective thinking (who matters), care (how to see each other), relationality (how to be together), and love (how to stay together) have brought me where I am today in my applied theatre practice.

Monica: I am a 60-year-old white, privileged upper-middle-class university professor who came to academic life mid-career. My prior career was in professional children's theatre, primarily with Toronto's Young People's Theatre, and then as a high school drama educator. My ongoing values and commitments are feminist (seeking equity and justice for girls and women and all other groups pursuing equity); politically socialist (interested more in collectivity over individuality and in engaged democratic and active citizenship); processual (decades of drama and theatre-making have taught me the central importance of the process); and presence-oriented (as a trained actor, I understand presence in an embodied as well as an intellectual way). I am also influenced by critical pedagogy that is rooted in the work of Paolo Freire and his pedagogy of the oppressed (Freire 1971/2014) and in Augusto Boal's transference of Freire's work into theatrical forms (Boal 1979).

Bertolt Brecht's work remains an influence for me on how theatre can move towards social revolution, as do works by Western English-language playwrights such as Henrik Ibsen, George Bernard Shaw, Athol Fugard, August Wilson, Tony Kushner, Suzan-Lori Parks, Caryl Churchill, and Edward Bond, among others. In other words, I believe in the sociopolitical and educational power of drama and theatre as a force for collective good. In the fields of drama and theatre education and applied theatre, I have been inspired by field founders Brian Way and Dorothy Heathcote, as well as by Gavin Bolton, Warwick Dobson, Carole Miller, John O'Toole, Cecily O'Neill, Helen Nicholson, Juliana Saxton, James Thompson, and Jonothan Neelands, among others.

Ethical Engagement

If being *presente* demands an ethical engagement, it seems that the terms of my presentness—racially, through social status, disciplinary training, and institutional location—calls attention to its many complexities. (Taylor 2020: 7)

Our goal in offering this up-front information about us, our identities and values, is to model the kind of ethical transparency we hope will follow across the chapters of this book. We also both work at the same academic institution in North America, which further dominates the voices we bring to this publication. What is our voice and where is it coming from? How is our presence implicated through the stories and words we have included in this book? That said, ethical practice demands that we be thoughtful about how we gather together and work collectively and creatively with participant groups. For example, when Kirsten collaborates with the Hul'q'umi'num' Language & Culture Society on Vancouver Island, BC, or Monica works in prison theatre settings, our "presentness" and lenses of "besides-ness" will inherently create complex situations which require ethical engagement.

It is these small decisions, often made in the moment, that drive ethics in applied theatre practice. This book, and its array of chapters from international practitioners/scholars, focuses on these moments— in the field and on and off the stage—that enact the ethics of our practice. Our intent is to capture both past and present thinking about ethics in applied theatre, while also gesturing towards "the *not yet* and the *not anymore*" (Tuck 2009). This future-facing position is hopeful and inspired by Eve Tuck's desire-based framework that seeks to look beyond the "frameworks that position communities as damaged" (416) and therefore simultaneously focuses on concepts such as self-determination, contradictions, and complexity: "Desire, yes, accounts for the loss and despair, but also the hope, the visions, the wisdom of lived lives and communities. It is involved with the *not yet* and, at times, with the *not anymore*" (417, original emphasis). Communities have so much more to offer than their internal "damages," as Tuck argues, and if we are foregrounding ethical engagement here, then our initial step should be inspired by desire. We hope you enjoy your journey through these pages.

Ethical Concepts: How to Do "Good," both Individually and Collectively Speaking

We are all responsible to the story. We are all responsible for the teachings we take from it and for how we will carry those teachings in our attitudes and behaviors. (Carter, Recollet and Robinson 2017: 218–19).

In this book, we offer multiple ways for scholars and practitioners in the field to think about the ethics of applied theatre as both a noun and a verb: ethics and "ethicking" (Laaksoharju 2008: 2) or "to act in an ethical way." As in the demanding art form we practice, the challenge is to move the noun form of ethics from the page to the stage—to put it into action.

The book is divided into two parts. In the first four chapters we describe, discuss, and analyze *our* findings regarding ethics in the field of applied theatre in conversation with foundational literature and pioneers, including fundamental reflections in interviews with Indigenous artists from the land that is now known as Canada. Foregrounding diversity and prioritizing the voices we do not hear from enough are two of the ethical considerations of this book, and therefore we have explicitly chosen to have those voices heard right at the very beginning.

In the second part we have gathered together an international array of authors from Bangladesh, the UK, Canada, Nigeria, Sri Lanka, the United States, and the Philippines. We invited these authors to articulate an ethical concept derived from their practice, and have elicited rich, diverse, and complicated understandings of ethical approaches in the work that we do as a result. Across this book you will encounter ethics in the form of care for the human and more-than-human world, ceremony and medicine, micropolitical dilemmas, responsibility for the "other," critical generosity, acceptance, vulnerability, courage, tensions, precarity, research ethics, colonial adventurism, embracing the essential void, and more. The fieldwork carried out in support of these chapters occurred within a wide range of settings, such as: in Indigenous communities (in

Duncan, BC, and Toronto, Ontario, Canada); in a Massachusetts, US playback theatre space; in an intergenerational project in a Victoria, BC, elder care home with applied theatre students and patients living with dementia; in a creative dance project in Liverpool, UK, with those recovering from addiction; in refugee camps off the Greek coast; in a Toronto, Ontario, police training project; in a child rights project for internally displaced children in Jos, Nigeria; in projects carried out in remote fishing villages in the Philippines, and in a self-reflexive artist's journey in Colombo, Sri Lanka.

For us as co-editors, throughout the process of inviting these chapters—and in reading, rereading, and editing them—we have identified three "red threads" (Fox and Dauber 1999) that interweave amongst and across this collection. As playback theatre founder Jonathan Fox and co-editor Heinrich Dauber (1999) define it, "The 'red thread' is a metaphor from weaving, in which the red thread allows the weaver to follow the pattern, and is a common phrase in German for the 'connecting element'" (65). These connecting ethical threads in applied theatre are *service, presence* and *care* (see Figure 1).

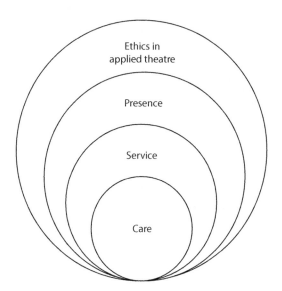

Figure 1 Key principles of ethics in applied theatre.

The first thread of *service* has been brought to our attention in our engagement with Indigenous artists: for example, with playwright, artist and director Kim Senklip Harvey, who began our first conversation with the question "How can I be of service to you?" The giving back of *service* to communities is a key ethical principle held by many Indigenous peoples that relates to the values in our work. We provide an arts-based service to the participant groups and larger communities in which we work. Yet seeing ourselves as service workers may not be an obvious connection that all of us automatically make. Our position here is that if we can begin to see the work we do as applied theatre artists as a form of service, we will develop a *cleaner* understanding of reciprocity and collaboration. That in itself may lead to thinking through how those who live lives of service (such as nurses, doctors, social workers, and teachers) model and behave in ethical ways. Syed Jamil Ahmed's chapter in this collection focuses on our shared responsibility to the "other" in ways that can be understood as service. Similarly, Anita Hallewas sees the notion of service expressed by the various arts groups working in refugee camps as exemplars in this regard. Also, in her contribution on the complexities of securing research ethics approval in our field, Sheila Christie urges for a revised process that serves the practice rather than limits it.

The second ethical thread of *presence* arises from Diana Taylor's *¡Presente! The Politics of Presence* (2020). Taylor's timely contribution has allowed us to see the ways that presence informs ethical practice. To be truly present, one must be open to listening to, learning from, and responding with others; as Taylor says, ¡presente! means to be "present among, with, and to, walking and talking with others" (4). Taiwo Afolabi's chapter on the *ethics of precarity* illustrates how the decisions made about his field research in Nigeria helped him to make fundamental ethical choices rooted in present circumstances. Dani Snyder-Young's chapter on *critical generosity* allowed the playback theatre troupe she observed to trouble notions of white discomfort in the improvisational choices made in stories captured in the present moment. And Dennis Gupa's fieldwork reflections from the Philippines clearly demonstrate the significance of being present during intricate research decisions. Led by his values, Gupa's research took a different turn which brought him exactly where he needed to be. Our presence is at the heart of what we do; if we allow ourselves to be distracted from the focus needed to listen, see, learn, and respond, *in the moment*, we are undermining our ethical positions and potentially weakening the work of collective theatre-making and sharing. Being present is demanding, both emotionally and intellectually, but we see it as a crucial aspect of ethical practice.

Finally, the third red thread woven into the fabric of this text is *care*. James Thompson, whom we regard as one of the pioneer ethicists in applied theatre, has focused much of his recent work on the ethics of care (Thompson 2014, 2015; Stuart Fisher and Thompson, 2020). As Stuart Fisher points out in the introduction to *Performing Care* (2020):

> Care emerges as being constitutively implicated within the concept of performance. After all, it is impossible to conceive of caring practice outside the parameters of how it is performed. In this sense, care, like live and theatrical performance, exists only as a live encounter and within a specific juncture of time and space. Furthermore, as with performance, care also involves forms of embodied knowledge. (7)

Here we see echoes of our notion of enacted ethics as a verb rather than a noun, and also the nested concepts of presence and service we have identified above. To care for others is to accept a responsibility for those others, ideally with a sense of reciprocity; a mutual giving and receiving that empowers rather than reinforces the simplistic notion of charity as a one-way power-over process. Stuart Fisher and Thompson helpfully remind us that caring holds political implications as well; as you will read in Chapter 4 in Kirsten's interview with Thompson, he considers ethics and care ethics as a series of "micropolitical dilemmas" (see p. 72). How we engage with and respond to these many dilemmas—which are part and parcel of any applied theatre project—reflect both our own sociopolitical and cultural positions and those of the group with whom we are working. In her chapter on the implications of the concept of vulnerability in her applied theatre practice with people in recovery from addiction, Zoe Zontou interrogates her own thinking on which modes of care are appropriate while working with lived experiences, in particular looking at the risks of reinforcing re-stigmatization. Trudy Pauluth-Penner's chapter focuses on the dilemmas that arose in an intergenerational project with senior participants living with dementia. Her sense of care infuses her writing, and informs the ethical concerns she experienced in staging a collaborative research-based play for her participants and others in a senior care home. Similarly, the role-play police training project that Yasmine Kandil presents in her chapter involves a level of care for those struggling with mental health issues. In its bold attempt to improve the sometimes violent and fatal outcomes that occur when police officers encounter people experiencing a mental health crisis, this project enacts a kind of sociopolitical care in its shared intent with the police officer participants to decrease the number of negative outcomes in these cases. Lastly, Ruwanthie de Chickera's reflections on her applied theatre practice during the pandemic explore ways of self-care and what they have taught her about the ethics around the essential void in personal and professional settings.

We invite you to consider how these ethical red threads of *service*, *presence*, and *care* underpin the work carried out and reflected on across this book. Next, we focus on what emerged from the literature review on the discourse of ethics in applied theatre that lies ahead in Chapter 3. In focusing on the questions highlighted in this review, we are better able to see how the discourse has morphed and become more complex over time.

Defining Ethics: How We Can Be and Do "Good" Together

In our gathering and selection of sources tracing the discourse on ethics in our field, outlined in Chapter 3 of this collection, we were struck repeatedly by the number of ethical questions posed by authors.

It appeared to us that ethical thinking in the midst of practice involves plenty of self-reflection, day to day, hour by hour, and moment to moment. Thus, what we offer here is a *found poem* crafted from the questions that emerged in our literature survey, presented as one way to begin to understand and appreciate the rich critical discourse on ethics in applied theatre (see Prendergast 2004, 2006). All words in the poem have been taken from the ethics literature review in Chapter 3, and although not included here (for aesthetic reasons), all sources referred to in the poem are listed in the References at the end of that chapter.

Questing for Ethics: A Q&A Found Poem

Q: whose standards?
interface with communities?
a sustained change in people's lives?
(should applied theatre workers
even be interested
in documenting
such change?)
is it ethical?
what moral authority
do applied theatre artists
share
other than
a commitment
to theatre?
implicated witness?
participant observer?
irresponsible responsible?
by asking for
witnessing
or
retelling stories
when does theatre
become implicated

in the horrors
of the situation
it displays?
what does it mean
to act ethically?
what do we
as practitioners
expect in return
for our labors?
artistic satisfaction?
the participants' acquisition
of skills or abilities?
(do we ask participants
to adopt new ways of thinking
or different political values?
do we expect them to change?)
in turn
how far might
our own perspectives
alter as a result?
how might
the voices
of participants
be represented?
aesthetics, ethics, or activism?
(who stands
to benefit most
from the research?)
how do we do this?

A: fidelity to the truth
speaking *with*, *for*, or *about*
participant communities
political tensions
at the heart of the stories
that are created
work sensitively

create a genuine climate
of dialogue and reciprocity
create impact
in diverse
unpredictable
and political contexts
challenge an 'aesthetic of injury'
proceed with
cultural sensitivity
and integrity

Q: (ethics and aesthetics—joined at the hip?)
what does the ethical act
really look like?
how are my ethics
different from
or
the same as
yours?
who or what
is being silenced?
how does identity matter?
what other
ethical questions
should we consider?

A: doing the social justice
and
anti-racist work
that we hope
to inspire others
to do
this empathetic gesture
[raising a hand to feed others]
animates
a life-affirming form
of ¡presente!

Q: (how i wondered
    might i/we
    be able to
    emulate
    replicate
    transform ¡presente!
    into sustained political practice?)

From an educational perspective, we might use this found poem as dramatic text and ask applied theatre students to collectively "stage" it with movement and sound. What does the poem *look like* when dramatized? What does it *sound like*? How does embodying some or all of these questions deepen our understanding and appreciation of them? We invite you to carry some or all of these questions with you as you read this book.

References

Boal, A. (1979), *Theatre of the Oppressed*, trans. C. A. and M. Leal MacBride and E. Fryer. London: Pluto Press.

Carter, J., Recollet, K., and Robinson, D. (2017), "Interventions into the maw of old world hunger: kinstellatory maps, and radical relationalities in a project of reworlding," in H. Davis-Fisch (ed.), *New Essays in Canadian Theatre*, Vol. 7. Canadian Performance Histories and Historiographies. Toronto: Playwrights Canada Press, pp. 205–31.

Fox, J. and Dauber, H. (eds) (1999), *Gathering Voices: Essays on Playback Theatre*. New Paltz, NY: Tusitala.

Freire, P. (1971/2014), *Pedagogy of the Oppressed: Thirtieth Anniversary Edition*, trans. Myra Bergman Ramos. London: Bloomsbury.

Laaksoharju, M. (2008), *Ethicking—Dealing with Ethics: Can Micro World Simulations Stimulate Ethical Competence?*, MA thesis, Uppsala University.

Prendergast, M. (2004). "'Shaped like a question mark': found poems from Herbert Blau's *The Audience*," *Research in Drama Education*, 9 (1), 73–92.

Prendergast, M. (2006), "Found poetry as literature review: Research found poems on audience and performance," *Qualitative Inquiry*, 12 (2), 369–88.

Stuart Fisher, A. (2005), "Developing an ethics of practice in applied theatre: Badiou and fidelity to the truth of an event," *Research in Drama Education: The Journal of Applied Theatre and Performance*, 10 (2), 247–52.

Stuart Fisher, A. and Thompson, J. (eds) (2020), *Performing Care: New Perspectives on Socially-Engaged Performance*. Manchester: Manchester University Press.

Taylor, D. (2020), *¡Presente! The Politics of Presence*. Durham, NC: Duke University Press.

Thompson, J. (2014), "Politics and ethics in applied theatre: face-to-face and disturbing the fabric of the sensible," in P. Mcneill (ed.), *Ethics and the Arts*. Dordrecht: Springer, pp. 125–35.

Thompson, J. (2015), "Towards an aesthetics of care," *Research in Drama Education: The Journal of Applied Theatre and Performance*, 20 (4), 430–41.

Tuck, E. (2009), "Suspending damage. A letter to communities,"*Harvard Educational Review*, 79 (3), 409–28. Available online: https://doi.org/10.17763/haer.79.3.n0016675661t3n15

2

Indigenous Perspectives on Ethics and Theatre

Ruby Peter, Kim Senklip Harvey, Deneh'Cho Thompson,
Thomas Jones, and Jill Carter with Kirsten Sadeghi-Yekta

Preface

This chapter is a summary of conversations that took place between 2019 and 2021 with Elders, artists, and scholars across Canada.

Since 2015 I have had the honor of collaborating with the Hul'q'umi'num' Language & Culture Society, comprising Elders, language teachers, and learners, and to find ways of using drama as a means to reawaken their endangered Coast Salish language spoken on Vancouver Island, BC, Canada.

The first time I entered this community, my firstborn was with me. He was only six months old. I was leading a theatre workshop with the group and suddenly I could not find my son. Realizing that he had soiled his diaper, one of our collaborators had taken him to a different room. They had found my diaper bag, changed him, and took extremely good care of him. Transparent care, with no hesitation.

Caring—taking care of each other, showing you/your care as a core value of this community—prompted the first conversation around care and ethics. And many more conversations about values, service, reciprocity, and peace with artists from different nations followed.

Stó:lō scholar Dylan Robinson calls for "non-Indigenous and settler scholars to stop instrumentalizing Indigenous world views, language, or stories for what they help you say, and treat them as the incommensurable things that they are rather than things that might be easily applied to your work" (in Carter, Recollet, and Robinson 2017: 229). I sincerely hope that the words in this chapter are treated as the "incommensurable" meanings they embody.

The following summaries have been approved by all authors after a range of consultations: Kim Senklip Harvey (Indigenous Theorist and Cultural Evolutionist); Deneh'Cho Thompson (Actor, Educator, Scholar); Thomas Jones (Artist, Carver, Hereditary Chief Kweyulutstun from Gabriola Island, part of the Snuneymuxw First Nation); and Artist-Scholar Jill Carter (Anishinaabe/Ashkenazi).

The first recorded conversation in this chapter is by Dr. Ruby Peter, Sti'tum'at (1932–2021), Hul'q'umi'num' language scholar, teacher, and advocate. Her work, knowledge, and contagious commitment to social justice and kindness will be a model for many generations to come.

Kirsten Sadeghi-Yekta

Ruby Peter, Sti'tum'at

What are some of the values that are really important to you for working in the community?
The most important thing that was taught to me was to teach our children to have them follow the proper examples. Respect. Respect yourself especially and respect other people and respect the land. That's what was stressed to me. How I should be and how I should bring up my children, how I should teach them how to respect themselves and look after themselves and other people. And when we started school, we were always told when we're leaving the door to go out, "You watch yourself, look after yourself and respect others. Respect yourself and respect the other children. Don't ever be mean, don't ever try to fight with anybody. Even if they're picking on you or getting mad, calling you names, walk away from them." And that's what I was taught, not to ever, ever be violent as a child. And this is something that was always stressed. You're going to be a parent. You watch yourself because

children copy your every movement, how you smile, how you talk, how you walk. Children copy you and that's what we were told. So that's what we had to follow.

What were some of the things that you had to do on the land?
Respecting things that are on the land. Things that you use. Things that you do on the land. Whether you're fishing, whether you're plowing or doing garden work, flowers, or things like that. But we respect by looking after things that we work on. What we do is with our hands and how we look after the land.

What are some of the things we should consider while we are using traditional stories?
Most stories are told as a parent, grandparent, tools to teach the young people. Behavior or hunting, fishing, whatever. They always tell you something about the land or what you do for officiating different things like that. It's always an example, it's never … it's never for destruction. It's always an example of what you do with life and how you look after things. How you take care of the things that you get from the land, the sea, or the rivers.

Every story that was told is an example of something. It represents something. Even behavioral. At least on the land or birds and fish. And yes, I think it is okay to stage traditional stories. I think that's what they are for. It's important for children to know and to see, and to hear those stories that were told, and for them to realize that they are such examples of how they should be or what they should be doing.

Most of the time, our people studied many things. I had a grandfather who was a weatherman. He was able to tell which kind of a year is coming up. Which kind of a year it was going to be next year. And I couldn't figure that out. We try to follow their example, but we don't know how they did it. My grandfather from Esquimalt [BC, Canada], he knew. He was a weatherman, and he knew everything how it was going to be. Even looking at the stars. He'll say, "Oh, it's going to be raining the next few days." And it always happened. And I look at the moon. I can't tell the difference. I really started pressing my grandfather how the moon stood or how it turned upside down. And I started really asking questions. Which was a no-no for our children. You can't be too much of a question box. But he was quite a person to be listening to me and he said, "You look at the moon. How it's sitting? If you really look at it, it's got water and it's going to turn over the other way and it's going to rain." So, I start watching the moon and trying to understand what my grandfather said. That it had water in it and it's going to turn over and it's going to rain. I just gave up and I quit.

[both laughing]

I should have kept on trying. No, it's very interesting to learn what the old people knew, how they'd study things. There are many things that we learned from them but could not complete.

It's already the end ... Middle of August. We already saw some leaves that were turning yellow. Yeah, my son and I were writing, and he said, "Mom, look, those leaves are turning yellow." Maple leaves. It's going to be an early winter.

Kim Senklip Harvey

What are your thoughts on ethics in theatre? What are some of the first things that come to mind?
I don't think we think about them enough. I think at the intersection of imperialism and Indigenous ontologies, we have neglected to construct and conjure an inter-national agreement around creation practices, and that disturbs me. Ethics—and from an Indigenous, like my Salish Plateau perspective—is the value-based ontological protocols of how we live in relationality to one another. A large part of my work is creating those structures of knowledge-sharing based on ethics and value systems that ensure our well-being is a part of the conversation. Without that, I can't participate as a good Salish Plateau person. I spent over ten years as an actor in unethical environments and I didn't have the language. I didn't have the methodology to express how violent that was in terms

of an extractive-based creation model. For me, if I don't have the same ethics as a collaborator, I can't work. Without a structure and a shared value system, a shared mandate of creation, I think everything suffers. The spirit, the mind, the body, the culture. But I try to say this to non-Indigenous people who are really product- and deliverable-based. The art also suffers.

The art suffers because nothing courageous can grow in an environment that isn't safe. That isn't anti-shame-based. That isn't in servitude. And the more I realize, I think a part of my contribution to Salish Plateau creation is around methods that acknowledge the ethics, values, and reciprocity of creating. That's why I say the process is the art. Not the product. The process has to be the artistic practice with the same emphasis, precision, and deliberateness. Because otherwise we bake into the art violence, oppression, theft, trauma, pain. And I cannot participate in those models because then I uphold and become complicit within imperialism and that dishonors my ancestors.

I think too often, Indigenous practitioners are positioned to have to fight for their ontologies and paradigms in violent colonial power structures that make it impossible for us to succeed. It's racist, it's violent, it's inequitable, and we're positioned to say thank you for unethical processes, which is unacceptable. I shouldn't meet these shocked faces with artistic leaders and producers when I want to hear what their values are. When I hear what their ethics of creation are. And for me, if you're not leading with your ethics, if you're not leading with your values, then there's something you're hiding. There's something that you're not able to embed into your practice and bring conscious, ethical, and practical attention to, and that's problematic.

Can you describe some of those key values for you, then?
When I think about my responsibilities as a storyteller, it's rooted in service. It's rooted in creating environments that allow every member of the community to have the opportunity at peace. I'm not trying to make peace, but I think every human being should be afforded the opportunity to decide whether or not they would like a peaceful life.

Whenever I'm feeling oppressed in situations, what nourishes me is to remind myself that I have the opportunity to choose peace, and I can't imagine what it would be like for people who haven't been afforded even this small dignity. Who have been so oppressed and traumatized by the system. So, when I think about that and I create a plan for how I can approach my creative practice, it's around my Salish Plateau values of service, respect, trust, humility, empathy, vulnerability, courage, and reciprocity. These core, alive nouns around care, around thought, around practice in protocol intersect with all parts of my life as a Salish Plateau woman. I have to be rigorous around how I embody those in the room. How I don't just put a values statement on a wall and that I don't just create a mission statement that I don't look at for twenty years after starting my theatre company.

I study Brené Brown and her research on vulnerability, and she talks about courage being her value. Courage as a discipline. Courage as an embodied practice. And I work on that every day. How can I make brave and bold decisions that decenter my egoic self of imperial ontology and center servitude? How can I root my practice in nourishing the connectivities between the people around me?

And so, how do you center all of the values that are specific to each nation? There are specific values to each Indigenous nation, and so it was also a matter of—as we internationally collaborated, which is how I create all my work—how do I honor the values and ethics and ways of being from all of these nations of the collaborators? Because they're not mine. All I can do is provide my Salish Plateau values and honor when somebody's saying, "I need more of this today." That's the respectful way for me to meet that practitioner and that artist in that moment. And that deep listening, that spiritual listening, that inter-national listening—any affective practice requires that deep listening.

How do I listen to the people who are arriving into the ceremony in a way that honors everything they have sacrificed? That honors the characters? That honors everything our ancestors did to allow us to get to that room? And I find when I move away from my value-based work, it's because I am not deeply listening to what's required of that moment.

It's also demanded a presence of my own. So, I'm also interested in creating processes that are self-sustaining and self-nourishing.

I do my best to nourish those moments when participants live up to these values, and that has worked incredibly well. In every experience that I've had, and I create a relationship that honors embodied values, those artists are more effective, they're more efficient, and they're more energetic, and I think that's also a reflection and a blood memory echo of how we survived for so long. Our systems of creation were self-sustaining and nourishing and consciously interrelational within the practice.

I'm still trying to figure out where and what methodology works in each situation, so I honor all of the values and ontologies of all the Indigenous and non-Indigenous practitioners coming to the table. I think that's how we traded. Co-lived. Shared for thousands of years, and that's what excites me most about the work.

Do you think that ethics can go hand in hand with a very strong aesthetics? Absolutely. I have a very strong aesthetic. And I think it is out of respect to your point of view and position as an artist to have strong ethical engagement practices to execute that vision. And I think that's where the art suffers, that we don't do that good methodological work, and therefore we're disappointed or people have problems. I have a very strong vision with regards to what a show will look like, and sound like, with a mixed team of different nations—Indigenous and non-Indigenous. If we don't have a clear blueprint of the bones of how this work will be founded and executed, it's just going to crumble. You need that structure to give people to hang on. I call them marks or to totem an idea so that you can have an artist hang on to it and pull them to the next idea. Otherwise, they're creating in quicksand, in mud, and it's uncomfortable. And again, the art suffers. The only way to create with a particular and specific and strong point of view is through creating structures that are rooted in Indigenous ontologies. I think people get concerned because we have such a scarcity mindset, and our cultures have been so taken from us and appropriated, that again people can get weary of sharing and evolving our cultural creation methods.

I don't think a lot of our artists have been positioned to assume that the Canadian Western way of making is how we all have to do it. And we can refuse that and create our own process, and I think it's absolutely necessary. I think all of our Indigenous artists will struggle until Canadian theatre really resources and makes space for Indigenous practitioners to create from an Indigenous paradigm and ontology. Otherwise, we'll have the same whitewashed, imperial-filtered Indigenous stories told by white people through a white paradigm. And I will say something bold. I don't believe that's Indigenous storytelling.

I think that's Canadian theatre telling an Indigenous story.

I owe my future ancestors, your children, your future ancestors, everyone—we owe them more. We owe them more than that. And for me, when people say, like, "How do you work?" I say, "It's my responsibility to create a better environment than the one we inherited." And environment and all the complexities and spherical nature of what that means—a better environment in the arts, a better environment in families, a better environment ecologically. And that I know even as troubled as this work can be—as I'm not getting the sleep I should right now—I rest all right at night knowing that it was in service to that work.

What are the things that I can do to be as respectful as I can in a community?
The more knowledge you have around my peoples, my ontologies, my epistemologies, our complex leadership systems, our current intersections with land, resources, the colonial state, the current social affairs. How many of our children are being apprehended? What are our language rates at? What is the incarceration rate? How many residential school survivors do we have? Do we have clean water? Just like I learn, I read people's executive summaries, interim reports. I read their books. I read as much as I can, because that's my job, so that when I try to meet them, I meet them. What I'm challenged by the most is people come and want to work with me and haven't done any of that work.

And it really hurts. It hurts because it is so disrespectful.

It would be like me going to your house, kicking off my shoes, eating some food, speaking the whole time and not engaging with you in any respectful way and then leaving. It feels violating. I would never invite a guest over to my house if they behaved that way. I would never arrive at someone's home empty-handed. I would never arrive not learning how to pronounce their names. I would not arrive without learning who their families were, knowing their offers and contributions. I am rigorous about learning about who people are so that I can respect them in our collaborative practice.

I remember hearing about how when the white people came, they asked a lot of the Indigenous people to take off their headdresses. For Indigenous people, we put on our regalia every day out of respect to the people we're meeting. I wear certain items on a first meeting because they are symbols and emblems of who we are in our communities so you can start to learn who we are. So, a Chief came in, or a respected Elder, with a long amount of eagle feathers, they're saying that's how many eagle feathers they were gifted. And so, they're piecing together how honored and sacred they are within the community. These stories within our regalia are our way of showing you who we are. We make generous offers to get to know us and yet, most people show up empty-handed saying, "how do I pronounce Squamish?"

You would never approach white practitioners with so little research work and capacity-building. And yet that's how so many come to us. So not only do we have to endure working in a model that's not built for us, I then have to also explain who I am to people who fail to show up doing basic and fundamental knowledge-gathering.

To not listen that deeply, to not know the nuance of my practice or whoever you're working with, is, I would say, the deepest disrespect. Historically, there were warrior songs that you would sing when you're coming to attack another tribe. That was out of respect so that you could hide your sacred items and put your sacred people in a safe place. I think in this day and age, we have to be singing songs to get to know one another and forewarn and learn and courageously investigate who we are to one another. And too often non-Indigenous people are showing up to communities expecting us to endure the oppression and explain it to you as well.

When I was younger, I too often accepted the bare minimum and I can't do that anymore. I work too hard to accept it, because if I do, then I normalize it and then that's what I steward in for the next generation, and I won't do that. The next generation deserves a lot of respect, and if that means I'm going to have to have uncomfortable conversations and engagements with non-Indigenous peoples now, I will do that. I will do that for them, because that means when they come up, those artistic leaders are going to be that much more prepared for them, and that is my service. So, I do get uncomfortable. I, my spirit hurts, my heart hurts.

This decolonial confronting work is exhausting. But courage is my value. Vulnerability is a discipline. And that ... those are hard moments when I think you know, "Should I have acted tougher? Should I put on more of a front?" I don't sleep well on those nights, but this is The Work.

I think about people's families a lot and the more precise and efficient we can be, the more time they get to spend with their families. I hope that we worked in a way that they were able to go back to their loved ones with a full heart and a nourished spirit. I work to end each creative day that way, knowing full well that sometimes it's not possible, but that notion is what I hold in my spirit.

I think about people and artists who might be able to create frameworks and ideas and theories to add to our cultural evolution and how I can support them, because that is what our ancestors did for thousands of years. I think because of the genocides and the 500-year war with the colonists, Indigenous culture has been in a bit of a stasis with regards to how do we meet the moment and evolve to make sure that all of our citizens are being taken care of. But I think when I have a breath and I really think about my responsibilities as a storyteller, I think about the most marginalized. I think about people who need more voice and how we can create to support their opportunity at peace.

Our ancestors were innovators. And I if, like my dad said, we weren't beating the same drum song for 10,000 years, we evolved our culture to ensure we met the moment, and I take that very seriously and I know that scares some artists and traditionalists. I am not here to undermine or disrespect the traditional ways but believe it's my Indigenous tradition and responsibility to evolve culture and practice to make sure we fucking stay alive.

I work to have strong relationships with people, to have each other's back. I think we had trade agreements like that from here. I think these strong networks, these relationships, require vulnerability, require service, require thoughtfulness that nourishes one another because then I feel productive. I feel effective. I feel of service. I feel like we created something together and I think it's hard to come by something that feels more nourishing than like-heart collaboration.

You know, whether it be in an intimate relationship, friendship, family member, when you have a moment where you're like making a meal and it tastes good together. You know, you're making love and it feels good. You and your friend are going on a walk and chatting and singing a song and singing harmonies, like I don't think there's much more this Earth can offer us than the peace and ecstasy of meaningful collaboration and that cosmic conjuring.

Lots of that in my life. I think that's what is nourishing, that is what is sustaining. That's the erotic sense of aliveness and vitality, and unpredictability, the mystery of life to be like, "I wonder what's going to happen today? I wonder if I'm gonna meet another mystic where we can have some alchemy together to create something new?"

I think about it a lot. It does consume me because the stakes are high. The stakes are really high. I think about the next generation. I think about our family members who are in jail right now, whose kids are being taken. About my reserves that are put on water advisories.

All of these urgent things that I—I hold in my heart to not keep me up but to nourish me to work hard that day. And the more I turn to joy, the more I turn to humor, the more I turn to nourishing relationships, I firmly believe the work gets done. The work gets done in a way that ignites other people to work in that way, and the feelings and experiences I have of investing in this way of being have given me the most amount of peace in my life.

I have worked in many environments that have attacked my dignity, my humanity, my spirit. And when you ask, how do I deal with it? You know, how do you help people meet you? I think if I respond with kindness, if I respond with gratitude. If I think about them, that embodiment ignites a reciprocation of that way of being. And so even when I feel like I'm getting kicked in the teeth, I have done the work to respond with kindness and courage. Always.

I think at the heart of almost every Indigenous nation is the sense of community and belonging and family systems within that, and I said in one podcast, I was like, "I'm just working so I can go home."

Home within my heart, home within my Indigeneity, home to my nations. A lot of us just want to go home and we need to create processes that allow that return and that peace to occur.

Deneh'Cho Thompson

What are your thoughts on ethics and theatre?
The Covid-19 pandemic has created a caesura in contemporary theatre, and I embrace the timeliness of conversations about ethics and theatre. Our current theatre systems and structures reward merit and capitalization, so the individual and the dollar become strong forces influencing our ethical structures. While these forces seem inescapable, I make efforts to use alternate frameworks towards ethics. In response to Black Lives Matter and Indigenous land defenders, several Canadian theatre institutions have made efforts to change their structures and ways of working to be more equitable, diverse, and inclusive ("Citadel Theatre" 2020; "Open letter" 2020). Bearing witness to these efforts has led me to interrogate my own complicity and participation in the status quo, and to use this moment of pause to reflect on my own practices and ethics.

During my theatre training I was constantly asked to justify my work through an intellectual lens of *why*: why did *you* choose this play? Why now? Why should *your* work receive public funding? Why should people buy tickets to *your* play? Why is *your* art important? Proving the consequence of one's art reflects the theatre industry's values: individualism and the production of capital. Darrah Teitel, playwright and activist, reminds us: "Oppression has many weapons, including racism, misogyny, colonial imperialism, and compulsory cis-heterosexuality, but all of these are wielded by capitalism. If a monster is stalking all of our lives, it is indeed a four-headed beast, but its body is capitalism" (2019: 40).

The axiology and worth of contemporary theatre is measured on a scale of either dollars (capital) or merit (individualism), principles that guide the ethics of the theatre, and I find this unsatisfactory. When I consider ethics and theatre-making, I first think about how my work is responsible to others, to my community and beyond.

Indigenous love, or "soft power" as defined by Jill Carter (2016a), provides a framework that prioritizes interpersonal and community relationships. Carter argues that the use of love expressed through soft power is a method for creating sovereign relational communities that Indigenous people have a responsibility to care for. A dynamic kinship network and relational responsibility are the foundations of a healthy community. Love, expressed this way, can also be understood as an aspect of *wahkohtowin*, a Cree and Métis concept that highlights the responsibility to connect in healthy and reciprocal ways. By choosing to be accountable to one another, it is possible to create a community that self-perpetuates because it becomes a community worth caring for.

The recent challenges to power systems at theatre institutions indicates a desire from the theatre community for new systemic models that account for the cultural shift being led by BIPOC, LGBTQ2S+, and other historically excluded members of the theatre community. Learning from Indigenous and other non-Western ways of creating and relating, we must consider how frameworks and methods can both interrupt the status quo and create support for the community as this cultural transition occurs.

Is it possible to be an ethical artist and create aesthetically compelling art? If so, how?

Several years ago, I worked on an Indigenous community-focused theatre piece where I helped lift a culturally specific story onto the stage with a group of non-actors. Culminating in a single performance, the house was full to bursting with community members of all ages. The audience made deep and complex connections to this relatively simple piece of theatre and it was transcendent to witness. What I saw that day evidenced the meaningful web of interpersonal, intergenerational, and community relations present in a community structure as *kinstellatory relations*, a term I borrow from Karyn Recollet, that "[is] based upon our reciprocity and radical relationalities" (Carter, Recollet and Robinson 2017: 214). Moreover, that moment embodied a spiderweb, a multidimensional weaving of relationships, each with its own meaning and strength. That day, I saw tendrils of hope, vulnerability, beauty, pain, fear, and perseverance pass through the room, extending beyond the performance, and beyond the theatre into the world as the audience carried that moment with them out the door. Words are incapable of fully capturing the embodied experience of that moment, but those transcendent moments of collectively existing as a community are my aesthetic.

My aesthetic preferences are grounded in making visible something that mainstream theatre deems *unseeable*. I contend that my community ethic deeply informs my aesthetics, thus eschewing Western taxonomy as my ethics are increasingly and unescapably woven into my aesthetics. It is when I am witness to moments of expressive kinstellatory web-making that I am aesthetically satisfied. As a storyteller, I have a responsibility to use an ethical aesthetic because stories, as many Indigenous scholars remind us, have the power to build community, to teach, and to heal. Stories are Indigenous law and they are knowledge systems and they must be used in a relationally responsible way (Archibald et al. 2019; Carter 2016a; Olson 2018; Simpson 2017; Smith 1999).

What would you recommend theatre artists from outside the community consider while working in community?

Cree scholar Willie Ermine proposes that when two distinct groups come together, three cultural spaces are present: that of community, that of the researchers/artists, and a third space created in the encounter of the two. This third space is not by default a safe space for all participants, but Ermine proposes the co-constitution of an "ethical space of engagement" (2007). The concept can be read as an oversimplification of the complex histories of two cultures and of broader social structures, but it is a potent analytical tool providing language to discuss encounters between researchers, artists, and community. The notion of the ethical space is supported by the broader field of community-based research. For example, *ethical validity* "is achieved when the research process is consistent with the ethical principles of *all* research partners" (Edwards, Lund and Gibson 2008: 19, my emphasis). Each project must manifest this space in response to differing and evolving circumstances.

To manifest a space of ethical engagement, I return to Carter's idea of the perpetual healthy community, the community worth caring for (2016a). The ethical space, a liminal community itself, must be crafted in a way that creates caring investment from all participants, regardless of their worldview or positionality. How this is achieved will vary, but I propose that there are at least two strategies that can assist in this work.

First, listen: current power structures inform a knowledge hierarchy that privileges Western educated or trained artists/researchers, disavowing that knowledge has many forms. Communities are full of incredible insights, strategies, and methods. It has become almost cliché to say this in research circles, but shut up and listen; know that you are not the expert.

Another crucial tactic is to remember that time might not function the same for a community as it does for your institution or from your position. Attending to time is a means of attending to community needs, and this may unsettle agreed-upon timelines and cause delays, extensions, fast-tracking, or even postponement or cancelation. When understandings about time diverge, ask questions, don't press for an absolute answer or solution too forcefully because there may not be a clear answer, and empower the community to be the authority on time if that suits their need.

Thomas Jones Kweyulutstun

What are the things that come to mind when you think about theatre and ethics?

When I think about it, ethics falls in the same place as stsuw'et, our teachings. How you conduct yourself in the situation. And already we're very theatrical people. If you've ever been to a ceremony when people sing and dance, you know, they're very, very theatrical. They go together well. And it's how we conduct ourself using stsuw'et or ethics that helps things proceed in a proper fashion.

We're always trying to move and conduct ourselves in the same way as our ancestors. We're always trying to uphold what they left behind first. When we get ready to do something or when we're doing something, it always comes up to ourselves or to each other. How do you think our grandmother would do this? How do you think our grandfather would do this? And are we doing it the way they would?

So, in theatre it's the same as a potlatch or a ceremony, we're really telling stories. You're trying to get something across to your audience. So, you have to be able to demonstrate and share things that are allowed to be demonstrated and shared. There are certain things that can and there are certain things that can't be. So, that comes into the teachings.

That knowledge would come from your own immediate family. Maybe it could go into your community, the knowledge and the stories and the things that can be shared publicly and can't be shared publicly. You would first off learn in your own home, with family, and then it would extend out into your community. And then you would learn from your community what is considered to be for the community and then what is a part of the bigger Salish world. Those stories that connect us all together.

Can you tell me a bit more about the content of the stories, how that relates to ethics?

You have to know your audience. Each story is aimed at a different audience, whether it's children, toddlers, newborns, or young adults coming into their own life. Young people who are becoming couples ready for marriage, or older people who are becoming Elders. All those different stories, they carry those teachings. As well as how it's passed on is important—who it's passed on to, and why it's passed on—because not everybody just gets any story at any time. It's all aimed at where they're at in their life. And I think it's that way even for when somebody has something to learn about themselves. With regular life struggles, you can always share a traditional story or an experience of your own life or your grandparent's life or your parent's life, you can share that experience with them to help them understand or maybe see their way through it. You have to be able to pick the proper contents. No matter what you are doing.

Do you think it is possible to work ethically and also create something really beautiful?

I think it's possible. And it's time and it's needed that we create things, but it's always important that we have the Elders involved with the process. Not only do we have them involved, but we also try and encourage open-mindedness, because a lot of the Elders, they come from a different time, where things just were a little bit different. And now we're moving forward in this educational world. We're trying to bring things to light and make them shareable. And we need their guidance. But we also want to encourage them to say, "we're doing this for us." Because there are a lot of fears—"what if this has been created and it's taken away," which is what happened with it, right? But if we encourage them that it's been created for us and for the future, their future grandchildren can jump in to see and use it. I think they'll be more open-minded to that.

What advice would you give an outsider working in the community with you?

I think it goes back to the last part. Just being open-minded to understand the community that you're going to work with. Just because every community is different, every nation is different in how they go about what they're going to share and what they're not going to share. And if you're open-minded to hear how those things need to be demonstrated and shared. A lot of people probably go into a community with their own ideas of how they want things to be done with their training. But when you know, when you come into our community and you think of why we do things the way we do things, I think it's really out of the protection of what we have. Because there was a time when you were thrown in jail for giving a speech or for having a dance. So, the way they operate is really to protect and shield what we have. And therefore, to really understand what's going on with each individual community that you're working with, I think that an open mind makes the work a lot easier. Not only if you have an open mind, but it also opens their mind up too to say, "okay, there's going to be some great things that come out of this, I think it's a good idea."

Jill Carter

What are some of the first things that come to mind when you think of ethics and theatre?

The act of making theatre is the act of communicating story. It is a ceremonial act (whether one chooses to acknowledge this or not). It is a catalyst for transformation—transforming teller, reshaping the lives of those of whom the story is told, and reconfiguring the beliefs and behaviors of those who come to bear witness. This is an age-old rite through which worlds are shaken, broken, re-made. The act of witnessing theatre is the act of receiving, holding, and activating, in our own lives (for good or ill), the stories that are being told. And those stories told, received, and retold sit with us always, nesting themselves ever more deeply into mind, heart, and blood. The ways in which we come to regard ourselves and others, the ways in which we operationalize that regard (through our behaviors and actions towards ourselves and towards other living beings) emerge from the stories, which we have come to believe, the stories we choose to tell, and the stories others choose to tell about us. Story carries immense power— the power to heal and create and the power to disrupt and destroy. And with such power, as Thomas King reminds us, comes immense responsibility (2003: 29).

This is an age-old rite through which worlds are shaken, broken, re-made.

Across millennia, princes and potentates have understood this. And today, those artists who insist on writing light onto corruption or imagining and w/riting into being new worlds in which such corruption has no place are and will continue to be imprisoned, murdered, or otherwise silenced by those who fear the possible worlds these tellers invoke. The powers that be and that wish to remain understand and take seriously this power.

Do we? As artists, do we understand the nature of the power we wield? As artists, do we *own* that power and all of the responsibilities with which that power invests us? Do we invest ourselves in these responsibilities with as much conviction as we invest ourselves in honing our skills in rhetoric or exercising our "artistic license"? Do we hold ourselves accountable? Do we tread softly—with care?

Indigenous artists, working in every genre, speak of art as medicine— the artist as healer. Indeed, many would agree wholeheartedly with the Métis scholar, storyteller, and theatre worker Maria Campbell that the primary task of those who exert themselves in the present moment to write possible worlds into actuality is the task of healing the present moment to ensure a healthy future: "If you're an artist and you're not a healer, then you are not an artist" (Campbell, quoted in Griffiths and Campbell 1997: 84). And the primary ethic that governs the calling to heal is "First, do no harm"—to ourselves, to our fellow artists, to those who come to witness our work and be healed. The operationalization of this ethic requires a bundle of principles and protocols (behaviors through which we activate these principles) that is scrupulously adhered to by all individuals who consider themselves to be members of "the body," which holds the privilege of practicing the discipline.

Is it possible to be an ethical artist and create aesthetically compelling art? Can ethics and aesthetics go hand in hand? If so, how?

> This story has given me a means to exploring my first question tonight … Am I an actor performing or am I a descendant of the great storytellers of our past? Or both? What is my responsibility to our stories?' (De-ba-jeh-mu-jig 2009: 186)

I am once again compelled to reflect upon Maria Campbell's assertion: "If you're an artist and you're not a healer, *then you are not an artist*" (Griffiths and Campbell 1997: 84, my emphasis). I believe quite simply that good process leads to good product. And I believe that good process (and, hence, the good product, which emerges therefrom) is a process that is woven through with ethical behavior—the sustained and mindful *doing* of wisdom, respect, humility, truth, bravery, honesty, and love. I did not arrive at this idea by myself: it's an idea that was communicated to me in childhood. It is an idea that has been passed down through the generations of Anishinaabe ceremonialists, artisans, orators, mothers, singers, dancers, medicine people, and world-builders. In the context of contemporary performance, I have learned throughout a lifetime of making and of witnessing that where harm (physical, emotional, or psychospiritual) is done —be it to the witness, to those charged in the communication of the story, or to those of whom the story is told—the story (and its creators) may enjoy a brief blaze of notoriety, exciting public interest, but it will prove of no lasting value to the generations that follow in the wake of its creation.

Personally, I have been momentarily swept away by many "aesthetically compelling" moments on the stage. But after that first gasp of wonder and delight, the memory has faded. I have witnessed wondrous illusions, but these have not affected in me a liminal transformation. Such moments have neither healed me when I was dis-eased, instilled in me crucial knowledge where I was ignorant, reminded me of what I should remember, or afforded a lasting light towards which I might turn in the darkness of despair.

Conversely, I have witnessed works that may, to some, seem less aesthetically compelling—works that, indeed, might be (and often have been) denigrated for the "flaws in their aesthetic." And yet, I can recount with perfect clarity and relive with utter joy the affective response they called up within me. Indeed, after many years, I continue to respond to the call of these works. Their lessons reverberate within me; the questions they have inspired continue to revolve in my mind. Perhaps, it is the flaw that compels, that worries the mind, that tugs at the heart.

Perhaps, such "flaws" are required to produce an enduring Affect. Indeed, many Indigenous artisans (weavers of rugs, crafters of molas, workers in beads, tellers of story) deliberately weave a flaw into their design to allow the spirit of creation to free itself from the finished work (see Carter 2016b: 11). I imagine that formless inspiritor circulating through communities of creators across genres and generations, inviting these artful humans to presence themselves in a never-finished, ever-growing communal "archive." In the telling of Indigenous story, an ending is not sewn up tightly and sealed with a moral lesson. And in that moment of telling, those to whom the story is told are charged with the task of co-creation. It is they who will make the meaning. It is they who will live the meaning they make into the world (see King 2003: 11). Likewise, in the crafting of the wampum belts that document nation-to-nation treaty relationships, the ends are traditionally left unfinished. And while some, like I, may find these texts all the more compelling precisely because of this irregularity, the Haudenosaunee artisans who crafted these belts did not make this choice to stir aesthetic sensibilities. The unfinished ends gesture towards their nations' ethical sensibilities: here we see the principles and protocols of brotherhood, tolerance, hospitality, and peace writ large in the space that is held on either side of the treaty belts to invite other nations into ancient agreements, to make peace with them, to make kin of them (Loft 2020).

"Can aesthetics and ethics go hand in hand?" I believe that they must. Why would they not? I have come to learn that Indigenous aesthetic principles are bound into the lifeways, principles, and protocols that begin with and are directed by the land and all her life-forms. The aesthetics employed to bead a moccasin, to weave a rug, to engineer enduring earthworks, to dance for healing, to sing to creation, or to tell a story are governed, I believe, by one overarching principle. For the Anishinaabeg, it is expressed as Minobimaatisiiwin—a way of living well. And while every Indigenous nation has its own way of articulating this principle, this "way," "path," "road," or "great law" places the preservation of all life at its center towards which each nation has laid out a series of actionable teachings/principles/ethics as processual pathways towards its achievement. Responding to a teaching of Leroy Little Bear, Kanien'kehaka multimedia artist and cultural theorist Jackson 2bears (2014) articulates his own processual journey with passionate sincerity: He creates, he tells us, through 'new media technologies, but [he utilizes these technologies] in a way that respects the "sacredness, livingness, and the soul of the world" (27). This is an Indigenous ethic. It is a directive for life. It is a prescription for art. It is a pathway towards healing.

What are the key values and aspects of ethics? How does this work within arts projects?

Every society (professional or political) has adopted its own set of guiding principles/ethics. For those of Judeo-Christian heritage, these are transmitted through the Ten Commandments carried down from Mount Sinai by Moses to the Israelites. For the Anishinaabeg, these are transmitted through the Seven Grandfather Teachings given to the people through prophecy and passed on to the people by the ceremonial specialists of the Midewiwin Lodge. Seven teachings. Seven verbs. Seven calls to action, which should be operationalized in every area of human life: we are called upon to cherish knowledge and so *do* wisdom; we are called upon to *do* love to all we encounter and so affect peace; we are called upon to demonstrate that we honor all of the created order by *doing* respect; we are called upon to *do* bravery, to *do* honesty, to *do* humility, to *do* truth, so that every *body* (human and other-than-human) in the creation will live well and fulfill the purpose for which it was invested with life. We are called upon to *do* these things in every area of our lives, in every era, in every situation—in our hunting, in our gathering, in our planting, in our harvesting, in our partnering, in our parenting, in our elder care, in our governance, in our treaty-making, and *in our artistry*. This is a recipe for care. This is a recipe for maintaining good relations. This is a recipe for upholding life and health—for ensuring that the works we produce lift up their makers and their witnesses, protect their health, and uphold their lives.

Do some of the traditional stories talk about ethics? In which ways?

> Every time I share this story or listen to it, I see how it directly relates to me, how I may be blocking the water up inside myself not even knowing that I am depriving not only myself. I am also depriving all those around me who need that water. (De-ba-jeh-mu-jig 2009: 186)

I don't think that traditional stories "talk about ethics"; they don't tell us what to do. Rather, they carry us on a journey throughout which it is our responsibility to perceive, reflect upon, and be influenced by "the way life moves" (Benton-Banai, quoted in Bell et al. 2010: 30). For me, this expression—"the way life moves"—connotes the principles and protocols which humans are to adopt and by which humans are to live in an ethical, balanced, and life-sustaining manner. These ethical teachings (and the protocols through which to activate these teachings) are actively modeled for us by all members of the created order within the biota into which we are born, with which we live, and by which we are sustained. The story, then, is a window into the heart of the created order, inviting us into the telling, investing all (witness and teller) with authorship/authority, and insisting upon our full accountability for the teachings we have taken up, the teachings we have ignored, or the teachings we have discarded.

Indeed, the very frameworks upon which Story is structured—through which the storied life moves—model the operationalization of these ethical teachings—teachings which we are invited to pick up and activate within our own lives (Simpson and Manitowabi 2013: 281; King 2003: 22–7). Because the "edge" is left unfinished, because the patterning allows for "intertextual facings" and "interfactual textings" (see Glancy 1999: 129), the autonomy of the sojourner as co-creator is respected; and hence, it follows that those who have grown up in this tradition—who have been lifelong sojourners on this learning path—understand what it is to respect the autonomy of others and, more importantly, have made the doing of that respect a daily, lifelong practice.

References

2bears, J. (2014), "My post-Indian technological autobiography," in S. Loft and K. Swanson (eds), *Coded Territories: Tracing Indigenous Pathways in New Media Art*. Calgary, AB: University of Calgary Press, pp. 13–29.

Archibald, J. A., Lee-Morgan, J., De Santolo, J., and Smith, L. T. (eds) (2019), *Decolonizing Research: Indigenous Storywork as Methodology*. London: Zed Books.

Bell, N., Conroy, E., Wheatley, K., Michaud, B., Maracle, C., Pelletier, J., Filion, B., and Johnson, B. (2010), "The ways of knowing guide." Ways of Knowing Partnership Turtle Island Conservation Programme, Toronto Zoo. Available online: https://www.torontozoo.com/pdfs/tic/Stewardship_Guide.pdf (accessed October 24, 2020).

Carter, J. (2016a), "Sovereign proclamations of the twenty-first century: scripting survivance through the language of soft power," in Y. Nolan and R. P. Knowles (eds), *Performing Indigeneity: New Essays on Canadian Theatre*. Toronto, ON: Playwrights Canada Press, pp. 33–65.

Carter, J. (2016b), "The physics of the mola: w/riting Indigenous resurgence on the contemporary stage," *Modern Drama*, 59 (1), 1–25.

Carter, J., Recollet, K., and Robinson D. (2017), "Interventions into the maw of old world hunger: kinstellatory maps, and radical relationalities in a project of reworlding," in H. Davis-Fisch (ed.), *New Essays in Canadian Theatre*, Vol. 7. Canadian Performance Histories and Historiographies. Toronto, ON: Playwrights Canada Press, pp. 205–31.

"Citadel Theatre commits to a more diverse organization by 2024–25" (2020), *Edmonton Journal*, September 22. Available online: https:// edmontonjournal.com/news/local-news/citadel-theatre-bipoc-women-non-binary-organization (accessed February 11, 2021).

De-ba-jeh-mu-jig (2009), "The gift," in J. Osawabine and S. Hengen (eds), *Stories from the Bush: The Woodland Plays of De-ba-jeh-mu-jig Theatre Group*. Toronto, ON: Playwrights Canada Press, pp. 169–88.

Edwards, K., Lund, C., and Gibson, N. (2008), "Ethical validity: expecting the unexpected in community-based research," *Pimatisiwin: Journal of Aboriginal and Indigenous Community Health*, 6 (3) 17–30.

Ermine, W. (2007), "The ethical space of engagement," *Indigenous Law Journal*, 6 (1) 193–204.

Glancy, D. (1999), "Further (farther): creating dialogue to talk about Native American plays," *Journal of Dramatic Theory and Criticism*, 14 (1), 127–30.

Griffiths, L. and Campbell, M. (1997), *The Book of Jessica: A Theatrical Transformation*. Toronto, ON: Playwrights Canada Press.

King, T. (2003), *The Truth About Stories: A Native Narrative*. Toronto, ON: House of Anansi.

Loft, A. (2020), "Come to one mind: consensus making in Haudenosaunee territory," University of Toronto, online workshop, 3 October.

Olson, M. (2018), "Braids of a river: memory and performance in the North," *Canadian Theatre Review*, 174, 62–4. DOI:10.3138/ctr.174.012

"Open letter calls for change at Saskatoon's Persephone Theatre" (2020), Global News, June 19. Available online: https://globalnews.ca/news/7086425/open-letter-change-saskatoons-persephone-theatre/ (accessed February 11, 2021).

Simpson, L. B. (ed.) (2017), *As We Have Always Done: Indigenous Freedom through Radical Resistance* (3rd ed.). Minneapolis: University of Minnesota Press.

Simpson, L. B. and Manitowabi, E. (2013), "Theorizing resurgence from within Nishnaabeg thought," in J. Doerfler, J. Sinclair, and H. Kiiwetinepinesiik Stark (eds), *Centering Anishinaabeg Studies: Understanding the World through Stories*. East Lansing: Michigan State University Press, pp. 279–93.

Smith, L. T. (1999), *Decolonizing Methodologies: Research and Indigenous Peoples*. London: Zed Books.

Teitel, D. (2019), "The theatre feminist: a manifesto," *Canadian Theatre Review*, 180, 36–41.

3

Ethical Discourse in Applied Theatre: A Historiographic and Curricular Literature Review

Monica Prendergast

Introduction[1]

For more than twenty years, applied theatre has been recognized as a branch of theatre practice interested in community-based interventions of many kinds. Scholars and practitioners in applied theatre come from a diverse range of backgrounds: some from theatre studies, others from theatre/drama education, theatre for development, theatre of the oppressed, and drama therapy. Ethics has been a key and necessary topic in the scholarship, but the multidisciplinarity of the field makes it more challenging to "pin down" ethical discourses because the wide variation in these subfields has a bearing on how ethics is both understood and addressed. This chapter endeavors to sort through the threads of this discourse in order to identify and recommend to readers (1) the most noteworthy published contributions to ethics over time (historiography) and (2) how these readings, presented as a proposed curriculum on ethics in applied theatre, could be seen as working towards a fuller understanding of the significance a considered ethical stance has for our practice.

I take a historical curriculum development approach to this ethical discourse review by selecting material that could be deemed suitable for an upper-level undergraduate or postgraduate applied theatre course on this topic. This review was carried out with sources up to

2020; of course, over time the discourse will continue to expand and new sources will need to be added. As in any literature review, the risk for the writer is always to miss key sources through oversight or through the author's positionality, as discussed in the Introduction (pp. 3–4).

Key Texts

The first two books from the Global North to appear in the field with the term "applied theatre" in the titles were Philip Taylor's *Applied Theatre: Creating Transformative Encounters in the Community* and James Thompson's *Applied Theatre: Bewilderment and Beyond*, both published in 2003. Like many others, Taylor came to community-based applied theatre practice with a background as a drama educator. In chapter 4 of his book, Taylor writes about ethics from this educational perspective, asking, "Whose standards is the applied theatre enforcing? How do these standards interface with the communities who experience applied theatre? ... What makes applied theatre an ethical theatre?" (76–7). He then looks at a number of applied theatre projects and considers their ethical positioning. One of these exemplars involves drama therapy (82–5), and although Taylor does say, "in the applied theatre there is a desire to transform the nature of the world in which we live, [but] teaching artists are not operating from a therapeutic perspective" (85), there is a concern here around including a drama therapy case study at all. This might cause some confusion for an emerging applied theatre artist, and the boundaries between *therapy* (requiring certified expertise) and *therapeutic* (the more universal benefit of art-making) need to be held with ethical care. Taylor goes on to look at more applied theatre-oriented projects, in particular one he led on domestic violence. The project made use of verbatim theatre techniques in which participants' words were crafted into dialogue and presented by teaching artists to a community audience affected by this issue (90–8). He concludes his chapter with some more questions that begin to define how applied theatre workers could think about ethics:

How do applied theatre artists document a sustained change in people's lives?

Should applied theatre workers even be interested in documenting such change?

Is it ethical for applied theatre workers to begin to construe their mission as one of creating social change?

What moral authority do applied theatre artists share other than a commitment to theatre as an aesthetic medium to help participants act, reflect, and transform? (100)

These questions come with a useful warning: "Applied theatre workers cannot be conned into thinking they are the saviors of the community" (99). Indeed, it is key for those in the field to recognize when applied theatre projects are offered as weak substitutes for real-world progressive sociopolitical policies and programs. As Augusto Boal (1979) says, theatre provides the space for "the rehearsal for the revolution" (122) but cannot be confused with real change brought about by much more complex processes than creating and performing a play. So what can applied theatre do for its participants? It can provide the space and the opportunities for communities to begin the process of understanding what lies at the base of the issues they are facing. In this way they may be better prepared when real opportunities for social change arrive.

In "Becoming Ethical," Chapter 5 of *Applied Theatre* (2003), Thompson begins by stating there are "problems of a value-based practice constantly tested by the flexibility demanded by context" (173). Ethics are inherently values-based, as are aesthetics; how our values (and those of participants) inform both what we do and how we do it are key to passing the "test" of being flexible within shifting contexts. He reminds scholars in the field of their ethical responsibility, in that, "[b]y putting pen to paper, we engage in the generation of ways of seeing the world" (175) and that "[a]ny ethnographic account of a theatre practice will ... at its heart be dealing with the ethics of knowing and seeing"

(178). The chapter reflects on three projects led by Thompson in Sri Lanka in which a range of ethical moments are addressed. The third of these reflections—on a project with former child soldiers living in a rehabilitation camp (which inadvertently led to a subsequent attack on the camp)—moves Thompson into an evocative poetic piece of writing "more jagged, with more questions and in note form" (190): "*Ethically my tattered wings were (are) flapping. / I have responsibility because I have searched out this work*" (191, emphasis in original). In a powerful postscript, Thompson relates that after the rehabilitation project, the camp was attacked and "29 young men were killed and many more were injured" (197). As Taylor does in his chapter, Thompson ends with questions: "Implicated witness? Participant observer? Irresponsible responsible? This is the place where it ends? Ethically my shattered wings clink and clank with their knives" (197). Thompson went on to become a central ethical thinker and writer in the field of applied theatre, perhaps based in part on learning that this horrific event followed his theatre-based intervention. Thompson's next two books also serve as ethical exemplars: both *Digging up Stories: Applied Theatre, Performance and War* (2005) and *Performance Affects: Applied Theatre and the End of Effect* (2009) offer much thoughtful reflection of benefit to applied theatre workers.

In *Digging up Stories*, Thompson expresses his ethical concerns around asking participants to tell and perform their stories in a war-torn setting:

> When creating theatre with vulnerable or marginal communities, the ethics of our practice must be a paramount concern, and I believe some of the most difficult issues arise within the structures through which groups tell stories or are invited to participate in that telling. [...] By asking for, witnessing or retelling stories, when does the theatre practice become implicated in the horrors of the situation it displays? (24–5)

He goes on to conclude that "[t]he digging up of stories in this context [in places of war] can become an act of exploitation rather than support" (39) and that, more generally in applied theatre, "[w]e must question our right to ask a community to participate in the creation of performances about the substance of their lives" (40).

By 2009, in *Performance Affects*, Thompson was able to crystallize his ethical approach by drawing on a diverse range of ethical philosophers: Michel de Certeau, Simon Critchley, Jacques Rancière, Elaine Scarry, and Emmanuel Levinas among them. He writes:

> Participatory theatre should focus on affect rather than effect. This would seek to avoid the anticipation or extraction of meaning as the primary impulse of an applied theatre process (both in execution of projects that communicate or teach and in the interpretation of those projects that report on effects, problems solved and things learnt). Working with affect awakens individuals to possibilities beyond themselves without an insistence on what the experience is—what meanings should be attached. (111)

Thompson concludes this influential book by suggesting that "[w]orking to keep people alive, to value their and others' lives, and to announce proudly that they are worthy of living and being valued for being alive, is then central to the politics proposed here. And happiness, joy and celebration are indispensable sensations in this act of redistribution" (179). Indeed, this shift in emphasis from effect to affect has led to what has been called the "celebratory turn" (Prendergast and Saxton 2020, 11) in applied theatre—a move, for the most part, due to Thompson's important writing on ethics.

Helen Nicholson's *Applied Drama: The Gift of Theatre* appeared in 2005 alongside Thompson's *Digging up Stories*. Here, Nicholson considers the praxis of applied drama (inclusive of performed work as in applied theatre) that "bears witness to a plurality of voices and experiences and maintains a commitment to radical social democracy" (157). She envisions applied drama/theatre as a form of "active performative citizenship … concerned with the ethics of how people interact with each other and with their environment" (36). Nicholson addresses ethical concerns throughout the book, particularly so in her final chapter where she poses, and attempts to respond to, a crucial question: "What does it mean to act ethically in contexts where there are 'competing conceptions of the good life' [citing Chantal Mouffe] amongst participants and practitioners in applied drama?" (157). In her reading of "gift theory" (citing French social anthropologist Marcel Mauss), which positions the act of gift-giving on a spectrum between disinterested and self-interested motives, Nicholson adds more questions:

> What do we, as practitioners, expect in return for our labours? Artistic satisfaction? The participants' acquisition of skills or abilities? Do we ask participants to adopt new ways of thinking or different political values? Do we expect them to change their behaviour in particular ways? In turn, how far might our own perspectives alter as a result of the work? What about the funders? Do they have expectations of a return? (161)

She goes on to consider Derrida's critique of gift-giving, concluding that "this theoretical reading of the gift relationship acknowledges the risks, contradictions and uncertainties of theatre-making in community settings" (163). Our role as practitioners is not to "*give* participants a voice ... but to create spaces and places that enable the participants' voices to be heard" (163, emphasis in original).

Next to appear as a key text for the emerging field of applied theatre was *The Applied Theatre Reader*, edited by Tim Prentki and Sheila Preston (2009). Introducing a section titled "Ethics of Representation," consisting of eight chapters, co-editor Preston lays out useful ethical questions:

- How appropriate is our preferred aesthetic for engaging with the politics of speaking *with*, *for* or *about* participant communities?
- How do we deal ethically with moral and/or political tensions at the heart of the stories and texts that are created?
- How can we work sensitively, and create a genuine climate of dialogue and reciprocity with participants and participant communities?

- How are issues of voice, authority and ownership reconciled in the process of constructing narratives and representations that result?
- How will representations that have been created impact in diverse, unpredictable and political contexts? (68, emphasis in original)

This set of ethical questions is followed by section chapters that are more theoretical than practical but do provide clear sociopolitical positions underpinning some (not all) applied theatre practice. These chapters—by Edward Bond, Chantal Mouffe, bell hooks, and Sue Wilkinson and Celia Kitzinger—make clear (although only Bond is addressing theatre practice as such) that applied theatre is a social practice with political effects involving critical, radical, feminist, and ethical positioning that must be clearly understood by all involved. Representing the "other" lies at the heart of ethics in applied theatre; as Amanda Stuart Fisher explores in her chapter "Bearing witness," "To enter into the confidence of ... testimony draws the listener into an *ethical* relationship with the other" (114, emphasis in original). Drawing on French philosopher Emmanuel Levinas (who is frequently cited across this literature), Stuart Fisher reminds us that "to become a listener or an audience member of testimony, is to encounter what Emmanuel Levinas describes as the 'infinite responsibility to the other person'" (114). Our ethical role as facilitators is to remember Levinas's words, echoed by Stuart Fisher:

> [T]he performance of testimony should perhaps always remain unsettling and never reassuring. This is because it brings before us our own vulnerability in the face of the incommunicable and allows us to glimpse the limits of our understanding of the world and of our place within it. In order to respond to the demands of testimony we must open ourselves up to this unsettling encounter with the other. (114)

We cannot assume a sameness between participants and ourselves, particularly when working with participants who have or are still experiencing trauma in their lives.[2]

The next book to appear that contributes to this review is *Theatre & Ethics* by Nicholas Ridout (2009). This short monograph is meant for a theatre generalist audience, not specifically an applied theatre reader. That said, the book makes an excellent addition to both this review and to a possible course on ethics in applied theatre; it is readable and offers a historical survey of ethical thinking in theatre, both offstage and on. Ridout begins with a line from Sophocles' play *Philoctetes*, "How shall I act?," which is, in essence, the key ethical question. He then traces a line through Ancient Greek philosophy (Aristotle, Socrates, and Plato) and drama (Sophocles, Aeschylus), with a focus on Plato's rejection of theatre in his ideal Republic. He reinterprets this rejection as, in fact, Plato's demand "that theatre ought to justify itself in terms of the contribution it might make to an ethical life" (24). Ridout correctly notes the Western Eurocentrism of his historical tracing—another important ethical reminder for applied theatre practitioners:

> Because this [modern European] theatre presents its values as "universal" and its culture as something to which the whole of humanity may aspire, it makes the implicit claim that anyone who does not participate in that culture (foreigners, people who do not go to the theatre, for example) is somehow defective. The universal concept of "human" which this theatre seeks to promote can easily lapse into "humans like me". (40–1)

In the third and final part of this all too brief monograph, Ridout notes Brecht's interest in the ethical dilemma, a stopping-point in many of his plays where an audience can wrestle with how a character may proceed, a tactic that is continued in the work of Augusto Boal and his Theatre of the Oppressed later in the twentieth century. He goes on to look at ethics post-Second World War, citing the works of Levinas, and reflecting usefully on some of the tensions that occur when trying to apply Levinas to theatre (53–6). Finally, Ridout moves into the twenty-first century in his consideration of Hans-Thies Lehmann's highly influential book *Postdramatic Theatre* (2006). Ridout sees contemporary artists' postdramatic works "as part of a long historical exploration of the relationship between the political, the ethical and the aesthetic" (63). He also invites us to ponder how these examples help us to "think about what it might mean to be there" (64):

> By this I mean three things: to be there is, first, simply to be present, to attend, as at the theatre; to be there is, second, to be part of it, to participate, as in politics, for example; and finally, to be there is to be there for someone, to engage in a relationship of care or support, to accept an ethical responsibility for the other. (64)

I will return to these key aspects of presence and care later in this chapter, but am grateful to Ridout for highlighting presence in his most useful and accessible short book. Ridout concludes his text by referring back to Plato and Levinas and proposing "that an ethical work or event of art would be one which demanded a labour of critical thought for its ethical potential to be realized rather than offering within itself anything of the ethical" (69). In other words, good ethical theatre contains the *conditions for prompting* critical ethical thinking rather than *doing the thinking* for participants or audiences.

Hazel Barnes's (2011) chapter "Mapping ethics in applied drama and theatre" in the book *Acting on HIV* (edited by Dennis Francis) offers a detailed overview of workshops held in Johannesburg in 2008 at the Drama for Life Initial Africa Conference in Applied Drama and Theatre hosted by Drama for Life at the University of Witwatersrand. These workshops on ethics invited participants to place themselves in relation to a range of ethical quotes representing ethical positioning in the field. This work led to the posting of a co-written Ethics Declaration on the Drama for Life website. The declaration reads:

> The Ethics working group considered that the following issues should be given serious attention by all practitioners of applied drama at all stages of the process of Intervention:
>
> 1. It is accepted that ethical principles as expressed through Human Rights declarations are fundamental to all research and intervention, but that their expression and lived experience is contingent and context bound.

2. There should be acknowledgement of the ideological basis of applied drama and theatre as embedded in Freirean principles of dialogue and empowerment, with the concomitant ethical principles.

3. It is recognised that applied drama interventions may have unequal power implications; practitioners should establish a spirit of mutual respect among all parties involved and all participants in the intervention should follow the principle of doing no harm.

4. There should be transparency about the purposes, intentions and methodology of the research/intervention wherever possible.

5. At all stages the participants' informed consent must be negotiated and a spirit of reciprocity and respect among all parties should be established.

6. There should be respect for intellectual property of and by all parties.

7. Practitioners should ensure that the research and intervention are culturally sensitive.

8. The results of the research should be returned to the community.

9. The benefits of the research should be shared with the community.
(141–2)

The field did not see the publication of many new books with ethical content until the appearance in 2015 of the Bloomsbury series in Applied Theatre, co-edited by Michael Balfour and Sheila Preston. One exception to the lack of books focused on ethics between 2010 and 2015 is a 2014 title *Ethics and the Arts*, edited by Paul Mcneill (2014a). Although encompassing multiple arts practices, this collection includes a reprinted chapter from James Thompson's *Performance Affects* (2009), "Politics and ethics in applied theatre: face-to-face and disturbing the fabric of the sensible," and two chapters by editor Mcneill (2014b, 2014c) that consider presence as a key aspect of ethical praxis across the arts: "'presence' is treated as 'presencing'—as something an actor does and not a metaphysical entity—as a verb rather than a noun" (151). I will return to this point in my conclusion, but do recommend these chapters, as well as one by Miles Little, whose contribution, "Ethics and aesthetics—Joined at the hip?," does some essential work in examining the philosophical linkages between aesthetics and ethics. As Little writes, "Aesthetics and ethics are linked because they represent the philosophies that underpin human judgement. In aesthetics, the judgement is directed toward the emotional responses that individuals have to sensory perceptions. In ethics, we are concerned with judgements of interactions between humans, and between humans and other entities in our environments" (185). When we separate ethics and aesthetics we risk missing this essential linkage: how ethics informs aesthetics and vice versa.

In 2017, Alice O'Grady's edited book *Risk, Participation, and Performance Practice* features a key contribution by Clark Baim. This chapter, titled "The Drama Spiral: a decision-making model for safe, ethical, and flexible practice when incorporating personal stories in applied theatre and performance," leads to Baim's 2020 publication *Staging the Personal: A Guide to Safe and Ethical Practice.* Baim's ethical contribution here is significant as he distinguishes between "*fictionalized personal stories, positive stories from the past* (stories of strength), *stories of resolved difficulties* (stories of survival, recovery, post-traumatic growth, resilience and overcoming adversity), and *stories of difficult and unresolved issues* (stories that are still traumatic or destabilizing)" (13, emphasis in original). The Drama Spiral model allows for a gradual movement inward by a participant group, from games and creative activities to fictional/distant stories to fictionalized personal stories to positive personal stories to stories of resolved difficulties to (finally) stories of unresolved difficulties (120). I believe that Baim's Drama Spiral in practice will prevent some of the worst ethical abuses of participants that might occur with a facilitator who pushes them to disclose traumatic stories in a non-therapeutic space. It should be noted that Baim is a trained and experienced psychodramatist. And, it is clear that one should never move towards the center of the Drama Spiral without thinking ethically (and practically) about how to support participants who may be triggered by sharing stories of trauma. Working with a therapist alongside the facilitator to provide additional support to those who may be triggered by sharing stories of trauma is advised.

A 2018 title, *New Directions in Teaching Theatre Arts*, includes a chapter, "Generating ethics and social justice in applied theatre curricula," (Fliotsos and Medford 2018) that focuses on the teaching of ethics in applied theatre, another important and perhaps neglected topic in our field:

> To effectively teach ethics in an applied theatre curriculum, there are two components to address. The first is for students to clearly understand ethical concepts, such as confidentiality, informed consent, or cultural humility, as they are not part of regular undergraduate theatre curricula. The second is to look at the various models of applied theatre to identify where inherent ethical dilemmas lie and to practice how to proactively avoid those dilemmas or deal with them when they do arise. (237–8)

The appendix of this worthwhile chapter provides an applied theatre code of ethics that makes an effective addition to Barnes's code presented above.

In 2020, as I write this, the world is facing the global challenge of the coronavirus pandemic. On the plus side, it was the year that saw the appearance of several new books, including Baim's (2020), along with *Performing Care* (Stuart Fisher and Thompson 2020). Here, Thompson describes the ethics of care:

> as a mode of enquiry that seeks to draw attention to interdependent human relations as a platform from which to enunciate broader conceptions of justice. The political aspirations for a fairer world should draw on the realisation that we are mutually reliant and that a better world cannot come about without a closer awareness of our reciprocal attachment to others. (41)

Further developing his ongoing interest in ethics, and its intertwining with both aesthetics and politics, Thompson states: "The care ethics expounded here, therefore, might be premised on the intimate moment of support exercised between two people, but it is insisting on a vision of politics that asserts a contract of mutual regard that extends far wider and demands a more fundamental realignment of human relations than one might at first assume" (43). Thompson's weaving together of ethics and politics is a hallmark of his scholarship that is also evident in Chapter 4 in this collection, where he defines ethics as a "series of micropolitical dilemmas" (p. 72).

I close this section on books and chapters that address ethics in the field of theatre/applied theatre with the third edition of D. Soyini Madison's *Critical Ethnography: Method, Ethics and Performance* (2020). Madison is not writing about applied theatre; rather, her work is in the field of performance ethnography. However, her chapter on ethics (99–129) is exemplary and I include it for its value to applied theatre students and practitioners. Madison reminds us again of the value of inquiry to building ethical stances. She begins the chapter by posing key questions: "What does the ethical act really look like? How are my ethics different from or the same as yours? What principles will guide the *means* or method for us to achieve the ethical ends that we desire? How do we determine what is ethical?" (100); "Where do our systems of thinking and theories come from? To what end are we employing certain regimes of knowledge, and who or what is being silenced?" (111–12). She continues in this broad-ranging and intellectually stimulating chapter by tackling topics such as advocacy and ethics (101–2); ethics and the significance of the ethical question (103); the relationship between ethics and religion (104); ethics, faith, and environmental activism (105–6); the question of freedom (106–9); the ethics of reason, the greater good, and others (109–20); and an examination of Maria Lugones: Contemporary ethics, ethnography and loving perception (120–7). In this final section Madison draws on Lugones' 1994 chapter, "Playfulness, 'world'-travelling and loving perception," to offer valuable and fresh ways to consider ethics:

> [W]hen we travel to other worlds, we open ourselves to the greater possibility of loving perception and dialogical performance because (a) we witness and engage cultural aspects of other worlds; (b) we witness and engage with others' sense of self in their own world; (c) we experience how we are perceived *through others' eyes*; (d) we are now bodies that must touch, see, and listen to each other because we are inhabiting a space in their world where distance cannot separate you; (e) we witness and engage the Other as a *subject* even as he or she may

be subjugated, and as a result, meanings of power and positionality begin to arise between us; (f) we are dependent on each other for the possibility of being understood. Traveling to another world threatens arrogant perception and makes loving perception possible. Loving perception evokes dialogical performance and sustains it. Loving perception is not sentimental or sappy, nor is it a romanticization of the other. (126)

Madison concludes her chapter with a text box on empathy, highlighting the importance of this emotional capacity to ethical practice. This text, written by an African-American woman scholar, and drawing on the work of a Latina scholar to examine ethics in performance, does some important work in offsetting the predominantly white Eurocentric voices found in most of the sources included in this chapter.

I turn now to journal articles on ethics in applied theatre.

Key Articles 1985–2020

No literature survey on ethics in performance contexts should exclude performance theorist and performance ethnographer Dwight Conquergood's much-cited and reprinted article "Performing as a moral act: ethical dimensions of the ethnography of performance" (1985). In order to address the moral and ethical concerns of his performances of ethnographic cross-cultural encounters, Conquergood outlines four "ethical pitfalls" (4) of performative stances towards a culture under investigation. He considers an ethnographic performance that corresponds to any of these four pitfalls as ethically problematic. The key to authentically conveying a culture is through "dialogical performance," "the moral center that transcends and reconciles" (5).

Conquergood's four problematic stances are: The Custodian's Rip-Off, or a stance of "strong attraction toward the other coupled with extreme detachment" (5); The Enthusiast's Infatuation, or the realm of the "quick-fix, pick-up artist" that is unethical because it "trivializes the other" (6); The Curator's Exhibitionism, or the practice of astonishing the audience rather than understanding, in which the ethical issue is sensationalism (7); and The Skeptic's Cop-Out, or the refuge of "cowards and cynics" who refuse to face up and struggle with the ethical tensions of performing culturally sensitive materials (8). Alternatively, the positive stance of Dialogical Performance (also cited in Madison's 2020 book) aims "to bring self and other together so that they can question, debate and challenge one another" (9), a critical discourse that extends beyond the stage to engage its audience.

The first decade (*c.* 2000–2009)

The shift to discourse more focused on the emergent field of applied theatre (in comparison to the sister field of drama education) can be seen in a *Research in Drama Education* special issue, "On ethics," from 2005. As Helen Nicholson (2005b) asks in her editorial for this issue:

> What are the ethical responsibilities of researchers when practice is developed collaboratively with participants? How might the drama be affected if participants know that they are part of a research project which might lead to publication? When is it ethically appropriate to ask participants for their consent? How might the voices of the participants be represented? What aspects of practice might be selected for analysis and opened for public scrutiny? (119)

She goes on to consider how ethics intertwine with both aesthetics and political activism, asking, "What motivated the research—aesthetics, ethics or activism? Who stands to benefit most from the research? How do researchers' moral sensibilities and activist commitments inform and transform each other?" (120). The issue contains a number of excellent articles that focus on a range of projects across many countries. Of particular interest are the essays by Bill McDonnell and Amanda Stuart Fisher. In the former, McDonnell calls for more "thick description" (127) of applied theatre projects, and more inclusive dialogues with participants in terms of capturing and relaying information about a project. In the latter, Stuart Fisher draws on French social philosopher Alain Badiou to consider that

> [O]ur task as applied theatre practitioners can be construed as one of generating an encounter or intervention that enables the truth process of a group or a community to emerge. But how do we do this? Perhaps more importantly how do we guarantee fidelity to the truth of the situation, whilst not shaping our actions by our own normatively inscribed morality and preformed sense of what is "good"? (249)

This entire issue has the potential for offering its readers (particularly students of applied theatre) a series of rich sources upon which an ethical practice might be built.

Finally, in this section, I include David Kerr's 2009 article "Ethics in applied theatre," which offers a welcome look at how ethical thinking plays out in various theatre for development projects in the context of a number of African nations. Kerr reflects usefully on various projects dating back to the 1980s and offers ethical insights such as: changing the lyrics and therefore the meaning of Indigenous songs (177–9); navigating through negative audience response (in this case, to a play on HIV) (179–80); the need to protect communities and students from authoritarian government attacks (including imprisonment and torture) in response to radical applied theatre projects (180–2); how ethics plays out in mediated settings such as television or radio dramas, and on the internet (182–5). He concludes that "ethics need to be flexible enough to adapt to different times, geographical locations of shifting social, political or economic circumstances" (186). These ethical principles of flexibility and adaptation are helpful to both emerging and established applied theatre workers.

We can see, through the first decade of the twenty-first century's questioning discourse on ethics in our field, the evolution of ideas about how to approach the work with principles of aesthetics, ethics, truth, and social justice, and the need for consideration of the tensions between individual and collective belief systems. The next decade continues to consider these ethical tensions and to add new thinking to this discourse.

The second decade (2010–2020)

In 2010, Fisher and Smith's article "First do no harm" offered important advice for theatre practitioners on how to gain informed consent from participants. The authors include a sample consent form (162), and of particular value is their advice to practitioners to be wary of stepping over the line into therapy or risking traumatizing others. As they say in the article's conclusion: "It is our hope that, through this proposal for informed consent, practitioners in applied theatre settings will develop an enhanced appreciation of the need to provide clear and open invitations to applied theatre work" (163).

Rustom Bharucha (2011) continues this critical discourse in his "Problematising applied theatre," in which he draws on philosophers Jacques Rancière and Elaine Scarry, among others, to argue that "what I have come to learn from my own experience of the theatre and of what lies beyond the exit of theatre is the recognition of the pain of the Other, which could be the first step in the beginnings of a radical sociality" (382). His key ethical point is that "we may have no other option but to be as vigilant and caring in our exploration of the pain of others, opening ourselves to our own pain in the process. Pain does not have to be locked in the other, any more so than oppression has to be designated outside ourselves" (381). The implications of this thinking involve applied theatre workers seeing themselves as bound up in the struggles of their participants, and that recognizing this entanglement, and the pain it may cause, is an ethical stance of some significance to our field.

Daniel Banks (2011), in his article "The question of cultural diplomacy: acting ethically," contributes to ethical discourse through his focus on how applied theatre practitioners can be "good guests" (112) when working in cultural contexts dissimilar to their own:

> Cultural diplomacy, at its most human and aware, would be self-reflective: constantly striving for better ways to interact; consciously working to deconstruct multiple levels of hierarchy in a room; and seeking the space of pure presence where participants paradoxically

celebrate the implicit humanity that connects all people, while learning
about significant differences. (119)

We work in a field that, although shifting over time towards increasing
diversity, remains dominated by white scholars working in Black,
Indigenous, or People of Color communities. Banks reminds us to
remain sensitive and aware of cultural differences *within* participant
groups as well as *between* facilitators and participants. What Banks calls
the "space of pure presence" (119) is a concept I will return to in the
conclusion to this chapter.

Next, in Leffler's (2012) article "Replacing the sofa with the
spotlight: interrogating the therapeutic value of personal testimony
within community-based theatre," we hear about a South African-
based project in which participants were encouraged by one of the
facilitators (not the author) to tell personal stories of frustration,
some of which were validated more than others as "stories of
harassment and emotional abuse" (347). Leffler's analysis of his
white middle-class discomfort with this approach allows him to
recognize how religion, and the process of confession, may be valued
by participants in ways that he does not share as a secularist. He
concludes his article with these ethical questions: "Should non-local
scholar-practitioners challenge an 'aesthetic of injury' out of our
own sense of what may be therapeutic, or should we accept it as local
knowledge which might constructively challenge our own academic
convictions? How can we proceed with both cultural sensitivity
and integrity?" (352). Here, Leffler echoes Banks's (2011) call for
the tactical skills of cultural diplomacy to navigate successfully in
cultures different from our own.

Kay Hepplewhite (2013), in "Here's one I made earlier: dialogues
on the construction of an applied theatre practitioner," considers how
applied theatre practitioners are trained, arguably an understudied
aspect of the field. In her interviews with twelve experienced applied
theatre artists, Hepplewhite draws out the key areas required in
educating future practitioners. She offers a model from nursing

called "ethical comportment" (52) as a framing for her interview analysis:

[Ethical comportment] combines aspects of expertise: having specialised techniques and an aptitude (skilfulness), the ability to make ethical judgements appropriate to context which consider the wider political impact of their practice choices and actions, and interactive "people skills" embodied in a demeanour (comportment). It offers a potential way to define what a "good practitioner" may look like, and also guidance on how to go about constructing one. (53)

She goes on to argue that

An applied theatre practitioner must also negotiate and assert their practice within a field of critical discourse, being reflexively aware of their own motivations whilst empowering the perceived concerns of the participants; championing a political vision and brokering wider social impact, whilst juggling the diverse agendas of others in the context, including stakeholders beyond the theatre participants. An ethically informed understanding of these issues is integral to informing good practice choices. (59–60)

Later in her essay, Hepplewhite warns that "It is bad practice to let theatre students loose in community contexts without full and proper preparation" (63), an important ethical consideration in training. She concludes by reminding us that "Applied theatre practitioners are complex and intuitive professionals who embody arts and social skills which are hard to identify and, consequently, to teach. Negotiation of this challenge presents an increasingly pressing task for educators" (70). It is becoming clear through this historical appraisal that the challenge to teach what is "hard to identify" is as much an ethical as it is an educational one.

Caroline Wake's (2013) article "To witness mimesis" makes a critical ethical contribution in its layered critique of a documentary refugee theatre production in Australia called *Through the Wire*. Wake considers the ethics of how this play was created and performed, and highlights what she calls the "traumatic reveal" (111), in which the audience learns that one of the four actors in the play was performing his own story, eliciting audible gasps from the audience that Wake considers to be sensationalist and voyeuristic. She also calls this production to ethical account for its use of "refugee as spectacle" under the gaze of audiences that "encourage the spectator to elide difference rather than come to terms with it" (120). Harking back to Conquergood's (1985) ethical model, this is a clear example of Curator's Exhibitionism (7) in practice, and a good reminder of how easy it can be to create unethical work even with the best of intentions.

The ethics of applied theatre resonates in many ways with the ethics of care (Gilligan 1982; Noddings [1984] 2013), and there is a marked increase in the discourse in the field of this and related concepts beginning around 2014. Indeed, *Performing Care* (2020) discussed above, offers a rich examination of the ways that other care professions—such as teaching, nursing, and social work—understand and practice the ethics of care. But let me now turn to Anne Smith's 2014 article "Maximizing empowerment in applied theatre with refugees and migrants in the United Kingdom: facilitation shaped by an ethic of care," which "highlights the necessity for all participants to be able to give as well as receive care and the impact of this upon achieving a sense of belonging" (177). Smith introduces readers to this key concept: "The ethic of care is a moral theory that foregrounds the interdependence of individuals and the salience of taking responsibility for particular others in a nuanced and individualized way which seeks to see those individuals empowered rather than maintaining a state of passive compliance and dependency" (178). The ethics of care as practiced in applied theatre can involve participants in seemingly simple ways such as: helping to set up or restore a rehearsal space, sharing food and drink with others, or doing the washing up (180). "Members of the group become host to one another, serving one another refreshments and demonstrating welcome and care to people arriving" (180). Here, participants engage in acts of generosity and hospitality rooted in reciprocity to create the sense of community so essential to making good theatre.

Kathy Bishop's 2014 article "Six perspectives in search of an ethical solution" surveys six applied theatre scholars (Johnny Saldaña, Jim Mienczakowski, Kathleen Gallagher, Tim Prentki, Anthony Jackson, and James Thompson) for what they view as the moral imperatives underpinning their practice. In analyzing these emailed surveys, Bishop identifies the five distinct approaches taken by her respondents as rooted in justice, critique, care, profession (or the artfulness of theatre-making), and moral integrity. She concludes with a "synergized moral imperative— Value the forms of theatre and research as you critique, care and choose with good character" (73–4) as her "guiding 'north star'" (74).

James Thompson's (2015) significant contribution "Towards an aesthetics of care" is reprinted in *Performing Care* (Fisher and Thompson 2020). In it, Thompson turns his attention to feminist theories on the ethics of care—led by Carol Gilligan (1982) and Nel Noddings ([1984] 2013)—that has had a significant impact in care professions such as education, child and youth care, social work, and nursing. The ethics of care is a response to a careless world, and as Thompson summarizes, "care ethics draws attention to our reciprocal relations with others, or reliance on others, as a source of ethical enquiry" (434). Thompson goes on to place this ethical notion within the larger framework of social justice:

> Care ethics, then, suggests we can learn about seeking justice and a practice that urges a fairer world from relationships where we are called to care for or have experienced the care of some other: where our interdependence and reciprocal needs are highlighted. ... The political aspirations for a fairer world should draw on the realisation that we are mutually reliant and that a better world cannot come about without a closer awareness of our reciprocal attachment to others. (434)

Thompson then applies this "closer awareness of our reciprocal attachment to others" to aesthetics in our field, concluding that "The shape and feel of the relationships at the heart of the project are its aesthetics—whether presented in front of hundreds or in a small circle in a rehearsal room" (439). Here, we see once more the vital connection between ethics and aesthetics; how we create theatre is infused with both aesthetic and ethical decisions made throughout the process.

The next entry focuses on the topic of how to better approach the uses of personal stories in applied theatre. Yasmine Kandil's 2016 article "Personal stories in applied theatre contexts: redefining the blurred lines," reflects on an applied theatre project in which she was a paid participant/actor. Kandil weighs the level of discomfort—the feelings of shame and embarrassment—that she experienced around how her story was shared and performed. These reflections lead her to some strong recommendations about "the exploration of an ethical way to elicit and utilise personal stories" (210). Her recommendations include assessing with participants the overall purpose and agenda of a given project, including how consent for the use of personal stories should be continuously returned to throughout the shifts and changes of rehearsal and staging. She also sees the importance of participant agency and autonomy, including the right to refuse to share a story at any point in the process. In her conclusion, Kandil poses a key ethical question: "How many novice participants engage in this type of practice wholeheartedly trusting the experience, and end up feeling isolated and alone in facing the overwhelming feelings sometimes associated with telling and sharing their personal narratives?" (212). I would follow this up with another question: How can we ensure this kind of experience of embarrassment, shame, and isolation is never experienced by participants in our projects?

In 2017, Nehemiah Chivandikwa published an article reflecting on his experiences of facilitating applied theatre projects with disabled students in Zimbabwe. As in Bharucha's (2011) contribution, Chivandikwa (2017) acknowledges the ethical necessity of exposing himself to the painful oppression experienced by his participants. He chooses to share an embarrassing personal story in a playback theatre session that allows his own vulnerability to build deeper and more trusting relationships with participants. In co-creating what he calls a "political-ethical approach," Chivandikwa advises that "both creative and political-ethical issues become the collective responsibility of everyone" (95) and suggests that "such an approach mandates non-disabled TfD facilitators to engage in multiple and potentially contradictory tasks and positions such as colleague, organizer, pedagogue, diplomat, learner, co-activist and adviser, in order to engage participants with disabilities in intensive encounters to advance radical disability politics" (95).

This section on ethics discourse from journals concludes with articles from Lazaroo and Ishak (2019) and Brown Adelman, Norman and Hamidi (2020). "The tyranny of emotional distance? emotion/al work and emotional labour in applied theatre projects" (Lazaroo and Ishak 2019) provides a look at how both facilitator and participants are required to carry out emotional labor, asserting that "Our research suggests that it is … important to see how emotion management and emotional labour affect applied theatre participants. This is especially important in a context that is informed by social justice, where participants have a high degree of emotional investment in creating awareness about social inequalities and are acting as agents of change" (75). There are clear ethical implications in requesting emotional labor from participants, and this article provides welcome guidance for our field. Brown Adelman, Norman and Hamidi (2020) explore identity issues in their article "Identity matters. All. The. Time. Questions to encourage best practices in applied theatre." They ask a series of questions as their subheadings and begin to answer them: "How does identity matter?" (16); "Should we use our own identities to engage with others?" (18); "How do we manage the intersections of identity?" (19); "Is it artistically necessary to think about identity?" (20); "How can we build awareness around identity?" (21); "What other ethical questions should we consider?" (23); and finally, "Should we personally be doing the social justice and anti-racist work that we hope to inspire others to do with our applied theatre performances?" (24)—to which the authors respond, "The answer here is quite simple. Yes." (24). Both of these articles present ethical entanglements of emotional labor and identity issues of consequence that are reflected on through practice.

Conclusion: Crafting a Curriculum on Ethics in Applied Theatre

Diana Taylor's 2020 book *¡Presente! The Politics of Presence* places the quality of *presence* at the heart of socially and politically engaged performance practice:

> ¡Presente!, with and without exclamation marks, depends on context. As much an act, a word, and an attitude, ¡presente! can be understood as a war cry in the face of nullification; an act of solidarity as in responding, showing up, and standing with; a commitment to witnessing; a joyous accompaniment; present among, with, and to, walking and talking with others; an ontological and epistemic reflection on presence and subjectivity as process; an ongoing *becoming* as opposed to a static *being*, as participatory and relational, founded on mutual recognition; a showing or display before others; a militant attitude, gesture, or declaration of presence; the "ethical imperative," as Gayatri Spivak calls it, to stand up to and speak against injustice.[3] ¡Presente! always engages more than one. Sometimes it expresses political movement, sometimes a being together, walking down the street or celebrating and enacting our response, position and attitude in our encounter with others, even when the other has been disappeared, or hides its face. (4, emphasis in original)

Across the book, Taylor documents her lived experiences with community groups fighting for liberation in the North, Central and South Americas (38–9). She closes with a powerful story from Mexico that manifests an ethics of care, of being present with, to, and for others (245). A woman named Leonilla Vasquez sent her two daughters out to buy bread and milk in February of 1995. On their way home, the girls encountered a train carrying migrant workers north. These workers were crowded onto the roof of the train and called out to the girls for food and water. With no hesitation, the girls reached up their arms to share what they had. This act of selfless generosity (from those who have little enough themselves) became a movement, led by the girls' mother, called Las Patronas that prepares food for hundreds of Central

American migrants to this day (246). Taylor reflects on this act: "The women hold up their hands with food and water. Not for themselves, not just for their ethnic or political kin, but for strangers. That's all. That's everything. If this empathetic gesture animates a life-affirming form of ¡Presente!, how, I wondered, might I/WE be able to emulate, replicate, transform it into sustained political practice?" (247).

For applied theatre workers and artists, the final line of Taylor's powerful book resonates as an ethical call to presence, service, and care, and the necessary entanglement of poetics and politics, aesthetics, and ethics: "¡Presente! Holding out one's hands to others, is the beginning of everything" (250). My hope is that this collection of readings on ethics in applied theatre will be utilized as the curricular foundation for courses on this topic, alongside the other chapters in this collection, requiring ongoing ethical entanglements in praxis that are rooted in the key ethical precepts of service, presence, and care.

Notes

1   I wish to thank Professor Emeritus Juliana Saxton for her very helpful critical edits and input on this chapter.
2   The second edition of *The Applied Theatre Reader* appeared in 2021, co-edited by Tim Prentki and Nicola Abraham. It contains both retained and new material in the section "Ethics of representation" (pp. 69–128).
3   See Spivak 2012.

References

Baim, C. (2017), "The drama spiral: a decision-making model for safe, ethical, and flexible practice when incorporating personal stories in applied theatre and performance," in A. O'Grady (ed.), *Risk, Participation, and Performance Practice*. New York: Palgrave Macmillan, pp. 79–110.

Banks, D. (2011), "The question of cultural diplomacy: acting ethically," *Theatre Topics*, 21 (2), 109–23.

Barnes, H. (2011), "Mapping ethics in applied drama and theatre," in D. A. Francis (ed.), *Acting on HIV*. Rotterdam: Sense Publishing, pp. 131–44.

Bharucha, R. (2011), "Problematising applied theatre: a search for alternative paradigms," *Research in Drama Education: The Journal of Applied Theatre and Performance*, 16 (3), 366–84.

Bishop, K. (2014), "Six perspectives in search of an ethical solution: utilising a moral imperative with a multiple ethics paradigm to guide research-based theatre/applied theatre," *Research in Drama Education: The Journal of Applied Theatre and Performance*, 19 (1), 64–75.

Boal, A. (1979), *Theatre of the Oppressed*, trans. C. A. and M. Leal MacBride and E. Fryer. London: Pluto Press.

Brown Adelman, R., Norman, T., and Hamidi, S. Y. (2020), "Identity matters. All. The. Time. Questions to encourage best practices in applied theatre," *ArtsPraxis*, 7 (2b), 12–25.

Chivandikwa, N. (2017), "A political-ethical approach to disability in a Zimbabwean theatre for development context," *Applied Theatre Research*, 5 (2), 83–97.

Conquergood, D. C. (1985), "Performing as a moral act: ethical dimensions of the ethnography of performance," *Literature in Performance*, 5 (2), 1–13.

Fisher, T. J. and Smith, L. L. (2010), "First do no harm: informed consent principles for trust and understanding in applied theatre practice," *Journal of Applied Arts and Health*, 1 (2), 157–64.

Fliotsos, A. and Medford, G. S. (eds) (2018), *New Directions in Teaching Theatre Arts*. New York: Palgrave Macmillan. doi:10.1007/978-3-319-89767-7_14

Gilligan, C. (1982), *In a Different Voice: Psychological Theory and Women's Development*. Cambridge, MA: Harvard University Press.

Hepplewhite, K. (2013), "Here's one I made earlier: dialogues on the construction of an applied theatre practitioner," *Theatre, Dance and Performance Training*, 4 (1), 52–72.

Kandil, Y. (2016), "Personal stories in applied theatre contexts: redefining the blurred lines," *Research in Drama Education: The Journal of Applied Theatre and Performance*, 21 (2), 201–13.

Kerr, D. (2009), "Ethics in applied theatre," *South African Theatre Journal*, 23 (1), 177–87.

Lazaroo, N. and Ishak, I. (2019), "The tyranny of emotional distance? Emotion/al work and emotional labour in applied theatre projects," *Applied Theatre Research*, 7 (1), 67–77. doi:10.1386/atr_00006_1

Leffler, E. (2012), "Replacing the sofa with the spotlight: interrogating the therapeutic value of personal testimony within community-based theatre," *Research in Drama Education: The Journal of Applied Theatre and Performance*, 17 (3), 347–53.

Lehmann, H-T. (2006), *Postdramatic Theatre*, trans. Karen Jürs-Munby. New York: Routledge.

Little, M. (2014), "Ethics and aesthetics—joined at the hip?," in P. Mcneill (ed.), *Ethics and the Arts*. Dordrecht: Springer, pp. 179–87.

Madison, D. S. (2020), *Critical Ethnography: Method, Ethics and Performance* (3rd ed.). Thousand Oaks, CA: SAGE.

McDonnell, B. (2005), "The politics of historiography—towards an ethics of representation," *Research in Drama Education: The Journal of Applied Theatre and Performance*, 10 (2), 127–38.

Mcneill, P. (ed.) (2014a), *Ethics and the Arts*. Dordrecht: Springer.

Mcneill, P. (2014b), "Presence in performance: an enigmatic quality," in P. Mcneill (ed.), *Ethics and the Arts*. Dordrecht: Springer, pp. 137–50.

Mcneill, P. (2014c), "Ethics and performance: enacting presence," in P. Mcneill (ed.), *Ethics and the Arts*. Dordrecht: Springer, pp. 151–63.

Nicholson, H. (2005a), *Applied Drama: The Gift of Theatre*. New York: Palgrave Macmillan.

Nicholson, H. (ed.) (2005b), "On ethics" (special issue), *Research in Drama Education: The Journal of Applied Theatre and Performance*, 10 (2), 119–25.

Noddings, N. [1984] (2013), *Caring: A Relational Approach to Ethics and Moral Education* (2nd ed.). Berkeley: University of California Press.

O'Grady, A. (ed.) (2017), *Risk, Participation, and Performance Practice*. New York: Palgrave Macmillan.

Prendergast, M. and Saxton, J. (2020), "Applied theatre and education: we are not-yet …, " *Canadian Theatre Review*, 181, 8–12.

Prentki, T. and Abraham, N. (2021), *The Applied Theatre Reader* (2nd ed.). New York: Routledge.

Prentki, T. and Preston, S. (eds) (2009), *The Applied Theatre Reader*. New York: Routledge.

Ridout, N. (2009), *Theatre & Ethics*. New York: Palgrave Macmillan.

Smith, A. (2014), "Maximizing empowerment in applied theatre with refugees and migrants in the United Kingdom: facilitation shaped by an ethic of care," *Journal of Arts and Communities*, 6 (3), 177–88.

Spivak, G. C. (2012), *An Aesthetic Education in the Era of Globalization*. Cambridge, MA: Harvard University Press.

Stuart Fisher, A. (2005), "Developing an ethics of practice in applied theatre: Badiou and fidelity to the truth of an event," *Research in Drama Education: The Journal of Applied Theatre and Performance*, 10 (2), 247–52.

Stuart Fisher, A. (2009), "Bearing witness: the position of theatre makers in the telling of trauma," in T. Prentki and S. Preston (eds), *The Applied Theatre Reader*. New York: Routledge, pp. 108–15.

Stuart Fisher, A. and Thompson, J. (eds) (2020), *Performing Care: New Perspectives on Socially-Engaged Performance*. Manchester: Manchester University Press.

Taylor, D. (2020), *¡Presente! The Politics of Presence*. Durham, NC: Duke University Press.

Taylor, P. (2003), *Applied Theatre: Creating Transformative Encounters in the Community*. New York: Routledge.

Thompson, J. (2003), *Applied Theatre: Bewilderment and Beyond*. New York: Peter Lang.

Thompson, J. (2005), *Digging up Stories: Applied Theatre, Performance and War*. Manchester: Manchester University Press.

Thompson, J. (2009), *Performance Affects: Applied Theatre and the End of Effect*. New York: Palgrave Macmillan.

Thompson, J. (2015), "Towards an aesthetics of care," *Research in Drama Education: The Journal of Applied Theatre and Performance*, 20 (4), 430–41.

Wake, C. (2013), "To witness mimesis: the politics, ethics, and aesthetics of testimonial theatre in *Through the Wire*," *Modern Drama*, 56 (1), 102–25.

4

A Dialogue with James Thompson: Paper Airplanes, Good Care, and Working *Alongside* Each Other

Kirsten Sadeghi-Yekta

James is in Lisbon, Portugal; Kirsten in North Vancouver, Canada. The following chapter was developed from a series of conversations, the first of which took place on Zoom in the midst of the second wave of the Covid-19 pandemic, in October 2020. James had been working in Portugal but had also been supporting an old friend and her son, providing some "hands on" care, at the same time as he'd been researching for his new book on *care aesthetics.*

In this conversation James reflects on how his thinking on ethical dilemmas has evolved and discusses concepts connected to ethics such as care, love, and aesthetics. Each section is a response to a question from Kirsten, summarized in its subtitle.

The First Time You Actively Started Thinking about Ethical Implications or Ethical Questions in Our Field

It is always difficult to reflect backwards on motivations for practice or writing. I don't want to smooth out what I wrote then—or make it more coherent than it was! So, these reflections are very much from where I am today in 2020, rather than a justification of past opinions. Back then I don't know if I would have called it ethics. However, one of the things that surprised me when I first went into a prison setting was that it challenged the assumptions that I had about theatre practice. I think I wrote in the original applied theatre book that the straightforward idea of theatre as a way of giving somebody a voice is challenged on walking into a prison, as you are immediately unsure if some of the people need a voice quite in the way you'd thought. You ask yourself exactly what sort of a voice does this person need? The experience disturbed a certainty that I brought with me—I don't know whether that's an ethical question, but I think applied theatre practice constantly challenged assumptions, and those challenges then reshaped the practices in which we were engaged. It is the relationship between an ethics brought to practice and an ethics forged through practice. Bringing theatre as a tool to give marginalized people a voice suddenly doesn't quite work out in a simplistic way when there are multiple voices of people in prisons; some of them might be abusive, some of them might be racist, some of them might be victims of racism. There are many different voices and therefore a practice presupposing an oppressed, single voice suddenly becomes problematic. I didn't call it ethics then, but it certainly made me go, "Okay, this ain't as simple as I imagine it to be." And I think back then I was maybe more excited about the work because of that sense of disturbance. This is, I suppose, the original bewilderment idea—so an original ethical principle was holding onto that sense of confusion. I wouldn't call it that now, but that sense of needing to constantly question what you're doing at the same time as being quite excited—again the wrong word—but quite in awe of the questions it provokes. So right at the beginning it was more about a dynamic of dilemmas I think I faced in some of those practices that provoked thinking about a sort of micropolitics, and I wonder whether ethics for me was a series of micropolitical dilemmas.

How Our Language is Significant for Ethics and the Problems of Using Terms such as "Marginalized" for Groups We Work With

I think war zones are the places where that is acutely true. We couldn't make assumptions about who was vulnerable or marginal, or who was powerful and who wasn't. If you have one group who self-identify as oppressed and are armed to fight against another (who might be a state but whose supporters also identify as "marginal" or "oppressed"), using these terms either makes you part of the discourse of the war—and therefore part of the war effort—or immediately identified as taking a side. Language involves you and you can't make claims that you are outside the problems of the context.

There is a sense that we have a deficit model of applied theatre where the artists have something and the communities or institutions lack something, and the meeting of the two is providing something to meet the deficit of that community. I've been part and parcel of this model, so this is not me saying something about those practitioners over there. It is absolutely part of the way I thought about bringing the arts to a community that doesn't have arts—it was immediately an assumption that we have something that they don't. And as you said, the language of marginal etc. falls into this model. We perhaps need to think about practice that is more mutual—a complementary learning or creative process.

In *Applied Theatre: Bewilderment and Beyond* (2003), You Say "Discussion of Ethics becomes More Acutely Problematic and Simultaneously More Necessary in the Context of War"

I still agree with this, to an extent. However, I also believe we shouldn't present certain contexts as fundamentally more challenging or difficult than other contexts; working in a Vancouver primary school might actually provide a huge range of ethical debates that are just as powerful. In war zones you meet a lot of people that are very clear about what's going on. People are really clear about their truth claims: about who's right, who's wrong, what the history is, what the history isn't, what sort of work should be done, what work shouldn't be done. And therefore, when you're in the middle of that, you get pulled along in that system and you need to be hyperconscious of it. I remember, when working in certain conflict contexts, hearing people explain what I was doing: "This is James, what he's doing here is this," and I sat there thinking, "Well, I don't think I'm quite doing that." And because you realize that you're in a place where people are competing for claims of truth, people kept on claiming and framing my practice to fit with particular perspectives. "This is theatre for the rights of community X," or, "This is theatre for reconciliation." And I go, "Well, yeah, sort of, but also not that." I think the ethical debate at that stage was how to keep practicing, staying true to what I believed, while also respecting the beliefs of the people I was working with and making the work that was being developed of use to those communities. It was in northern Sri Lanka in the early 2000s where some of those dilemmas were really spelled out to me. It was difficult at times, very difficult.

There was one moment mentioned in the applied theatre book, where we did a Forum Theatre piece on a roadblock. It was a young woman trying to get through, but she doesn't have her ID card. The group solution was to kill the soldier manning the roadblock. I thought maybe that is their answer, but I just don't believe in it even as it was being played out outside the workshop room. In that community many did support armed violence as a legitimate response to their situation. The snag for me was a commitment to creating theatre work that enables a community to interrogate its own problems and develop solutions at the same time as not believing their solution. So, my internal dialogue was going, "Yes, it's a great principle for applied theatre"—but in that moment I thought that it was just wrong. I didn't believe killing someone was the solution (and we perhaps don't have space here to explain whether this was particular to my view of the Sri Lankan civil war, the Sri Lankan civil war at that moment in its history, or wars more generally). All said, I think in that moment I did go, "Fine, okay, right that's the solution," but I didn't really know what to do. In terms of ethics—whether they are principles brought to or forged through practice—here I am suggesting that I had a position that could not shift, and I didn't want it to be hidden. It was not a claim that it was right. But in this context, I wanted to find a way to feel confident enough to say that I don't believe killing people is a solution. I wanted to find a way not to deny the position that I held—while acknowledging it could be wrong.

If I could speak to my younger self, I would probably criticize my use of Boal's Forum Theatre in this setting—which demands antagonists and protagonists in a situation where those roles are already clearly delineated—with one community claiming to be the protagonists and another community contradicting them and saying, "No you're not, you're the antagonists." I had presented a Theatre of the Oppressed framework into a situation where those terms were already under dispute, and I allowed one community to adopt them unproblematically. Perhaps what I should have done is say, "Let's not use those terms because they are the terms that are already at play in the violent confrontations that shape this conflict." So, it'll be more interesting to say: "I'm not going to work with you using a form that frames the scenes we create as an absolute opposition between two forces, because that's what is part of the problem here. Can we speak about what's going on in your lives in a different way?" I still hold the Boal training I had really dear. I still love that work, but there's something about the Theatre of the Oppressed model and particularly Forum Theatre, in a highly conflictual situation, that just doesn't work.

The Challenges of Staging and Witnessing Stories in War Zones

I think staging stories can be an amazing, reflective learning process. What I've noticed is that it changes whether the witness is a co-community witness reflecting on a story that's part of all their lives, or whether it's a group with representatives of different communities and they present a story that is contested. Also, I think the nature of the witness is a real test. There is a difference if a witness is part of the community or the witness or audience is someone to whom you're making a plea. Is it "let's listen to our story," or "will you listen to my story"? The latter makes a claim—it is trying to convince you of a certain truth or feel a certain way about me. I think that is a powerful relationship but also a potentially problematic one. What claim is made and what demand is made of the witness are confusing and you have to be really clear what you're doing. So, for example, if it's a community of people with a particular history and they're making an appeal to a group of medical professionals. The proposal is that this community is being treated badly by health services and they're going to create a piece that reflects on that and it's going to be performed for medics. You know what the claim is: you're making an appeal to them. But we have to be really clear on that relationship. Are we petitioning people who actually have the power to hear and then act on that petition?

Some of these questions came out in my *Digging up Stories* book [2005], where someone created a story which half the group said just wasn't true. A participant read a mural image as a massacre that had happened to the Tamil community, and a section of the group simply said that the massacre did not exist. For a number, the massacre story was a crucial part of their identity. It wasn't a story of something out there; it was an embodied or felt part of their history. To have it denied, to have people go, "It is a fiction, it never really happened," felt to a number of the participants like an attack on their bodies. The person telling the story of the massacre was someone who wanted to have the story witnessed, but in fact he was also deliberately using the telling of that story as a challenge to the people present who he knew would deny its existence. The person telling the story had a right to have that story told, but they weren't an innocent storyteller having their truth denied. A victim telling this story of the oppression of his community. He was making a claim to a truth of that story that he knew would provoke some of those present, and therefore he was cleverly working with the dynamic of the challenge that storytelling can make to a witness. He knew exactly how provocative this story was in that environment. Again, it goes back to your question about language. Rather than seeing this as a workshop with "vulnerable" people, we need to frame them as sophisticated theatre makers who knew the physical impact a story can have on people, either affirming or denying its reality.

Interestingly, a piece I wrote about the London Bubble Theatre piece *Grandchildren of Hiroshima* [Thompson 2017] is also very much about witnessing. It draws from the political scientist Norman Geras's work on the role of the bystander during the Holocaust and what he calls the "contract of mutual indifference." This, for him, was the social contract through which bystanders didn't stop Jews from being taken from their communities and sent to the concentration camps in the Second World War. I argued that basing moral action (or lack of moral action) on the notion of the bystander, the witness to the arrest of Jewish people, was problematic for a piece of theatre that was focused on the bombing of Hiroshima. My case is there were no bystanders to nuclear war— Hiroshima and Nagasaki were massacres where everyone was killed. The bomb dropped on everyone, so it raises the question of how do you stage a piece about an event that wasn't witnessed? It didn't have one group who failed to act—who failed as witnesses. Everyone was targeted. The article was trying to work out what it means not to have a witness—for an ethical appeal to the witness not to be the structure around which the play can be built. A contemporary play on a historical incident that is not making the point that there was a "contract of mutual indifference" and the moral action would involve the witness taking action through a "contract of mutual regard." The play was performed to an audience of people in Hiroshima—from Hiroshima and in the city for the commemoration of the nuclear bombing. My point is that it was not an appeal based on witness—but on our duty as a participant in the history of the event. We aren't "watchers" who are appealed to act—we are either targets of the American bomb, or, in the case of Western viewers, its beneficiaries. I prefer to see ourselves as participants in events in this way, rather than witnesses, which feels less involved—less implicated.

The Connection between Affect and Ethics in *Performance Affects: Applied Theatre and the End of Effect* (2009)

The start of that book was an account of the evenings' singing and dancing in Sri Lanka and me thinking we're going to get back to the workshop tomorrow morning and then realizing the singing and dancing in the evening is so much better than anything I was doing in the daytime. And simply asking the question, why did we think this wasn't the important bit and the daytime workshops were the important bit? I suppose it was something about the importance of the arts to those communities and registering that rather than searching for something else. So, there might be something ethical in trusting in the performance and creative arts skills of communities that are already in place. I suppose the bigger ethical question was who has the power to determine what is seen in these circumstances. Usually, it is the white guy who gets invited to go there, write about the workshops and what they did or did not achieve. My shift was to admit that this misses a huge amount of the work, and in many ways, this reorientation was the origin of the *In Place of War* project. When I first read about the arts work in northern Sri Lanka, there was one book by Ranjini Obeyesekere which said—and I am unfairly summarizing—"There is no artwork in the north because of the war." I then went to the north and found this diverse, vibrant arts community. So, I suppose, affirming the importance of affect was a response to it being ignored, and there is an ethics in that act of redirecting attention. I also think my focus on affect was an affirmation of the importance of the aesthetic experience that shapes applied theatre practice. And an aesthetic experience is by no means something detached from an ethical experience.

If you accept that aesthetics can be relational, that it can be a sensory experience between people in a process, then the distinction between an aesthetic experience and an ethical relation is really hard to untangle. Once you say aesthetics isn't a picture on the wall, but it is a set of relations between people over time, then you're dealing with ethics and aesthetics simultaneously. It is simultaneous, as it has a sensory quality—it has a form, it has beauty and all those things—but it also has politics, so they are embedded in each other. The basic instruction that we all know in a drama workshop—please stand in a circle—is simultaneously an ethical and aesthetic demand. A circle has an aesthetic and a pedagogical ethic—the democracy of the circle is seen and felt. It many ways—jumping forward many years!—it would be the opening gambit in a workshop that has an aesthetics of care.

A Shift to Aesthetics of Care

My first article on care aesthetics came from a hunch [Thompson 2015]. I was thinking care could be considered a craft, but I didn't quite know what it was. It was an invitation to go looking. And that's what I'm currently working on. If we think about care as an embodied, sensory craft practice and then talk to a nurse, with a potter, or with one of your students who is designing a theatre workshop, we can find connections across these conversations. Care aesthetics is suggested as a language for discussing our practice that doesn't distinguish between artists and care workers. In a hospital, I'm interested in the aesthetics of care that might be executed by a person cleaning the floor as they make it shine in such a beautiful way that it provides an environment in which people will feel more nurtured, and safe. It permits a conversation between the cleaner and the artist about why you do your work and what skills you bring to it. This all has an echo of the work done by the artist Mierle Laderman Ukeles in the 1960s and 70s in the United States which she called *Maintenance Art*. It aims to challenge assumptions as to who's the creative person in that relationship. I'm writing a book on care aesthetics, so I will see where it goes. Covid has produced some real challenges to care aesthetics because a lot of the intimate bits of care aesthetics are touch and are the opposite to social distancing. It's about being close to people, and the art of touch, of bearing the weight of another (literally and metaphorically)—Covid has driven right through this. But at the same time, it has made us realize just how important physical human relations are. It has made the desire for the aesthetic experience of caring for each other even more pronounced. Covid, on the other hand, has created many everyday care aesthetic responses— so we've seen people cooking amazing food for isolated neighbors and making displays in their windows for children—creating extraordinary acts of microsolidarity which I would argue operate in the care aesthetics register.

One of the problems with care aesthetics is that it is happening all the time in everyday life. In caring for my friend's child here today, if I chose to prepare him some food with particular attention to detail, we might argue this to be my care aesthetic practice. I've been mentoring children with additional needs during lockdown and this might be classified as my care aesthetic work. The everyday practices are rich, but they are also somewhat hard to write about. In some ways it is easier in the arts to locate care aesthetics in the work of certain companies or individual artists. So, for example, Fevered Sleep in the UK do work that is just beautiful and careful. There's stunning work around the arts and dementia—Anne Basting in the US, or Small Things in the UK, and many more. In the long term, I would like to create some kind of lab where people are trying to explore what it means in practice. It would be an exploratory space that could be with healthcare professionals, social care professionals, applied theatre people, artist folks, and students working together. In small and larger scales to experiment—trying to discover what care aesthetics was about. You might put a very specific disciplinary group together—so what would happen if physiotherapists and choreographers work together on how you work with human bodies. You give them a task: it might be a one-day workshop, or it could be a series of meetings over a longer period of time to look at how those disciplines work together. It's the idea of putting different professional groups, student groups, learning groups, research groups together to try and work out what it is. This could be part of student teaching as well. I've been reading about care workers: people who are going for twenty minutes to someone's home to do something for them, come out, and go to the next one. And when they talk about their work, there's an amazing intuitive embodied set of skills and capacities that they have which is hidden because they've not been given the opportunity to talk about what they do because it is so undervalued. But they've got a range of intuitive storytelling, relational and embodied capacities—a range of skills that are extraordinary, and if they happened in a biennale, we would call their work "intimate one-to-one immersive theatre"!

So, when I am trying to think about the lab, I would love one of these care workers to come to talk about their work to performance artists who do intimate theatre, for example. These combinations of different practitioners are needed to push a concept that, as I said earlier, is still really only a hunch.

Good Care

Care is a problematic word, because it is both normative and descriptive. The care of one human for another—that sentence doesn't automatically say whether it was good care or bad care. I care for you, however, sounds like something positive. It doesn't mean I care for you badly. So, when you say good care, it is because you realize there is bad care. Good care happens in many different settings, it happens at all levels, from an institution caring for its staff down to interpersonal relations as you care for your family member or your neighbor. It is important to realize that all of us have experienced care in some shape or form, so it's something we have in common. Good care needs to happen to everyone in order for them to live. Ideally, good care is mutual, it's done with consent, and it's done with respect and dignity; but at times it might be unequal, because when you're caring for your 2-month-old baby, they can't democratically agree whether to have a nappy change or not. The baby will be changed without consent!

Good care is very dependent on the situation in which you're doing it. It is firmly embedded in a microrelational moment between carer and cared for. And the shape of good care is radically different in different contexts. You can have good care between a parent and their child, between a friend and another friend, between a paid care worker and a wealthy elderly patient. There is the possibility of good care in these moments—when it can be nurturing and mutually respectful, but then it might not be these things. You see incredibly good care in hospitals even though there might be financial or managerial constraints that mitigate against it. Stereotypically, there are many Filipino care workers in the UK. They are often poorly paid, working far from their family members, and often quite isolated. However, they're really skilled and often do amazing work. I think recognizing their good care isn't accepting of the injustices they face. It is just giving them value for the skills they have. It's really important to recognize them as a workforce that isn't just straightforwardly oppressed and vulnerable. Care aesthetics wants to find a way to recognize that they are highly skilled people who should be valued.

Good Care in Participatory Arts Practices

There are times when you notice really poor care of participants, when you realize this is more about the ego of the director, or the level of inclusion and support for the people present isn't as great as it should be—people forget things like food and water, or they forget things like proper access. Good care in participatory arts is structured around the whole way that a project is designed: it is as much about what time of day it is happening, whether people can really get there, or can afford to get there, or when they get there is the place safe for different people in terms of mobility needs, language needs, whatever it might be. Then there is good care in a process, because some practitioners have an assumption that arts work has to be set to a default of risky. People use words such as "challenging" or "it is going to be disturbing," and you think, "yeah, maybe, but we need to think through how the experience is a caring experience even if it is challenging and it makes people think." Working in participatory practice, through the framework of care aesthetics, means you consider the shape of the drama work, the context of the place you are in, and what factors exist beyond the room that shape the lives of those involved. You may need to care in particular ways because of what's happening outside—and "particular ways" suggests this is an aesthetic and ethical question. The forms chosen, feelings worked with, and physical practice choices made are ethical-aesthetic choices.

Another point is that we need good care for the people who are running projects as well. I think for years all of us have been going to work in challenging situations without considering how people can get exhausted. Applied theatre folk haven't been great at looking after each other either. So, I think there's a bit of care for each other as participatory arts workers as part of good care as well.

Applied Theatre in a Careless Society

At its best applied theatre has been exploring how we are present with each other in the room in a way that makes sure people are acknowledged, that they can grow, can learn to accept each other, can learn to create with each other. These are all qualities that a process generates and outcomes of a process that can celebrated. I just think that has to be a model for a more care-ful society—one that in Shannon Jackson's words we can "actively produce." And the way you construct an arts experience for a group is often about realizing the creative power of our reliance on others—about human dependencies in a workshop space that rather than be disavowed are accepted as a model for how society could be working. There is of course a model of the artistic genius or the avant-garde performance artist who thinks they have no responsibility to the world because they're autonomous or free and they should be able to cajole or confront their audience-participants as much as they like. A care-ful practice is the antithesis, because what you're doing is saying that I'm not denying our mutual interdependencies. The independent artist hides the social securities and delegated care that make their work possible. Care aesthetics points to how we all need embodied relations with others to make life possible.

One of the problems with what I'm suggesting here, however, is how the workshop of care—the mutually rewarding, powerful process—actually transfers beyond the moment. For example, you're a great parent and you know how to nurture and care for your child. Some care ethicists then make this leap that says that you will therefore have the capacity to be a better citizen of a caring democracy. Care for an intimate—workshop friend, parent, child—shifts to a care for the world. I'm less sure. One of the questions for care aesthetics and ethics is how you jump from one zone of practice to the other: you're sitting in a workshop room; you're working with a youth theatre where they all learn to care and respect each other and work brilliantly together. How do we know those capacities to be mutually respectful, supportive, nurturing will in any way enable them to be more nurturing citizens? For me, there is perhaps a hint of an answer in some writing on Japanese aesthetics about the way care shifts across different worlds—and is continuous between the micro and macro of your everyday practice. So your care for the environment is exercised in the smallest details (your relations to small objects, to your neighborhood, your neighbor) and it's a practice of a culture of care that starts with a continuity between, for example, flower arranging, wrapping presents, dealing with children and the special arrangements in a classroom. But this is of course an oversimplification. How the aesthetics of care becomes a practice—or whether there is a training—is a question I don't have an answer for.

"To applied theatre, with love" (2021) and New Directions

"To applied theatre, with love" is a kind of love letter to applied theatre. The article is about why I fell out of love with the field and how perhaps care aesthetics has become one of my routes back in. The article is about how we've become a bit embarrassed about talking about the positive, beautiful, and breathtaking parts of our practice when we want to say,

"It's just bloody brilliant and it was just amazing." I probably spent too much time saying to students, "Stop what you're doing and be a bit more critical." Now I just think, "Oh, what you're doing is amazing, creative, inspiring and you deserve to be excited by it." I want to remember there are amazing things that happen in those projects—and the article is asking how we might create a language for that.

bell hooks is asking this same question when she writes about how come we can speak of loss so much more fluently that we can speak of love. In my original applied theatre book, there's a chapter there about Burkina Faso. I can't remember it much now. When I worked there, there was a Burkinabé woman called Pauline who was a great arts worker, and our host. I remember being in this really crummy bar with rickety tables, on an uneven muddy floor. Burkina Faso is one of the poorest countries in the world. And I said, "Pauline, tell me a bit about this place, tell me more about your city." And she said, "James, just look around you." And I looked around at the rubbish everywhere, kids in rags, mosquitoes flying, and she said, "It's marvelous, isn't it?" I was taken aback and just said, "Yeah, yeah, it is." And I just thought, "All right, James, stop being such an idiot." And we drank beer and there was lots of dancing. I wasn't trained to have the language to see or speak of the good in a place. Then I thought I should just shut up and stop making assumptions about the quality of Pauline's life. Now I think we need a language to speak of what is *marvelous*. Of course, that word sounds better in French!

In the article I discuss three shifts in our field: (1) from eulogy to criticism; (2) from vocation to professionalism; and (3) from solidarity to impact. And perhaps, just naming them for me, was to remind myself of why I started in applied theatre. It is a bit of a nostalgic old man moment, thinking how practice used to be about loving this stuff, about misbehaving, not filling in those forms and just doing it. Years ago, I remember teaching prison theatre when a bunch of students were planning a session, and I remember thinking this is going to be a disaster—some really risky bunch of games. With my body I was trying to say just don't do this, this is going to go down like a ton of bricks. But they went in there and did it and had one of the best sessions ever. I was completely wrong, and this was years ago. I realized that even then I started to censor through fear. You get so caught up in sort of ethical dilemmas you lose the willingness to take the odd risk, and this is the danger I am using in this article to explore, because you can do really good work with your students and make them think carefully about their work but also lose something. We need to remember the rebellious side of ourselves, why we're doing this work in the first place. The article is reminding me that I started out in applied theatre because I liked being with people. It asks whether we can stop thinking of ourselves as researchers, stop thinking of ourselves as academics and scholars, and to start thinking of ourselves as artists who want to be with people. The first time I went into a prison I just thought these people are amazing—I've never met this diverse a group of people in one place and done these stupid things with them. It made the work more exciting and probably more impactful than other more considered work. There is something about the vocation of it that needs to be remembered. I've seen some people do work and I think you are very good at this, it's very professional, but probably a bit boring. If you aren't driven by something vocational—something like a calling (although I don't like the word)—what is motivating us to do the work?

There's something about the language that's really important. If we go into a community thinking about the distress and oppression of the community, it does color the way we think about that community. Now we know communities have been distressed and suffered and have been hurt with awful things, but there's something that happens when that distress becomes the creative resource we're working with. Yes, it produces really powerful work and it produces work that's really important. I'm not denigrating it, I'm not saying it shouldn't happen, but if that's the only resource which we're drawing on, it's very difficult to articulate the future we're looking for with people we work with. If it is only articulated through responses to suffering, trying to come up with words about joy, beauty, love, passion, compassion (all really difficult words), let alone trying to imagine worlds filled with these things, is really difficult. If you start with suffering, it can hold the work in that place. If you say that we're actually working to imagine something better with this community, we want to be with this community as they imagine a vision of a different world, then some of the language focused on the capacities that people have for love, joy, beauty, passion, compassion, solidarity, celebration need to be articulated—they need to be a resource from which we might start.

Ethical Principles

There is the disavowal of principles existing prior to the work that you do, since one "principle" is the idea that principles emerge from the way you commit to the work in the situation that you are in. That's not really an ethical principle, it's more a fear of ethical principles, because I think there is a negotiation of principles as you meet people in a particular place. There is something that comes from the Quaker tradition of "you're probably wrong" or "you might be mistaken." You have to start working with other people from the position that any principles you hold might be wrong. I like the way Quakers use this for their peace-building work. It's really challenging when you are meeting people whose opinions you do not like. If you're working with racists or violent people and you start with that position that you might be wrong, it's really challenging, so thinking "I might be mistaken" is not just a nicety. It's actually a really, really tough thing to hold true in the way you respond to other people.

The other principle I was thinking about is being alongside people—not outside or inside—you are there with people. And if you're there with people, *you* are there as well. You're not hiding yourself; you are part of that situation you're in, and therefore you also have a voice in that situation. You are a participant not just a witness. I know you said according to some communities you are there to be silent and work, but then you reach the point where you must say that I'm largely here to shut up but I'm also here. I'm here. Otherwise you just go away; otherwise you don't turn up. Your presence alongside that community in some way doesn't mean that you have something that you're offering. It might just be your physical presence—in solidarity—when you don't say a word. But it might be the fact that you know how to make paper airplanes and the kids there don't. You bring something to that community. There might be an access to power which is much more awkward. You are a member of staff of the university, and you might say I have the power because I'm in the university and therefore I bring that. And we accept that's what you bring, but not to impose.

Things Brought to a Community that had Nothing to Do with Theatre

I said once to Helen Nicholson when I was in Sri Lanka, I think I'm probably just a glorified children's entertainer who happened to then write books about applied theatre. I know lots of small games to help entertain kids. I realized that in serious meetings I'd find myself trying to keep the kids distracted in order to do something else. I know how to make a picture of an elephant with one movement of my hand in the sand! I can't do it on Zoom (!)—you put your hand in the sand flat down, then in one movement it makes the shape of an elephant for the person looking at you. There are other tricks you can do drawing on the ground. So much war-zone stuff is waiting around: the workshop is going to start in an hour's time and like four hours later someone says, "We're now going to cook a meal," and you say, "Okay, let's cook a meal instead," and then two hours later you do the workshop, so you get used to waiting. Songs, blowing my cupped hands to make tunes, that's all I really did in war zones, none of this theatre stuff. It's just dressed-up children's entertainment. Then I got the job as an academic and got paid more than a children's entertainer. I was lucky. That's all it is, really.

References

Thompson, J. (2003), *Applied Theatre: Bewilderment and Beyond*. New York: Peter Lang.

Thompson, J. (2005), *Digging up Stories: Applied Theatre, Performance and War*. Manchester: Manchester University Press.

Thompson, J. (2009), *Performance Affects: Applied Theatre and the End of Effect*. New York: Palgrave Macmillan.

Thompson, J. (2015), "Towards an aesthetics of care," *RiDE: The Journal of Applied Theatre*, 20 (4), 1–12.

Thompson, J. (2017), "No more bystanders—grandchildren of Hiroshima and the 70th anniversary of the atomic bomb," *TDR—The Drama Review: The Journal of Performance Studies*, 61 (2), 87–104.

Thompson, J. (2021), "To applied theatre, with love," *TDR—The Drama Review: The Journal of Performance Studies*, 65 (1), 167–79.

Part 2

Examples of Togetherness

5

Towards a "First Philosophy" of Applied Theatre: Practice of Freedom Embedded in Responsibility for the Other

Syed Jamil Ahmed

Creatively rereading the critical purchase of a Levinasian radical move insisting that "ethics is first philosophy," and thus suggesting that "at the bottom of any account of human existence lie these matters—about right and wrong, good and bad, just and harmful" (Morgan 2011: 4), if only because "my ethical character precedes all else that I am, and ethics is the ground of language and community" (ibid.: 74), this theoretical undertaking attempts to outline a "first philosophy," i.e., an ethics, of applied theatre. If "to say that ethics is first philosophy is to say, well, that nothing else comes first" (Drabinski 2011: 3), then, for applied theatre, ethics should come before efficacy, aesthetics, transformative agendas, theoretical underpinnings, and all else, because a few acknowledgments from the nodes of knowledge production have emerged of late exposing how applied theatre praxis has now been conditioned by competitive funding in a grant-driven market and numerous forms of personal gain. Three snippets are excerpted below to justify this observation:

(i) "the necessity of funding for applied drama work, and the increasingly competitive grant-driven market, has [sic] required applied drama workers to make their work 'useful' in order to gain funding." (Finneran and Freebody 2016: 21)

(ii) "status, job security, profile in the field, grant money, flexibility, ability to recruit desired students and collaborators—these too, are *real* things that artists *get* [but] they do not benefit project participants and do not help make the world more just." (Snyder-Young 2013: 27, emphasis in original)

(iii) "applied drama as an industry, rather than a practice, sources much of its income and sustenance from its working in marginalised communities." (Finneran and Freebody 2016: 22)

Given the conundrum as exemplified above, this theoretical undertaking proposes an outline of a "first philosophy" for applied theatre. It proceeds in two parts. The first explicates Foucauldian ethics as the practice of "freedom that is transgressive of modern knowledge-power-subjectivity relations" (Bernauer and Mahon 2005: 160). The second part unpeels Levinasian phenomenology of ethical responsibility as face-to-face confrontation with the Other as a necessary precondition for ethical action. It concludes by discussing the implications of Foucauldian ethics as practice of freedom, and Levinasian acknowledgment that "the Other is my responsibility" (Levinas 1998: 103), for any praxis of applied theatre. Before proceeding further, it is necessary to insert a disclaimer. For the purpose of this theoretical endeavor, the *sine qua non* for applied theatre is Freirean dialogue as an epistemic relationship involving a two-way process of learning and knowing in any performative event that disavows top-down teaching. Importantly, the process is conjoined with praxis, i.e., "reflection and action upon the world in order to transform it" (Freire 2005: 51), deriving stimulus from the philosophical legitimation for engagement famously articulated in the Eleventh Thesis on Feuerbach as: "the philosophers have only *interpreted* the world in various ways; the point, however, is to *change* it" (Marx 1845, emphasis in the original).

Foucauldian Political Ethics as Practice of Freedom

Drawing a distinction between two meanings of the word "subject," Michel Foucault (1983b) observes that one can be "subject to someone else by control and dependence," or "tied to his [*sic*] identity by a conscience or self-knowledge," and that "both meanings suggest a form of power that subjugates and makes subject to" (212). Although a subject, in Foucauldian analytic, "is not universally given, but is in fact socially constructed by forms of knowledge and techniques of power" (Butler 2011: 210), Foucault nevertheless grants that "the subject [is] both constituted and self-constituting" (Robinson n.d.), and recognizes that the subject can struggle "against subjection, against forms of subjectivity and submission," which ties it to submission to others (Foucault 1983b: 212). Foucauldian ethics is located here, in this struggle of the subject against subjection to control and dominance.

Always suspicious of the notion of liberation as normalization, and at the same time rejecting any universally applicable system of ethics as catastrophic, Foucault engages ethical inquiry with an activist's political concern. In this pursuit, he institutes ethics as one of the three principal components of morality. One of the three components, as explained in *The Use of Pleasure* (Foucault 1990), is the moral code, i.e., a set of values and rules of action that is recommended to individuals through various social institutions and assemblages. The second component is the actual behavior of individuals in relation to the moral code, and it designates the manner in which the individuals comply with, obey, resist, respect, or disregard a moral value. The third is "the manner in which one ought to 'conduct oneself'—that is, the manner in which one ought to form oneself as an ethical subject acting in reference to the prescriptive elements that make up the code" (26). Thus, acknowledging the importance of moral code and the actual behavior of individuals, the Foucauldian theoretical toolkit serves to shift attention to "the kind of relationship [one] ought to have with [one]self, [...] which determines how the individual is supposed to constitute himself [*sic*] as a moral subject of his own actions" (Foucault 1983a: 238). Hence, the distinctive purchase accruing from Foucault's substantive ethics "conceived independently of the structure of the moral code" (Davidson 1986: 232) is that "there are different ways to 'conduct oneself' morally, different ways for the acting individual to operate, not just as an agent, but as an ethical subject of this action" (Foucault 1990: 26).

Foucault elaborates the third component of morality, "the manner in which one ought to form oneself as an ethical subject," by a four-part theoretical framework (1990: 26–8) that Davidson aptly describes as a "grid of ethical intelligibility" (1986: 232), which can be deployed to interpret any system of ethics. Firstly, the determination of the ethical substance, in other words the behavior or aspect of self, that is morally problematic and needs to be transformed. The aspect of the self could include feelings, desires, or intentions; it could also concern a part of one's self. Secondly, the mode of subjection—that is, "the way in which people are invited or incited to recognize their moral obligations" (Foucault 1983a: 239). Foucault suggests the following modes as examples: divine law that has been revealed in a text, natural law, a cosmological order, a rational rule, the attempt to give one's existence the most beautiful form possible (239). Thirdly, self-forming means by which one can change oneself in order to become ethical subjects. It involves ethical work or techniques "that one performs on oneself, not only in order to bring one's conduct into compliance with a given rule, but also to attempt to transform oneself into the ethical subject of one's behavior" (Foucault 1990: 27). The techniques may include exercises, practical tasks, various activities, care of the body, health regimens, physical exercises without overexertion, the carefully measured satisfaction of needs, meditations, readings, notes that one takes on books (51). Fourthly, the telos of the ethical subject—that is, the kind of being to which we aspire when behaving ethically. In other words, it seeks to answer: "What is the goal to which our self-forming activity should be directed?" (Davidson 1986: 229). The examples of telos that Foucault cites are "to become pure, or immortal, or free, or masters of ourselves" (Foucault 1983a: 239). These four parts of the grid of ethical intelligibility work with "both relationships between them and a certain kind of interdependence" (240).

Briefly, then, morality for Foucault is a tripartite system consisting of moral code, actual behavior or action of individuals in relation to the moral code, and a four-part framework by means of which one ought to form oneself as an ethical subject. As Foucault explains, "there is no specific moral action that does not refer to a unified moral [code of] conduct; no moral [code of] conduct that does not call for the forming of oneself as an ethical subject; and no forming of the ethical subject without 'modes of subjectivation' and an 'ascetics' or 'practices of the self' that support them" (Foucault 1990: 28).

The critical purchase of Foucauldian ethics must be recognized here, in its objective of fashioning of the ethical subject who is to work to subvert the modes of subjectivation—that is, the technologies of domination by which one may be subjected to control, by practices of self (in the ancient sense of *askēsis*, or ascetic practice),[1]—namely, subjectification or technologies of the self that must be mobilized to resist the mechanics of domination.

Foucault excavates technologies of the self, such as *parrhesia* (frank-speech on one line)[2] and *epimeleia heautou* ("taking care of one's self")[3] from Hellenistic and Roman periods, not to resuscitate an ancient cultural practice, but to articulate an ethics for modern times, the guiding thread of which is "constituted by what one might call the 'techniques of the self,' which is to say, the procedures, which no doubt exist in every civilization, suggested or prescribed to individuals in order to determine their identity, maintain it, or transform it in terms of a certain number of ends, through relations of self-mastery or self-knowledge" (Foucault 1997c: 87).

The techniques of the self are to be fashioned, argues Foucault, "not to discover what we are but to refuse what we are," so as "to imagine and build up what we could be to get rid of this kind of political 'double bind,' which is the simultaneous individualization and totalization of modern power structures" (Foucault 1983b: 336). It is here that Foucauldian ethics situates itself in a triangulated structure with "power" and "knowledge" at the base, and the "self" at the apex.

What characterizes Foucauldian notion of power "is that it brings into play relations between individuals (or groups)" (217), and what defines a power relation is that "it is a mode of action which does not act directly and immediately on others. Instead, it acts upon their actions: an action upon action, on existing actions or on those which may arise in the present or the future" (220). Because exercise of power guides the possibility of conduct and puts in order the possibility of outcome, it opens the prospect of government, understood as "the way in which the conduct of individuals or of groups might be directed" (221). The second basal node of "knowledge" is an epistemic field that is dynamic, heterogeneous, temporal, and shaped by ongoing conflict. No element, technique, or practice in the field, solely by itself, is recognized as knowledge, unless, by the way it is used, and thereby its increasing connectivity to other elements over time, it accrues for itself epistemic significance (Rouse 2005: 110). By examining the discursive traces left by the past, Foucault demonstrates how the techniques of surveillance, elicitation, observation, and documentation were mobilized by disciplinary establishments (most notably prisons, hospitals, army camps, schools, and factories) to produce knowledge that constructed normative behaviors, and mobilized such knowledge as a means of domination. Because "a more extensive and fine-grained knowledge enables a more continuous and pervasive control of what people do, which in turn offers further possibilities for more intrusive inquiry and disclosure" (Rouse 2005: 96), numerous technologies for knowledge extraction are deployed to simultaneously optimize "the body's capacities, skills and productivity and to foster its usefulness and docility" (Armstrong n.d.). Foucault proposes a connection between power and knowledge by arguing that "the exercise of power perpetually creates knowledge and, conversely, knowledge constantly induces effects of power" (Foucault 1980: 52). These two nodes of power and knowledge, acting in the conjunctive form of power/knowledge, work as technologies of domination for the subjectivation of the subject situated on the apex of the triangulated structure mentioned above, subjecting the subject into, as observed above, a "subject to someone else by control and dependence."

Acknowledging that the subject is both constituted and self-constituting, Foucault focuses on the triangulated structure, where "discursive practices and power-relations dovetail with ethics" (Robinson n.d.), in order to locate strategies for subjectification so as to refuse what we are—in other words, locating technologies of the self that must be mobilized to resist the mechanics of domination. This he accomplishes by a deft move to argue that because power may be defined as "as a mode of action upon the action of others," wherein the action is characterized "as the government of men by other men," it is inevitable that the notion of freedom is embedded in the conceptual formulation, if only because "power is exercised only over free subjects, and only so far as they are 'free'" (Foucault 1983b: 221). Instead of a face-to-face and mutually exclusive all-or-nothing confrontation between power and freedom, Foucault observes a complex interplay between the two notions, such that freedom may well appear as a precondition "for the exercise of power" (221). As he further argues, "the power relationship and freedom's refusal to submit cannot therefore be separated. The crucial problem of power is not that of voluntary servitude (how could we seek to be slaves?). At the very heart of the power relationship, and constantly provoking it, are the recalcitrance of the will and the intransigence of freedom" (221–2).

If the Foucauldian project discussed herein is recognized as fashioning of the ethical subject who is to work to subvert the modes of subjectivation, and if the techniques of the self are to be fashioned by refusing what we are by locating strategies for subjectification, then his "ethics is essentially a mode of self-formation, the way we fashion our freedom" (Bernauer and Mahon 2005: 151). Acknowledging that a person begins with limits instead of liberty, Foucault argues that "the encounter with the limit creates the opportunity for its transgression" (151). As Foucault asks quite unceremoniously, "what is ethics, if not the practice of freedom, the conscious [*réfléchie*] practice of freedom?," he follows up with this explanation: "freedom is the ontological condition of ethics. But ethics is the considered form that freedom takes when it is informed by reflection" (Foucault 1997a: 284). At this instance, where the subject's practice of freedom is a politics of his/her self, in that it is the struggle against modes of subjectivation enforced by the conjunctive form of power/knowledge as technologies of domination, Foucault's discourse emerges as a political ethic.

Levinasian Phenomenology of Ethical Responsibility

Emmanuel Levinas's ethics as responsibility for the Other needs to be read against two important contextual threads. One of these is biographical: his life was "dominated by the presentiment and the memory of the Nazi horror" (Levinas 1990: 291). The second is perceptual: his cognizance that "all Western philosophy, whether metaphysical, epistemological, or ontological, [is] totalizing or imperialistic" because it "acknowledges nothing transcendent to the philosophizing self, no *Other*" (Morgan 2011: 98, emphasis in original), and, in consequence, it "reduc[es] to the Same all that is opposed to it as Other" (Levinas 1993: 91). Against this background, Levinas sets off from phenomenological ground to devalue the classical Greek-Renaissance-Enlightenment philosophical tradition that marks the self "as autonomous and given prior to relationship with other people" (Nooteboom 2012: 164). He argues that the autonomous self does not relinquish its privileged sovereignty readily, not even in subjective death, which merely demonstrates "the derisory nature of its selfishness" (Simmons 1996: 77). Only a confrontation with another person, the Other (or "other," from the French *autrui*, translated as "the other person," "someone else"), calls into question the autonomy of the self. Since humans "live together with and in interaction with other persons," the confrontation is inevitable in the social condition which has "within it something that is irreducibly other"—an other that is neither an idea nor a concept but is "utterly particular—a unique and concrete living human" (Morgan 2011: 3). As Levinas responds in an interview, "with the appearance of the human—and this is my entire philosophy—there is something more important than my life, and that is the life of the other" (Wright, Hughes, and Ainley 1988: 172).

Levinas elucidates the relationship with the Other by invoking a Platonic distinction between "need" and "desire." "Need" belongs to the domain of the Same and can be satisfied by the ego by appropriating the world. However, "desire" is constituted by a dual structure of transcendence and interiority. It originates in the interiority of the ego but longs for the unattainable, pulling the ego away from the

Same towards the beyond (Simmons 1996: 80). This longing for
the unattainable beyond is desire—"desire for the absolutely other"
(Levinas 1979: 34). Qualifying desire as metaphysical, beyond "the
hunger one satisfies, the thirst one quenches, and the sense one allays,"
Levinas further asserts that it is "beyond satisfaction, where no gesture
by the body to diminish the aspiration is possible," for "it desires
beyond everything that can simply complete it" (34). Drawing on the
formal structure of Descartes' argument that employs the notion of
infinity as a proof of God's existence, Levinas claims that "the infinite
can participate in the finite without being subsumed under the Same"
as both "infinite and in-the-finite" (Simmons 1996: 86), to conclude
that the infinite is the human Other (91). Hence, the self cannot
totalize the Other into the Same, not because of insufficiency of the
self, but because of "the Infinity of the Other" (Levinas 1979: 80).
Agreeing with Descartes that the "infinite overflows human thought,"
Levinas "asserts that the concrete form of this overflowing is not a
direct relationship with God, but the face-to-face relationship with
the human Other" (Simmons 1996: 91–2). As he argues, "the Other
is not the incarnation of God, but precisely by his [*sic*] face, in which
he is disincarnate, is the manifestation of the height in which God is
revealed" (Levinas 1979: 79).

The confrontation of the self with the Other, the face to face, is a
performative enactment in daily life, where the Other, as already
observed, is utterly particular. As Levinas explicates:

> The relationship with the Other, the face-to-face with the Other, the
> encounter with a face that at once gives and conceals the Other, is the
> situation in which an event happens to a subject who does not assume
> it, who is utterly unable in its regard, but where none the less in a
> certain way it is in front of the subject. (Levinas 1987b: 78–9)

In such daily-life encounters, "what is occluded, hidden, or forgotten
[…] is not some idea or value; it is this presence of the other's face to
me—and my responsibility to and for this person" (Morgan 2011: 59).
By this argument, Levinas's philosophy attempts "to replace all accounts
of the human condition that fail to appreciate our essential social

existence with one that does so," and thus revolutionizes philosophy, and in so doing discloses "the deepest structure of human social existence," yielding a remarkable "conclusion that, as he often puts it, 'ethics is first philosophy'" (3). By this assertion, Levinas insists that ethics is self-grounded, in that "there is nothing more primary to human existence than the ethical" (7), and that "ethics is something that occurs between every two particular persons in terms of their face-to-face encounter with one another" (8). When daily-life performances-as-encounters are cognized as such, the Other dismantles any philosophical and political thought that lays primacy of the self (Simmons 1996: 79).

Levinas argues that in the face-to-face encounter with the Other, concretized in the face of another human, "the face, the countenance, is the fact that a reality is opposed to me, opposed not in its manifestations, but as it were in its way of being, ontologically opposed" (Levinas 1987a: 19). But this opposition is "not the opposition of a force," or "a hostility," but is "a pacific opposition," and if there is violence, it "consists in ignoring this opposition, ignoring the face of a being, [and] avoiding the gaze" (19). Levinas further argues that the face is not a representation, but "the presentation of an entity as an entity, its personal presentation" (20). Importantly, "the face of the Other has a paradoxical dual structure," since it is, on the one hand, extremely frail, and on the other, commands ultimate authority (Simmons 1996: 94). It presents itself "prior to any particular expression, and beneath all particular expressions," with "the nakedness and destitution of the expression as such, that is to say extreme exposure, defencelessness, vulnerability itself" (Levinas 1989: 83). By its expression, asserts Levinas, "the face before me summons me, calls for me, begs for me, as if [it is] the invisible death that must be faced by the Other" (83). It is "precisely through the way the face summons me, calls for me, begs for me, and in so doing recalls my responsibility, and calls me into question" that "the Other becomes my neighbour" (83).

The face of the Other as self's neighbor, Levinas asserts, cannot be grasped by the eyes, the hand, and the mind, but nevertheless the face can emerge as an epiphany that determines a relationship "different from that which characterizes all our sensible experience" (Levinas 1979: 187), by "the banal fact of conversation," which, because it "quits the order of violence," is in effect "the marvel of marvels" (Levinas 1990: 7). "To speak, at the same time as knowing the Other, is making oneself known to him [*sic*]. The Other is not only known, he is *greeted* [*salué*]. He is not only named, but also invoked. […] I not only think of what he is for me, but also and simultaneously, and even before, I *am* for him" (7, emphasis in original). The commerce that the speaking implies by applying a concept, by calling, and even by appealing to the other person, "is precisely action without violence," because "the agent, at the very moment of its action, has renounced all claims to dominance or sovereignty" (8). For Levinas, "speaking and hearing become one rather than succeed one another. Speaking therefore institutes the moral relationship of equality and consequently recognizes justice. Even when one speaks to a slave, one speaks to an equal" (8).

A distinctive feature in Levinasian ethical philosophy is that responsibility is a form of recognition, an acknowledgment of a claim, and, most importantly, a bond with an imperative order, the locus of which imperative is articulated in "the other who faces—the face of the other" (Lingis 1991: xiii). As Simmons demonstrates, Levinas's theory of responsibility does not annihilate the ego as it confronts the Other, but maintains it by means of the dual structure of desire (constituted by transcendence and interiority), albeit the ego is now in a subordinate position, because "without a responsible self, responsibility loses its meaning" (Simmons 1996: 96). Levinas forces one to rethink the very notion of responsibility for the naked face of the vulnerable Other by insisting that it "goes beyond what I may or may not have done to the Other," submitting in devotion to the other "before being devoted to myself," submitting with "a guiltless responsibility, whereby I am nonetheless open to an accusation which no alibi, spatial or temporal, could clear me" (Levinas 1989: 83). Indeed, this notion of responsibility is so extreme that it defines subjectivity of the ego as subject to the Other, for he argues that "the I is not simply conscious of this necessity to respond, [...] rather the I is, by its *very position*, responsibility through and through" (Levinas 1996: 17, emphasis in original). Indeed, "the face of the Other calls the ego to respond infinitely," not allowing respite in the comfort of having done with being responsible, because the more the ego responds to the Other, the more is it responsible (Simmons 1996: 98). Furthermore, the responsibility to the Other is asymmetrical, because, argues Levinas, "the tie with the Other is knotted only as responsibility" (Levinas 1985: 97), to the extent that the ego is "responsible for the Other without waiting for reciprocity" (98). He extends the notion further by insisting that "responsibility for my neighbour dates from before my freedom in an immemorial past, an unrepresentable past that was never present" (Levinas 1989: 84). In effect, the extent of this responsibility extends to all humans, as he quotes Dostoyevsky to drive home his argument: "we are all responsible for all, for all men [sic] before all, and I more than all others" (Levinas 1985: 101). This responsibility of absolutely unflinching commitment to the Other that Levinas calls for needs to be read "as something like a necessary precondition for ethical action, not a complete description of what such ethical action is" (Achtenberg 2012: n.p.).

In recent times, Levinasian ethics as a face-to-face encounter with the Other has been debated spiritedly from both postcolonial and anticolonial critical perspectives, justifying the arguments by observing that "colonial structures continue to persist today—through neocolonial policies abroad and through neoliberal capitalism domestically—[as] the Manichean structure of traditional colonization has merely changed form, rather than ended" (Anderson 2017: 171). Among the critics, Anderson presents anticolonial reading of Levinasian ethics of responsibility for the Other against Fanon's psychoexistential account of colonial subjectivities to demonstrate that "there are serious impediments to bringing Levinas's phenomenology into the colony, for his historical consciousness is incomplete and his phenomenology fails to describe the zone of nonbeing" (Anderson 2017: 171). On the other hand, there is indeed a racist and xenophobic agenda in Levinas, for he has gone on record saying "humanity consists of the

Bible and the Greeks. And all the rest can be translated: all the rest—all of the exotic—is dance" (Mortley 1991: 18). In another interview, he asserted that "when I speak of Europe, I think about the gathering of humanity. Only in the European sense can the world be gathered together" (Levinas 2001: 138). Acknowledging "Levinas's insight into the ethical, that sense of responsibility to the Other who accuses and obligates *without prior measure*, is critical for thinking in a postcolonial context," Drabinski calls for "decolonizing Levinas" as "crucial for the project of an ethical postcolonial cultural politics […] uncoupled from a staggeringly naïve and problematic conception of Europe" (2011: 2, emphasis in original).[4]

These critiques of Levinas are not entirely unfounded. For example, when Levinas claims the commerce that speaking implies "is precisely action without violence," because "the agent, at the very moment of its action, has renounced all claims to dominance or sovereignty" (Levinas 1990: 8), he is making ahistoric claims, entirely oblivious of physical as well as epistemic violence wrought on the colonized. Indeed, because colonialism has not been erased from the earth but has merely changed its guise to nuanced subtlety, one can question who actually is the Levinasian Other when he asserts that speaking "institutes the moral relationship of equality and consequently recognizes justice" (8). In claiming that speaking to a slave is speaking "to an equal" (8), Levinas stands accused of destroying the very ethical ground he has so painstakingly constructed. As Franz Fanon would argue back to Levinas's claim, "to speak a language is to take on a world, a culture," so much so that if a Black person "wants to be white," which is another term for a "human being," s/he will gain that status proportionate to his/her gain to "greater mastery of the cultural tool" that the language of the white person is (Fanon 2008: 25). Because a Black speaks "jabber" (16) when s/he speaks his/her own language, "nothing *is* more astonishing than to hear a black man express himself properly, for then in truth he is putting on the white world" (23, emphasis in original). Indeed, a Black person "who quotes Montesquieu had better be watched," for s/he may be dangerous (22). To be very clear, "Fanon uses 'white' as a generic term for *European civilization and its representatives.* In contrast, 'black' refers to the non-West in general" (Sardar 2008: xv, emphasis in original). From the perspective of feminism, Levinas's philosophy is overwhelmingly aligned to the patriarchal penchant for deploying masculine pronouns to stand for the entire humanity (a practice for which Foucault too should be held responsible). To be fair, Levinas does acknowledge that "the feminine is other for a masculine being not only because of a different nature but also inasmuch as alterity is in some way its nature" (Levinas 1985: 65). Nevertheless, as this theoretical endeavor demonstrates, Simone de Beauvoir is justified in rebutting Levinas for "deliberately tak[ing] a man's point of view, disregarding the reciprocity of subject and object," and "assert[ing] masculine privilege" (Beauvoir 1953: 16, fn. 1).

Notwithstanding these "red flags," the outline of Levinasian precondition for ethical action underscored by responsibility for the Other, as deliberated upon earlier, may be strategically deployed by appropriating the supposed self of the European master race (constituted by, as he says, "the Bible and the Greeks"), and the Other as the Jew scarred by the inscription of the Holocaust, and redeploying both the self and the Other as individuals of any race, color, or ethnicity. Perhaps, here lies the value of Levinas in a world where hybridity, mimicry, and syncretism are ubiquitous and pervasive. Let us not forget, contra Levinas and his fondness for the Bible and the Greeks, that Homo Sapiens, emerging from Africa some 60,000 years ago, migrated to Europe concurrently as the Neanderthals, who once dominated Europe, disappeared completely (*The Guardian* 2013). Although Greek science became the basis for the development of medicine in Islamic civilization (de Bustinza 2016), the latter in turn "had a huge impact on the development of medieval Western Europe," so much so that "the Islamic world provided the foundations for developments in western civilisation" (BBC Bitesize 2020: n.p.). Hence, what is any identity in the world but a continuation of hybridity and syncretism that has been going on from the time humans began to emerge on the earth?

Conclusion

Having explicated a two-part proposal as discussed above, it is now necessary to indicate how it may be employed in the field of applied theatre. It is suggested that Foucauldian ethics as practice of freedom may be employed as the academic/practitioner's principle for fashioning the self when faced with the necessity of funding, status, job security, and profile in the field. Indeed, the choice is clear: whether to be subjectivated or subjectified. If s/he chooses to attempt subjectification, the fourfold grid of ethical intelligibility may help devise possible options by determining the ethical substance, identifying a possible mode of subjection, ascertaining the self-forming means in order to become an ethical subject, and establishing the telos. Proceeding by the fourfold framework, the applied theatre practitioner/academic may fashion him/herself as an ethical subject who can subvert the modes of subjectivation, and thus engage in the practice of freedom. S/he may even choose to practice *parrhesia* or frank-speech (see endnote 2), and abandon the "necessity" of critical understatements, half-truths, and false praise-speech, expecting reciprocal praise-speech by the same measure. The applied theatre practitioner may even employ the notion of "practice of freedom" as a critical underpin for devised performances, in that the performance itself may incite or invite the spectators in the practice of freedom. One may also engage in the practice of freedom by devising ways and means to engage in applied theatre praxis by refusing funding from neoliberal institutions, if it entails subjectivation. Such refusals are not unknown in the history of world theatre—Mukta Natak in Bangladesh was one such example (see Ahmed 2011). One may also be reminded of Bertolt Brecht's *The Life of Galileo* (scenes 1–3), where the trickster-academic Galileo Galilei, too poor even to pay his milkman, swindles the Republic of Venice by claiming to have invented the telescope, and with the money obtained engages in scientific experimentation that proves the Copernican System. However, if the two nodes of power and knowledge subjectivate the subject as a subject to someone else by control and dependence, and if there is no way out for whatever reason, the academic/practitioner, instead of making excuses, needs to make an explicit declaration regarding this, and follow the moral code prescribed in his/her society, and act in compliance with it. Indeed, it may not be possible to win all the battles in a lifetime.

Subjectivated or subjectified, the applied theatre practitioner or academic needs to confront the participants anywhere in the world as his/her Other, not necessarily the European Other that Levinas may have had in mind. It is this Other, marked by any racial, ethnic, religious, gender, age, or national identity, that calls into question the autonomy of the applied theatre practitioner/academic as the self. It is this Other that needs to emerge as the infinite and an epiphany, or even epiphany of the infinity, concretized as a body of utterly particular, unique, and concrete human beings. Ontologically opposed to the self of the applied theatre practitioner/academic, not in hostility but in pacific opposition, the Other as the body of participants that is both extremely frail and at the same time commanding ultimate authority cannot be ignored, for that would imply violence. It is this Other that the self of the applied theatre practitioner/academic needs to acknowledge as his/her neighbor, and as his/her equal. Responsibility for the naked face of the vulnerable Other must be acknowledged by the practitioner/academic as asymmetrical, beyond what the self may or may not have done to the Other, submitting in devotion with a guiltless responsibility, acknowledging that the self is, by its *very position*, responsibility through and through.

There is yet a secondary level at which the same responsibility applies to the same conception of the Other. Here, it is among the applied theatre academics themselves. They need to always remember that the epistemic field they are located in is dynamic, heterogeneous, temporal, and shaped by ongoing conflict. What they generate is not knowledge unless it gains epistemic significance by increasing connectivity to other elements of knowledge. Here lies their trickster-like field of possibilities. For they need to forge increasing connectivity among those elements of knowledge that are located in the peripheral counterdiscourse. It is their responsibility to find ways and means so as not to produce knowledge as tools for constructing normative behaviors and disciplined living. Instead, they need to find ways and means, by trial and error, to forge networks between themselves so as to subvert technologies of power that subjugate. And in the networks that they forge, they need to recognize each Other, wherever the Other's location may be, by calling into question the autonomy of the self of the academic. This Other is the epiphany of infinity. Both extremely frail and at the same time commanding ultimate authority, this Other, be s/he located in the Global North or the South, cannot be ignored, for that would imply violence. Acknowledging this particular Other as the self's neighbor, and as his/her equal, the self must acknowledge responsibility for this particular Other, allowing no respite in the comfort of having done with being responsible, because the more the self responds to the Other, the more is it responsible.

Undoubtedly, for us who are all swept into neoliberal life and living, this is a tall order. But then, dreams are made of stuffs that are difficult.

Notes

1 "*Askēsis* means not renunciation but the progressive consideration of self, or mastery over oneself, obtained not through the renunciation of reality but through the acquisition and assimilation of truth. It has as its final aim not preparation for another reality but access to the reality of this world" (Foucault 1997b: 238–9).

2 "A particular ancient practice of caring for the self [was known as] parrhesia (alternatively, parresia) or frank-speech. Parrhesia is the courageous act of telling the truth without either embellishment or concealment for the purpose of criticizing oneself or another" (Robinson n.d.).

3 *Epimeleia heautou* "does not mean simply being interested in oneself, nor does it mean having a certain tendency to self-attachment or self-fascination. [...] For example, Xenophon used *epimeleia heautou* to

describe agricultural management. The responsibility of a monarch for his fellow citizens was also *epimeleia heautou*. That which a doctor does in the course of caring for a patient is *epimeleia heautou*. It is therefore a very powerful word; it describes a sort of work, an activity; it implies attention, knowledge, technique" (Foucault 1983a: 243).

4   In all fairness, though, as Deborah Achtenberg (2012) observes, the ethnocentrism is found in Levinas's minor works, and may not affect most of his major works.

References

Achtenberg, D. (2012), "Review of J. E. Drabinski, Levinas and the Postcolonial: Race, Nation, Other," *Notre Dame Philosophical Review.* Available online: https://ndpr.nd.edu/news/levinas-and-the-postcolonial-race-nation-other/ (accessed May 25, 2020).

Ahmed, S. J. (2011), "Revisiting a dream-site of liberation: the case of Mukta Natak in Bangladesh," *Research in Drama Education: The Journal of Applied Theatre and Performance,* 16 (1), 5–27.

Anderson, P. D. (2017), "Levinas and the anticolonial," *Journal of French and Francophone Philosophy,* 25 (1), 150–81.

Armstrong, A. (n.d.), "Michel Foucault: Feminism," *Internet Encyclopaedia of Philosophy.* Available online: https://iep.utm.edu/foucfem/ (accessed May 25, 2020).

BBC Bitesize (2020), "The Islamic world in the Middle Ages." Available online: https://www.bbc.co.uk/bitesize/guides/zx9xsbk/revision/8 (accessed May 27, 2020).

Beauvoir, S. de (1953), *The Second Sex,* trans. H. M. Parshley. London: Jonathan Cape.

Bernauer, J. W. and Mahon, M. (2005), "Michel Foucault's ethical imagination," in G. Gutting (ed.), *The Cambridge Companion to Foucault.* Cambridge: Cambridge University Press, pp. 149–75.

Butler, N. (2011), "Subjectivity and subjectivation," in M. Tadajewski, P. Maclaran, E. Parsons, and M. Parker (eds), *Key Concepts in Critical Management Studies.* Los Angeles: SAGE, pp. 210–14.

Davidson, A. (1986), "Archaeology, genealogy, ethics," in D. C. Hoy (ed.), *Foucault: A Critical Reader.* Oxford: Blackwell, pp. 221–33.

De Bustinza, V. P. (2016), "How early Islamic science advanced medicine," *National Geographic History*, November/December. Available online: https://www.nationalgeographic.com/history/magazine/2016/11-12/muslim-medicine-scientific-discovery-islam/ (accessed May 26, 2020).

Drabinski, J. E. (2011), *Levinas and the Postcolonial: Race, Nation, Other*. Edinburgh: Edinburgh University Press.

Fanon, F. (2008), *Black Skin, White Mask*, trans C. L. Markmann. London: Pluto Press.

Finneran, M. and Freebody, K. (2016), "Tensions and mythologies in the liminal space between drama and social justice," in K. Freebody and M. Finneran (eds), *Drama and Social Justice: Theory, Research and Practice in International Contexts*. Abingdon, Oxon: Routledge, pp. 15–29.

Foucault, M. (1980), "Prison talks," in Collin Gordon (ed.), *Power/Knowledge: Selected Interviews and Other Writings*. New York: Pantheon Books, pp. 37–54.

Foucault, M. (1983a), "On the genealogy of ethics: an overview of work in progress," in H. L. Dreyfus and P. Rabinow (eds), *Michel Foucault: Beyond Structuralism and Hermeneutics*. Chicago: University of Chicago Press, pp. 229–52.

Foucault, M. (1983b), "Subject and power," in H. L. Dreyfus and P. Rabinow (eds), *Michel Foucault: Beyond Structuralism and Hermeneutics*. Chicago: University of Chicago Press, pp. 208–26.

Foucault, M. (1990), *The History of Sexuality*: Vol. 2: *The Use of Pleasure*, trans. R. Hurley. New York: Vintage Books.

Foucault, M. (1997a), "The ethics of the concern of the self as a practice of freedom," in P. Rabinow (ed.), *Ethics: Subjectivity and Truth: Essential Works of Foucault 1954–1984*, Vol. 1. New York: The New Press, pp. 281–301.

Foucault, M. (1997b), "Technologies of the self," in Paul Rabinow (ed.), *Ethics: Subjectivity and Truth: Essential Works of Foucault 1954–1984*, Vol. 1. New York: The New Press, pp. 223–51.

Foucault, M. (1997c), "Subjectivity and truth," in Paul Rabinow (ed.), *Ethics: Subjectivity and Truth: Essential Works of Foucault 1954-1984*, Vol. 1. New York: The New Press, pp. 87–92.

Freire, P. (2005), *Pedagogy of the Oppressed*. New York: Continuum.

Levinas, E. (1979), *Totality and Infinity: An Essay on Exteriority*, trans. A. Lingis. The Hague: Martinus Nijhoff Publishers.

Levinas, E. (1985), *Ethics and Infinity: Conversations with Phillippe Nemo*, trans. R. A. Cohen. Pittsburgh, PA: Duquesne University Press.

Levinas, E. (1987a), *Freedom and Command: Collected Philosophical Papers*, trans. A. Lingis. Dordrecht: Martinus Nijhoff Publishers.

Levinas, E. (1987b), *Time and the Other* [and additional essays], trans. R. A. Cohen. Pittsburgh, PA: Duquesne University Press.

Levinas, E. (1989), "Ethics as first philosophy," in S. Hand (ed.), *The Levinas Reader*. Oxford: Basil Blackwell, pp. 76–87.

Levinas, E. (1990), *Difficult Freedom: Essays on Judaism*, trans. S. Hand. Baltimore, MD: The Johns Hopkins University Press.

Levinas, E. (1993), "Philosophy and the idea of the infinite," in A. Peperzak, *To the Other: An Introduction to the Philosophy of Emmanuel Levinas*. West Lafayette, IN: Purdue University Press.

Levinas, E. (1996), "Transcendence and height," in A. T. Peperzak, S. Critchley, and R. Bernasconi (eds), *Emanuel Levinas: Basic Philosophical Writings*. Bloomington: Indiana University Press, pp. 11–32.

Levinas, E. (1998), *Entre Nous: On Thinking-of-the-Other*, trans. M. B. Smith and B. Harshav. New York: Columbia University Press.

Levinas, E. (2001), "Being-toward-death and 'thou shalt not kill,'" in Jill Robbins (ed.), *Is It Righteous to Be? Interviews with Emmanuel Levinas*. Stanford, CA: Stanford University Press, pp. 130–9.

Lingis, A. (1991), "Translator's introduction," in E. Levinas, *Otherwise Than Being or Beyond Essence*. Dordrecht: Kluwer Academic Publishers, pp. xi–xl.

Marx, K. (1845), *Theses on Feuerbach*. Available online: https://www.marxists.org/archive/marx/works/1845/theses/ (accessed May 30, 2020).

Morgan, M. L. (2011), *The Cambridge Introduction to Emmanuel Levinas*. Cambridge: Cambridge University Press.

Mortley, R. (1991), "Emanuel Levinas," in R. Mortley (ed.), *French Philosophers in Conversation*. New York: Routledge, pp. 11–23.

Nooteboom, B. (2012), *Beyond Humanism: The Flourishing of Life, Self and Other*. Houndmills, Basingstoke: Palgrave Macmillan.

Robinson, B. (n.d.), "Michel Foucault: ethics," *Internet Encyclopedia of Philosophy*. Available online: https://www.iep.utm.edu/fouc-eth/#SH6b (accessed May 15, 2020).

Rouse, J. (2005), "Power/knowledge," in G. Gutting (ed.), *The Cambridge Companion to Foucault*. Cambridge: Cambridge University Press, pp. 95–122.

Sardar, Z. (2008), "Foreword," in F. Fanon, *Black Skin, White Mask*, trans. C. L. Markmann. London: Pluto Press, vi–xx.

Simmons, W. P. (1996), *An-Archy and Justice: An Introduction to Emmanuel Levinas's Political Thought*, PhD disseration, Graduate Faculty of the Louisiana State University and Agriculture and Mechanical College, Baton Rouge. Available online: https://digitalcommons.lsu.edu/gradschool_disstheses/6374/ (accessed May 23, 2020).

Snyder-Young, D. (2013), *Theatre of Good Intentions: Challenges and Hopes for Theatre and Social Change*. Houndmills, Basingstoke: Palgrave Macmillan.

The Guardian (2013), 'Why did the Neanderthals die out?' Available online: https://www.theguardian.com/science/2013/jun/02/why-did-neanderthals-die-out (accessed May 24, 2020).

Wright, T., Hughes, P., and Ainley, A. (1988), "The paradox of morality: an interview with Emmanuel Levinas," in R. Bernasconi and D. Wood (eds), *The Provocation of Levinas: Rethinking the Other*. London: Routledge, pp. 168–80.

6

For an Ethic of Critical Generosity: Facilitating Productive Discomfort in Applied Theatre Praxis

Dani Snyder-Young

A white playback actor steps forward and looks into the eyes of the twenty white people and three Black people who have assembled for a playback theatre workshop on white fragility facilitated by True Story Theater in the rec room of a suburban church in the northeastern United States in the autumn of 2019. Contemporary race relations in the United States are fraught with tension and conflict. White supremacist legacies including settler colonialism, enslavement, lynching, segregation, and restricting access to mechanisms of wealth accumulation such as property ownership have created a nation of deep racialized inequalities. Whiteness, in its dominance, frequently goes unmarked as a social position, and in the United States white people have often been raised with conspicuous silences and taboos surrounding direct engagement with race and racism. White people who want to help dismantle white supremacy as a dominant system of power frequently find ourselves hobbled by our ignorance of how racialized power operates on and through our white bodies (Rankine 2014; Snyder-Young 2020; Sullivan 2014; Yancy 2016).

In playback theatre, an ensemble of actors attentively listen to stories told by volunteers from the audience and then empathetically dramatize the stories, using scenes, movement, metaphor, and music to capture the essence of what they heard (Ellinger 2020; Salas 1983; Rivers 2013; Rowe 2007). In this workshop, audience members watch as the actor enacts a section of a story a workshop participant has talked about, taking responsibility for their own racialized discomfort. The actor breathes deeply; her gaze confronts the audience. "I will stand here *(breath)* before you *(breath)* in this discomfort." As she says the word "discomfort," she gestures to her feet, as if fanning the flames of a pyre. "Come on; like, add some wood. Add some wood," she invites the other actors on stage. A white man in the ensemble obliges, grabbing two stools, which he dismantles and sets at her feet. "I'm not literally going to burn," she tells him, and then shifts her gaze back to her audience, "It just feels like it sometimes." She closes her eyes and lifts her head to the skies, honest and open, "I could say I'm sorry a thousand times. I could say 'I'm sorry, I'm sorry, I'm sorry,' and I know that will not … " (she pauses to confront the fire at her feet as the actor who builds it drapes a red scarf over the pyre) " … change it." The fire builder waves the scarf; the flames leap. She shares a smile with the audience that quickly changes to a grimace, as she touches her chest. "There's that discomfort." She looks down and around her, taking in the growing intensity of the fire, breathes sharply, and exclaims, "Oh! Love that heat!" The fervor and determination on her face grows, exploding in a "Yeah! HA-AH!" She looks back to the audience, spent, and speaks with sincerity, "I can stand here. For the rest of my life, I will have to stand here, and do something." In another context, the imagery of martyrdom might be read as performing white moral superiority, transmogrifying racial discomfort into dangerous pain the white figure at the center of the enactment publicly accepts as proof of moral goodness. However, this assembled audience makes sense of this representation in relation to the story told by the teller, and reads it as a metaphor for accepting responsibility and tolerating discomfort. This contextual interpretation is rooted in *generosity*; audience members make sense of the enactment in relation to their understandings of the artists' goals.

Robin DiAngelo (2018) draws attention to the problem that racialized privilege and unmarked segregation frequently buffer white people from racial stress. She offers, "Given how seldom we [white people] experience racial discomfort in a society we dominate, we haven't had to build our racial stamina" (1–2). In this playback workshop, we white people—me, the True Story Theater ensemble members facilitating the workshop, and most of the assembled participants—have gathered with the express purpose of learning to better understand and tolerate the discomfort of racial stress, increasing our awareness of racism and capacity to be more open to learn and change in response to feedback on our uninterrogated biases and unwitting participation in racism. This three-and-a-half-hour workshop was produced by interracial dialogue group Beloved Community Team, which was founded in 2014 by three white women and four Black women from an episcopal church in a racially diverse town whose congregation is roughly half white and half Black. In 2015 this small group joined with a predominantly white congregation from a nearby town that is predominantly affluent and white; the group expanded to include additional white people interested in dismantling racism. The group spent several months studying DiAngelo's book *White Fragility: Why It's So Hard for White People to Talk About Racism* in advance of this workshop, which was attended by sixteen Beloved Community Team members and four others who were not part of the group (Patmon 2020).

This workshop is explicitly framed as a space for white people to interrogate whiteness; the three Black women in attendance from Beloved Community Team operate primarily as witnesses who have ongoing social and intellectual relationships with a number of the white people in attendance. One of them gives introductory remarks introducing the history of Beloved Community Team, and all three women participate in an opening warm-up exercise; beyond this, they watch but do not otherwise participate in workshop activities. In the opening warm-up exercise, participants are asked to identify with our bodies along a physical spectrum of the room where we fell in terms of our understanding of racism. The three Black women move all the way over to one end of the room, using their physical placement to express that they understand racism deeply, while the white facilitators and white participants scatter from the opposite end of the room to the middle, self-reporting with our bodies our limited to moderate understandings of racism. Facilitators and participants of both races acknowledge that the Black women have never had the privilege of *not understanding* racism and the structural systems of power. After this exercise, the three Black women sit down and watch the white participants engage in the day's activities; the purpose of the workshop is to help the white people better understand their own white fragility, and that is not work for the Black women to do.

I studied this workshop as part of a larger examination of the work of True Story Theater. The study was designed to exclude the details of the stories tellers share as part of their performances, and I received formal consent from tellers to analyze the performed enactments the ensemble created of their stories. I made this choice because tellers share stories within the intimate context the playback theatre engenders; to record and report out on the details would feel, ethically, like a violation of the social contract of the performance event.[1]

In this chapter I draw upon examples from True Story Theater's workshop on white fragility to examine why an ethic of critical generosity is essential in applied theatre praxis. I selected this case study to focus on because this event is designed to surface the discomfort white people have been taught to suppress; participants attend explicitly to work on tolerating the flames of racial stress. Discomfort activates tensions between what Claire Bishop characterizes as "an ethics of interpersonal interaction" (25) and a politic of social justice. This chapter highlights the necessity of discomfort in processes that dismantle hegemonic oppression and illustrates how critical generosity can amplify the learning potential of a moment of productive discomfort in helpful ways.

Productive Discomfort, Critical Generosity

Michalinos Zembylas (2015) describes how "discomforting feelings are important in challenging dominant beliefs, social habits and normative practices that sustain social inequities and they create openings for individual and social transformation" (163). The status quo is fundamentally comfortable for people benefiting from social inequities, particularly when those benefits are largely unmarked. The smooth operation of business-as-usual draws no attention to itself; hegemony naturalizes its comforts. Foucault (2007) advocates an *ethics of discomfort* that troubles the status quo, arguing for the necessity to make the familiar landscapes of our everyday lives strange:

> Remember that, in order to give [certainties] an indispensable mobility, one must see far, but also close-up and right around oneself. One must clearly feel that everything perceived is only evident when surrounded by a familiar and poorly known horizon, that each certitude is only sure because of the support offered by unexplored ground. (127)

Everything we know about the world we have learned in our own bodies, saturated in the social and ideological contexts through which we move. To borrow from Norman Denzin (2008), that world has been, for me as a white person raised in the US, "a white imaginary world" (97); a white supremacy cloaked in meritocratic myths and steeped in uninterrogated assumptions about white superiority and entitlement. The certainties of that world have been made possible by gaping chasms in my knowledge of how the status quo actually works. As I come to recognize the conspicuous gaps in my understanding—an ongoing process I do not pretend to have perfected or completed—I experience feelings of shame and guilt. Such discomfort is a necessary part of the process of disinvesting from oppressive ideologies that have made my life easier by making the lives of others more difficult. Even when I intellectually understand that, the feeling of discomfort is far from fun.

DiAngelo defines *white fragility* as:

> a state in which even a minimum amount of racial stress in the habitus becomes intolerable, triggering a range of defensive moves. These moves include the outward display of emotions such as anger, fear, and guilt and behaviors such as argumentation, silence, and leaving the stress-inducing situation. (103)

White people are frequently insulated from racial stress. The unmarked nature of whiteness means that most white people do not think of ourselves as racialized beings and often do not recognize how our race shapes our perception of the world. Whiteness's dominance means that we feel racial comfort in spaces of status and prestige; we are surrounded by narratives quietly affirming our racial superiority. This racial comfort is punctured when we are challenged racially. An example of a racial challenge is when a white person is asked to look critically at our complicity in supporting racist structures. Understanding racism as conscious individual acts of cruelty motivated by racialized hate and investment in a racist system we benefit from and misrecognize as meritocratic, white people frequently respond defensively to racial challenges. White taboos against direct discussion of race frequently leave us racially ignorant; white fragility is an obstacle preventing us from developing a clearer view of how racism works. It pushes back against the productive discomfort white people need to experience as we make strange the familiar experiences of benefiting from white supremacy.

Many artists want to use participatory performances and applied theatre practices to intervene in racism. Claire Bishop (2012) critiques how, in discourses surrounding participatory art, "an ethics of interpersonal interaction comes to prevail over a politics of social justice" (25). Such ethics foreground mutuality, consent, the decentering of authorial authority, and participant agency in matters of representation. I have written elsewhere (Snyder-Young 2011) of the tensions between participant agency and progressive political activism in my own applied theatre praxis. In that essay, I navigate tensions between privileging the political— using my authority as an artist/facilitator/teacher-like adult to insist on a sharper analysis of the influence of patriarchal values in a moment of Theatre of the Oppressed work— and privileging the relational— building trust with a teenager by giving her agency to author an artistic moment in the way she wanted to. In the moment, I privileged the relational; the trust built by ceding authority was essential to the success of the larger project. Ultimately, in so doing, I provide evidence of the ethos Bishop critiques. I am neither better than nor outside of this problem.

Bishop argues, "sensitivity to difference risks becoming a new kind of repressive norm— one in which artistic strategies of disruption, intervention or over-identification are immediately ruled out as 'unethical'" (25). An uncritical embrace of *sensitivity to difference* risks flattening differential relationships to structural systems of power. Bishop advocates projects in which "intersubjective relations are not an end in themselves, but serve to explore and disentangle a more complex knot of social concerns about political engagement, affect, inequality, narcissism, class, and behavioral protocols" (39). The "complex knot of social concerns" cannot be untangled by respecting difference in a way that erases differential relationships to structural systems of power.

I contend that a balance between an *ethic of interpersonal interaction* and an *ethic of discomfort* is required to untangle such knots. Too much discomfort can cause stakeholders to disengage. As I indicate earlier, the term *white fragility* describes disengagement in response to racialized discomfort. In order for anyone to put themselves in a position to risk possible discomfort, they need to trust that the discomfort is not dangerous. To borrow from the playback workshop described at the beginning of the chapter, they need to feel safe that they will not literally be burned to ash. John Fletcher (2013) defines how *an ethic of critical generosity* "holds that even negative criticisms should stem from deep empathy for and understanding of" a project's goals and context (28). Critical generosity can help people feel understood, even if they are not agreed with.

The act of naming racism—that is, highlighting its presence in an action—can cause the white person who has performed the action to feel racialized discomfort in the form of shame. However, that is not to be confused with *shaming*. Critiques of racist actions can be wielded as weapons, denigrating, insulting, or scapegoating. Monica Prendergast (2019) describes how a kind of "hyper-negativity" pervades our media landscape, which is saturated with "insults and derogatory remarks shared widely" via social media and formal political discourse

(100–1). A great deal of social media discourse about racism follows these hypernegative patterns. Critical generosity can help provide a counterbalance to such hypernegativity. Good antiracist facilitation focuses not on the moral badness of the individual performing a racist action, but on the action itself, its impact(s), and its relationship to larger structural patterns of oppression. White fragility makes it difficult for many white people to disentangle feelings of shame in response to such naming from acts of shaming or bullying. Critical generosity can help them navigate the difference.

From Judgment to Empathy

For Sianne Ngai (2007), "ugly feelings" (or negative affects) are generated by "a general state of obstructed agency with respect to other human actors or to the social as such" (3), which is "charged with political meaning regardless of whether the obstruction is actual or fantasized, or whether the agency obstructed is individual or collective" (3). Ngai focuses on minor, unattractive emotions—disgust, envy, paranoia— for their non-cathartic qualities. The playback workshop includes representations of the feeling of powerlessness and guilt, making explicit the sense of obstructed agency. As participants tell the stories, they construct this obstructed agency as individual in nature, but the playback event draws attention to their collective nature as performers explicitly affirm them and audience members overtly respond in ways demonstrating that they share the expressed feelings. To borrow from Ngai, the ugly feelings emerging from white fragility "are saturated with socially stigmatizing meanings and values"; they are "organized by trajectories of repulsion" and provoke instincts to get away from them (12). The workshop's purpose is to intervene in the instinct to push ugly feelings away, and participants encourage each other to tolerate the discomfort of these shared feelings, learn from them, and work to channel them into concrete actions. However, one participant seems unable to channel her ugly feelings in this sort of way; instead, she tells a story that she does not see skin color, distancing herself from racism by denying her participation in it. Eduardo Bonilla-Silva (2003) describes how *color-blind discourse* negates the social reality of race, supporting white supremacy by cloaking racial inequalities in myths that racialized differences do not exist. Color-blind frameworks imagine that people of different races do not have different experiences of the world, rendering the mechanisms reproducing racial inequality invisible and implicitly rationalizing inequality as attributable to individual failings.

The playback theatre performers enact her story in this way:

A bell rings twice; a voice cries, "We're all God's children. We are ALL God's children." A white man, bewildered, spreads his hands wide and asks, "But all human beings are so precious." He looks around, disoriented, confused, and trying to register the audience's disapproval, "Are you ... Are you saying something different?"

A white woman kneels in front of him, placing her hands over her eyes (as if evoking the concept "see no evil"), and says, "I was raised right." She moves as if to look around her, but her vision is blocked by her hands, insisting, "I was taught not to see it. Why do I ... ?" She shrugs her shoulders dismissively, keeping her hands in front of her eyes. "I was raised right." Offstage, a string instrument plays two notes quickly in succession, building a feeling of suspense. The woman apologizes, "I don't see color." The man shakes his head in confusion, "I don't get it,"

A younger white man climbs onto a step, positioning himself above the other two. "We're just feeding into more toxicity." He looks around the audience, slightly exasperated, and implores, "We just need to see each other as human beings." A younger white woman wraps herself in a translucent white scarf and kneels at the front of the vertical stage picture. She looks to the audience and says firmly and clearly, "I don't want to see anyone in pain. I can't believe it. I won't believe it. I don't want to see anybody in pain." The bell rings through the space again, and the actors freeze as the enactment concludes.

This enactment manages to balance the perspective of the teller and a critique of her story. The piece operates from an *ethic of critical generosity*, grounding her hope to spare pain and recognizing her stance as coming from a place of moral goodness, both in the overt religious framing at the start (recognizing that the performance is in a church, sponsored by a church-based group) and her hope to spare pain. This framework is at odds with the ways racism is constructed as individual moral failure, as moral philosopher Shannon Sullivan (2014) notes, with a sharp line drawn between *good white people*, who know and act in adherence to the rules of appropriate antiracist behavior, and *bad racist white people*, who do not (4). The enactment establishes that the teller is not a morally bad person, and in so doing performs an *ethic of interpersonal interaction*, supporting her perspective as it recognizes the difference between her understanding and the understandings held by the rest of the people in the room. It balances that recognition with a clear critique of her refusal to see and believe, which firmly situates this story within the shared antiracist framework held by the rest of the audience.

The social aspect of audience response amplifies the collective nature of the problem, animating the "trajectories of repulsion" (Ngai 2007: 12), as other workshop participants distance themselves from the implicit biases in the color-blind discourse in her story. One of the Black women in the audience catches the eye of another Black woman and makes a shooing gesture, as if to communicate, "brush it off." White audience members physically recoil, catch each other's eyes, and make faces demonstrating disapproval, showing that they are uncomfortable with the story and do not agree with the teller's framework and analysis.

Amber Esper, the conductor (facilitator) of this moment of performance, critiques the color-blind racism in the story, challenging the teller, "You say you don't see racism, but also you are at an event where people are describing the impacts of racism, and that racism is real. So you say you don't see race but also here you are hearing us say race is real." In so doing, she refuses to privilege the comfort of the teller over the imperative to intervene in her ignorance. The critique within the enactment and in this overt comment performs *an ethic of discomfort*, attempting to unsettle the teller's certainty of her understanding of what it means to see race and racism. It is important to note that Esper critiques the action and names racism and its impacts without calling the teller *racist*. The teller might feel racialized discomfort at the critique, but Esper does not *shame* her.

In postperformance surveys distributed three months following the event, this is the moment participants report as the most salient to their ongoing antiracist learnings. Several comment they were impressed by the ensemble's delicate handling of the moment and look to it as a model as they work to intervene in instances of white fragility when they appear in other contexts. One remembers how the teller "seemed angry at being challenged and for a moment it seemed things might turn ugly, but the skill of [True Story] members prevented that. (I, like many others, am somewhat conflict averse, which that moment also confirmed to me.)" Another "was mesmerized by Amber's ability to connect with the audience member and redirect her so calmly and evenly. It was like magic. I wish I could do that." Audience members recognize how the moment of intentional discomfort could devolve into conflict and use the language "skill" or "magic" to describe the ways Esper and the ensemble employ *critical generosity*. In Theatre of the Oppressed, "magic" solutions to problems disregard or wish away obstacles embedded within given circumstances. Critical generosity is the opposite of such "magic," in that it fully acknowledges the obstacles present, diffusing potential conflict by demonstrating understanding of adverse points of view.

Meghan A. Burke (2016) calls for the examination of color-blind racism to center on "the social relations of individuals who express them in concrete, material settings" (105). After the performance, when I went to recruit the woman telling the story for the larger study from which I have excerpted these examples, she explained her social relations to me. She told me that she lived with a Black man, the love of her life, for sixteen years, and that this means she is not racist. Aware that I planned to write about the workshop, and the enactment based on her story, she contextualized it for me. I think she elaborated upon her story because she felt discomfort at the way it had been received by workshop participants and hoped the additional context would help me receive it in a spirit of *critical generosity*.

When the ensemble ground their representation of her story in an empathetic understanding of her perspective and goals, they open up new understandings in audience members, inviting us to stay curious about our own instincts to respond with "trajectories of repulsion" (Ngai 2007: 12). One audience member reports, three months later, how the way the ensemble translated "'I don't see race. I just see the divinity of each person' into 'I don't want to see anyone in pain' move[d] me from potential judgement to empathy." The ensemble's modeling of critical generosity helped audience members suspend their instincts to distance themselves from the teller. The teller may not have been ready to embrace racialized discomfort, but the moment of discomfort in the workshop helped audience members take Foucault's advice to "Never consent to be completely comfortable with your own certainties" (127) and to embrace an ethic of discomfort when so doing can advance the goals of social justice.

Ethical Principal: Critical Generosity

When I began writing this essay, I initially focused on an *ethic of discomfort*, inspired by Sara Ahmed's (2016) invocation to lean into the role of the feminist killjoy, strident in my commitment to unsettle the status quo. But as I wrote my way through this concept, I had to recognize that, in real life, this is rarely my method of engagement. I find that when my instinct is to put the screws of discomfort to someone who has revealed an uninterrogated bias, that instinct tends to be rooted in a desire to distance myself from an action I find shameful. That instinct of *repulsion* comes from my own shame of recognition that I too hold uninterrogated biases, and that the biases I have been able to identify and work to dismantle were once biases informing my social behavior. Racist ideas surround all of us; they seep in through the skin and rattle around in our heads. It is the work of a lifetime to identify and dismantle them. The foundation of my *critical generosity* begins with the knowledge of my own human failings.

Critical generosity relies on understanding the context within which actions are taken and decisions are made. I understand the world from within the limits of my own lived experiences; there is much I cannot see from where I stand. I am frequently baffled by the decisions and actions of others, and when they hurt me or I see them hurt others, I get angry. That anger can be a productive source of energy, but my instinct when angry can be to lash out *to hurt* in retaliation. I try to keep that instinct in check; it rarely helps to soothe the initial pain. Instead, I try to ask real questions to better understand context and motivation. I try to listen generously to the answers. Frequently, when someone makes a decision or takes an action I find hurtful, they are responding to features of a landscape I cannot see, just as they cannot always see (or recognize the importance of) features of the landscape to which I have access. The process of asking and listening frequently opens up a productive dialogue, and within that dialogue I can situate my critique in relation to the full context and motivation of the action in a way that enables the person whose actions I do not understand to feel seen and heard. Sometimes such dialogue enables me to sway actions and policies. Sometimes it makes no immediate material change but the process of opening up dialogue strengthens the relationship, which in turn opens up opportunities for me to be better heard at a later time. Sometimes it results no change, but allows me a better understanding of a perspective I had not previously understood, and I can use that learning in another context where I can make more impact.

To be sure, this approach has been shaped by my socialization as an upper-middle-class white woman to avoid conflict and smooth over rough edges. But listening openly gives me an opportunity to slow down an encounter, breathe into my emotional responses to use them as a source of power, and give myself time to think through my responses and arguments. As I write this essay in the summer of 2020, racial conflict in the United States has reached boiling point. Inequalities have been amplified by the Covid-19 pandemic, as low-income BIPOC communities bear the brunt of an incompetent governmental response to the public health crisis. A vocal minority of white people refuses to participate in simple public health measures such as the wearing of masks to mitigate the spread of the virus. The Movement for Black Lives rises up in civil unrest against the state-sanctioned murder of an ever-growing list of Black people. The need for *critical generosity* as we attempt to listen to each other's motivations, hurts, and needs is more urgent than ever.

Note

1   This study has been approved by Northeastern University IRB #19-08-10.

References

Ahmed, S. (2016), *Living a Feminist Life*. Durham, NC: Duke University Press.

Bishop, C. (2012), *Artificial Hells: Participatory Art and the Politics of Spectatorship*. London: Verso.

Bonilla-Silva, E. (2003), *Racism without Racists: Color-Blind Racism and the Persistence of Racial Inequality in America*. Lanham, MD: Rowman & Littlefield.

Burke, M. A. (2016), "New frontiers in the study of color-blind racism," *Social Currents*, 3 (2), 103–9.

Denzin, N. K. (2008), *Searching for Yellowstone: Race, Gender, Family, and Memory in the Postmodern West*. Walnut Creek, CA: Left Coast Press.

DiAngelo, R. (2018), *White Fragility: Why It's So Hard for White People to Talk about Racism*. Boston, MA: Beacon Press.

Ellinger, C. (2020), Email communication with the author, March 24.

Fletcher, J. (2013), *Preaching to Convert: Evangelical Outreach and Performance Activism in a Secular Age*. Ann Arbor: University of Michigan Press.

Foucault, M. (2007), "For an ethics of discomfort," in S. Lotringer (ed.), *The Politics of Truth*. Los Angeles: Semiotext, pp. 121–7.

Ngai, S. (2007), *Ugly Feelings*. Cambridge, MA: Harvard University Press.

Patmon, H. (2020), Email communication with the author, March 27.

Prendergast, M. (2019), "Generosity in performance," *NJ: Drama Australia Journal*, 43 (2), 100–13.

Rankine, C. (2014), *Citizen: An American Lyric*. Minneapolis, MN: Graywolf Press.

Rivers, B. (2013), "Playback theatre as a response to the impact of political violence in occupied Palestine," *Applied Theatre Research*, 1 (2), 157–76.

Rowe, N. (2007), *Playing the Other: Dramatizing Personal Narratives in Playback Theatre*. London: Jessica Kingsley Publishers.

Salas, J. (1983), "Culture and community: playback theatre," *The Drama Review*, 27 (2), 15–25.

Snyder-Young, D. (2011), "Rehearsals for revolution? Theatre of the Oppressed, dominant discourses, and democratic tensions," *Research in Drama Education: The Journal of Applied Theatre and Performance*, 16 (1), 29–45.

Snyder-Young, D. (2020), *Privileged Spectatorship: Theatrical Interventions in White Supremacy*. Evanston, IL: Northwestern University Press.

Sullivan, S. (2014), *Good White People: The Problem with Middle-Class White Anti-Racism*. Albany: State University of New York Press.

Yancy, G. (2016), *Black Bodies, White Gazes: The Continuing Significance of Race in America*. Lanham, MD: Rowman & Littlefield.

Zembylas, M. (2015), "'Pedagogy of discomfort' and its ethical implications: the tensions of ethical violence in social justice education," *Ethics and Education*, 10 (2), 163–74.

7

Off the Record: Can We Just Have a Conversation? An Ethics of Acceptance Approach for Applied Theatre Practice and Research

Trudy Pauluth-Penner

Introduction

This chapter highlights key ethical dilemmas that arose in one interdisciplinary, intergenerational reminiscence theatre research study that explored the impact of such engagement upon dementia-specific institutionalized older adults' quality of life. Although many ethical scenarios are pertinent to applied theatre practice (autonomy, informed consent, power-over, duality of roles, insider/outsider issues), these are not elaborated upon here. In this chapter, the focus is on one central ethical aspect that lay at the core of the reminiscence theatre study—an all-too-common binary of aesthetics versus the ethics of research participant representation. An argument is made for an applied theatre *ethics of acceptance* framework, influenced by emergent research designs (Bruce et al. 2016; Campbell and Lassiter 2015).

The chapter opens with a summary of the reminiscence theatre study. This is followed by an exploration of aspects of ethics relevant to dementia-specific applied theatre healthcare contexts. Finally, applied theatre aesthetics are reviewed, emphasizing the aesthetics of experience in everyday life as it pertains directly to the study's dementia participants' representation. Connections are made between experiential aesthetics and the ethics of acceptance.

Note that this chapter reflects the opinion of one applied theatre artist/health researcher, the author; it is not intended to be representative of applied theatre professionals as a whole.

Setting the Context: Study Synopsis

The reminiscence ethnotheatre study, entitled "Moving forwards backwards: exploring the impact of active engagement in reminiscence theatre with older adults in residential care with mild to moderate cognitive impairment" (Pauluth-Penner 2018), considered the impact of such on the psychosocial quality of life for older adults with dementia. The intent was to honor each participant's lived experience. Study participants comprised eleven adults aged 65 years and older residing in a dementia-specific residential care facility and thirteen applied theatre devisors/actors, all of whom were University of Victoria (Canada) applied theatre undergraduate and graduate students. Qualitative ethnotheatre methods (older adult life interviews, transcriptions, field notes, drama/storytelling workshops, theatre devising, performance, and post-project evaluations) were integrated with quantitative pre- and post-program health assessments. The study culminated with a devised theatre production entitled *The Artist and Her Daughter*, performed for participants and invited guests.

The project was successful in enhancing quality of life and reaffirming the older adults' capabilities while reducing social isolation. Older adult participants' activity levels increased long after the study completion. However, the study was not without strife. Balancing aesthetics and study participants' ethically principled representation during the devising process became problematic.

Next, I describe key aspects of ethics, linking dementia ethics with applied theatre practices. This is followed by an exploration of the specific ethical challenges I experienced that emerged in the reminiscence theatre study.

Ethics of Applied Theatre in Healthcare Contexts

Shifting perceptions of dementia. Although this chapter draws extensively on a dementia-specific study, dementia per se—a neurodegenerative condition—is not elaborated. However, it is beneficial to briefly note shifts in care practices and dementia ethics principles as these directly correlate with the study's intentions.

While much focus is placed upon accumulated loss in dementia, an increased awareness of abilities that are retained despite cognitive decline is gaining attention (e.g., Kontos 2010; Nicholson 2011; Tuokko and Smart 2018). Unfortunately, stereotypes of declining abilities in dementia still prevail. These need to be altered to truly advance a dignified quality of life, an ethical right for all human beings.

Ethics in dementia care. The ethical framework for dementia care is based primarily within the biomedical health model that is concerned with the principle of "do no harm," questioning the morally right choices when faced with ambiguous situations. It prioritizes how to optimize safety and freedom, deciding what is in the best interests of the person with dementia, and balancing the person's needs with the needs of others. The Nuffield Council on Bioethics (2009) offers methodological approaches to guide professionals through the complexities inherent in dementia care practices. The dementia ethical framework is primarily concerned with autonomy, dignity, solidarity, quality of life and well-being, and recognizing personhood.

Parallels of applied theatre and dementia ethics. There are several ethical nuances in applied theatre that resonate with dementia ethics. At the core of each lies "a set of moral principles that seeks to guide researchers from harming those they research ... to protect humanity, establish and sustain a progressive value system that respects and promotes human dignity" (Afolabi 2018: 3). These values, for me, are rooted in concepts of social justice, education, relational interactions, moral imperatives, equitable care, autonomy, giving voice, representation, integrity, accountability, responsibility, informed consent, community respect, and individual rights. Afolabi asserts that a key guiding principle for applied theatre is relational interaction, emphasizing other over self.

In applied theatre, ethical conduct requires delicate, responsible sensitivity to the truthful negotiation of power imbalances embedded within relationships. Ethically sound practices in applied theatre and dementia care focus on creating safe, positive spaces and avenues to develop relationships that consider the cultural values and ideologies of the individuals involved. Ultimately, ethical consideration emphasizes methods answerable to the ethics of representation, participation, power relations, privacy, confidentiality, and acceptance of various ways of knowing (Afolabi 2018).

Ethical dilemmas. The term *ethical dilemma* is defined as essentially "a choice between mutually conflicting principles" (Simons 2006: 244). Ethical dilemmas involve making complex choices between alternative courses of action in which multiple factors (social, political, personal, cultural) must be taken into account for the specific context.

The ethics discourse in applied theatre (Gjaerum 2013) acknowledges that difficult dilemmas will occur, but with no clear solution for responding to these emergent ethical questions. At the core are applied theatre practitioners' intentions and roles. Researchers agree that the ethics discourse is a moral and difficult minefield (e.g., Bishop 2014; Dalrymple 2006; Kerr 2009; Neelands 2007; Nicholson 2005; Stuart Fisher 2005). Bishop (2014) emphasizes the need for a flexible set of ethical principles in applied theatre research. She advocates for a *multiple ethics paradigm* with principles rooted in justice, critique, care, profession, and moral integrity.

Duality of roles/ethics of representation. Dilemmas of duality of roles were significant to this study. My own roles as researcher, applied theatre facilitator, and healthcare provider held both explicit and implicit intentions that inevitably overlapped. For example, the applied theatre artist primarily aims for theatrical aesthetics, while the researcher's healthcare role in reminiscence theatre is to ensure that the participants' stories are inclusively and equitably represented. At times during the course of a project, particular roles take precedence: for example, a dramaturge may prefer choices that are in the best interest of producing an aesthetically pleasing, theatrically sound production. For the researcher the challenge lies in achieving the study's goals while balancing artistic autonomy with participants' inclusivity.

The roles of the researcher are clear—guided by research protocol as designed, to conduct health surveys and life history interviews, transcribe the interviews verbatim, gain consent for the use of material, analyze the material, document and track all aspects of the study, and finally to report on the findings. In any given context or phase of the study the researcher is cognizant of the responsibility to stay true to the overall research study intent, in this case honoring and paying tribute to the older adult participants' lived experiences, memories, and stories.

For healthcare professionals, the primary role is to support older adults' health and well-being to ensure their safety, addressing any care needs that emerge physically, socially, emotionally, or psychologically. If signs of discomfort or trauma emerge (which sometimes occurs in reminiscence practice), it is mandatory to refer any such concerns to the facility coordinator of therapeutic services, social worker, or administrator (e.g., signs of depression, anxiety, agitation, or other health issues). Herein, the role is to defuse difficulties to reassure or redirect participants.

The role of the reminiscence theatre facilitator/devisor is twofold: to ensure that all of the older adult participant stories are included in the final performance (study intention), and to convey the stories aesthetically. Ultimately, the intent is to facilitate the development of an equitable, reciprocally collaborative environment where actors are both challenged and supported in their devising practice while honoring their autonomy and artistic contributions. The challenge lies in creating a sustainable balance between research study intentions—honoring the older adult participants—and autonomous artistic aesthetic integrity.

The task at hand in this study was to create a theatrical framework to best reflect the essences of participants' stories aesthetically, and to figure out how to represent each story as recognizable to the older adults without falling prey to constraints of verbatim re-enactments. The aim of applied theatre, as articulated by Dobson and Goode (2002), is to create a fictionalized theatrical play with fictionalized characters reflecting the study participants, so as to construct a metaphoric representation of their stories while protecting anonymity. Stories are given by older adult participants but shaped by the applied theatre devising team and playwright into the theatrical production.

In this study, although collaborative devising theatre processes were intended, a traditional mainstage theatre rehearsal process took precedence for practical reasons. The original concept of co-creating the play with all study participants—older adult residents, the theatre devising company, and applied theatre facilitator/researcher—did not play out as anticipated, and that in turn compromised older adult participants' contributions while contradicting dementia ethics principles.

The ethics of representation—a core concern. Applied theatre practitioners are inevitably faced with the challenge of how to ethically and equitably represent others theatrically. Depictions of real-life experiences and stories of older adults with dementia raise critical ethical questions. Delicate choices are made regarding aesthetic quality and authentic representation of participants' life stories. Decisions reflect whether the theatre piece speaks *for, about,* or *with* individuals or communities. Questions arise: Whose story is it? Who has the ethical right to tell the story? Who can justly speak for whom? What stories are selected for script development and why—for dramatic aesthetic pleasure or authentic consensual representation? How are these decisions made and by whom? What stories are selected for script development and how are these best represented?

Wilkinson and Kitzinger (2009) prioritize efforts towards self-advocacy where people speak for themselves rather than the playwright unilaterally speaking for them. The interpretations of others' stories may fall prey to projections or transferences of our own agendas, thereby unintentionally misrepresenting participants' stories or intentionally discounting those deemed not sufficiently dramatic or aesthetically pleasing. As noted by Beck et al. (2011), artists and researchers engaged in arts-based research are involved for different purposes and focused on different audiences, and approach the research from backgrounds of diverse expertise and experiences. Tensions between aesthetics and representation became key ethical issues in this reminiscence theatre devising process.

Of central importance to this study was the representation of older adults' stories—to pay tribute, to honor each participant's story and life experiences. The task of the dramaturge, devisors, and researcher was to explore creatively how to best represent stories from all participants. In our reminiscence theatre devising process, stories were selected for the final play that were interpreted as holding the most dramatic aesthetic potential; these were subsequently prioritized over others. As a result, out of eleven older adult participants, four did not have any part of their stories included in the script.

An aesthetics versus ethics of representation binary developed. Aesthetic quality is central to applied theatre; however, it should not overrule authentic participant representation. While I am cognizant that it is impossible and undesirable to include all aspects of all stories in their entirety, I assert that in this particular situation with dementia participants, essences of each participant's stories needed to be visibly represented within the play, to be clearly felt and recognizable concretely by the older adults. While I was pondering these tensions between aesthetics and the ethics of representation, my considerations led me to an emergent sense of an ethics of acceptance.

An ethics of acceptance. The *Oxford Dictionary of English* (2018) defines *acceptance* as a willingness to tolerate a difficult situation, that it is a willful choice. As pointed out by Hayes et al. (2004), the etymological meaning is to take what is offered. Acceptance is not to be confused with the passive positions of resignation or surrender; rather, acceptance is an active stance of non-judgmental awareness and related to purposeful action in willingly accepting what is, doing what is needed and workable in the given situation. As clarified by Eifert and Forsyth (2005), it is not about approval, condoning wrongdoing, or being "right" but about acknowledging and experiencing *what is*, and being proactive rather than reactive.

An ethics of acceptance framework may have alleviated the reminiscence theatre study's aesthetics versus participant representation binary. With an acceptance of the constraints in dementia patients—of distorted, fragmented memories—and acceptance of a commitment that all participants' stories be represented, future devisors may be more inclusive.

In the reminiscence theatre devising process, despite my repeated intention to include the essences of all participants' stories, the dramaturgical choices took precedence. It became necessary to choose between aesthetics and the interests of the study and participants' ethical rights. As in many applied theatre contexts, decisions are made for the betterment of the whole project versus individual preferences. In this situation, the choice was made to acknowledge the constraints and accept the reality that some compromises had to be made to bring this project to fruition. I have no doubt these were the right decisions at the time for the play and devising company; however, I felt I had let down some of my participants by not including their voices, thereby compromising both my goals and applied theatre ethics.

Applied theatre may benefit from an ethics of acceptance approach to theatre devising as it has the potential to diffuse ethical conflicts. By honoring and accepting the diversity of needs and intentions between intersecting disciplines, contexts, and populations from the onset, the pathway for reciprocal open dialogue can be mapped out. Such principles are essential to move projects forward in a manner that addresses collective aspirations. The binary of aesthetics versus research intent could shift towards a more cohesive discourse wherein both objectives can be met. Authentic understanding and respect for each other's perspective would promote collectively agreed-upon intentions rather than one taking precedence over the other.

Applied theatre artists often face difficult devising decisions while navigating conflicting agendas. The task, challenge, and ultimate reward are in the creative process of selecting from an array of dramatic and theatrical conventions to authentically represent the essence of participants' stories. The aim of devised theatre is to configure these in a manner that is both aesthetically vibrant and authentically meaningful to participants. Rather than discount stories that do not fit neatly into a creative vision, the focus instead would be on determining how to creatively include elements identified as important to the older adult participants themselves.

An ethics of acceptance in applied theatre would invite careful consideration of the realities, conditions, and constraints (whether social, administrative, or political) embedded within our environments. Our task as theatre devisors is to find a balance of aesthetic quality and ethical representation. I strongly assert that for this study's play script many of the stories left out did hold considerable dramatic potential; elements could have been briefly integrated into existing scenes. This raises a fundamental ethical question: Who has the power and artistic control in interdisciplinary, collaboratively devised theatre in a healthcare context—the dramaturge or the researcher? Therein lay the challenge.

Aesthetics

The "aesthetics discourse" identified by Gjaerum (2013) involves the tensions between focusing on maintaining aesthetic quality of performance versus compromising on quality of productions in service of other agendas. In applied theatre the term *aesthetic* often implies a broad category of what is considered artistic or art-like, and also may relate to specific aesthetic languages, and references that suggest aesthetic attitudes or an aesthetic experience beyond art (White 2009).

Cohen, Varea, and Walker (2011) elaborate on the term more specifically, referring to features of *aesthetic experience*: First, it involves people "in forms that are bounded in space and time" (6). For example, study participants were comprised of older adults with dementia living within a secured residential care facility, each bound to live by institutional protocols, confined to the building, with limited social contact with the general community, and little choice in how they spent their time. Activities and care routines were tightly structured, with regulations designed to keep individuals safe, free from accidental harm (e.g., wandering, becoming lost in the outside environment). Researcher and applied theatre artists and students were also limited by such regulations; all activities needed to fit within the existing schedules and structures.

Second, there is engagement "on multiple levels at the same time—sensory, cognitive, emotive and often spiritual—so that all of these dimensions are involved simultaneously in constructing meaning and framing questions" (Cohen, Varea, and Walker 2011: 6). The older adult participants in the study were engaged at multiple levels. Their sensory, cognitive, psychological, and emotional responses were all impacted by the disease (Alzheimer's and related dementias) itself. Many were navigating through their days in various states, adjusting to life moment by moment, at the same time negotiating intermittent memory lapses, emotional confusion, and bodily symptoms in unfamiliar environments while trying to make sense of their circumstances among the flurry of activity around them—all of which may contribute to anxiety or agitation. Theatre devisors also had to simultaneously absorb various aspects of the environment—accommodating institutional constraints, administrative protocols, participants' needs, and balancing these with aesthetic theatre-making.

Third, through engagement in aesthetic experience, people can "acknowledge and mediate certain tensions, including those between innovation and tradition, the individual and the collective" (Cohen, Varea, and Walker 2011: 6). In this study, applied theatre devisors within the healthcare context were acknowledging the need to mediate tensions between traditional theatre or formulaic devising practices and innovative forms of reminiscence theatre that authentically represent participants, and between their own individual creative aspirations and those of the collective. The aim was to create a sense of reciprocity among artist/devisor, health researcher, administrators, and participants.

Sadeghi-Yekta (2015) refers to four types of aesthetics in applied theatre: the aesthetic sphere, aesthetic practice, aesthetic criteria, and aesthetic evaluation (159). The aesthetic sphere relates to art in general. The reminiscence theatre art form encompassed several art genres, all representative of essences of participants' stories: for example, music from their era, script devising, dance/movement to transition and enliven scenes, story narratives, photography for drama/storytelling workshops (pretexts), a short video on the production, and participant story booklets.

Aesthetic practice is also referred to as aesthetic object; it is the artistry itself—the activity of making and appreciating art. The reminiscence theatre production was devised collectively in the following manner. First, I carried out life history interviews that were transcribed verbatim and reviewed with older adults to select stories to be adapted for the play. Then, I analyzed the transcripts and coded them for themes. The dominant theme of pride was selected. The devising company of applied theatre students—along with me as the researcher and my older adult participants—then participated in facilitated drama/storytelling workshops, with photography prompts through improvised still image, and in-role writing processes. I video-recorded these workshops and then analyzed the results. Post-workshop discussions were held with devising company actors to reflect and further document stories. Once the workshop series was completed, I compiled all story-related materials—reviewed three times—into condensed stories and related themes. The devising company came back together with myself and the dramaturge/theatre director/playwright for a series of scene-devising workshops. Scenes were improvised from older adults' verbatim transcript sections. Through a *reminiscence rodeo* style, the story transcriptions were literally cut up into various lines and phrases, tossed into the air and actors one by one picked a piece of paper at random and improvised further. These workshops were also video-recorded and were transcribed verbatim for final script development.

The original intent was to create the script collectively. Given time constraints, the content was shaped into the final script by the dramaturge/director/playwright, then rehearsed in the traditional theatre manner of read-through and staging the blocking. The play was performed for study participants and invited guests, video-recorded, and followed by a post-show musical social with all involved. The older adult study participants received a story booklet with the script and photographs.

Aesthetic criteria, also referred to as aesthetic terminology, are concerned with "how we describe an art form, whether formal (composition, line and color, innovation), extrinsic (content) or subjective (beauty, grace, connotation, pleasure)" (Sadeghi-Yekta 2015: 159). The reminiscence theatre production was staged as a minimalist, stylized fictional play incorporating the essence of participants' stories into fictional characters, names, and locations. The play was set in a nursing home with an artist poised at her easel. As she painted, she arose and told the stories of participants as if they were random people passing by her window. Window story scenes were played out, introducing each character by holding a large empty frame over the character's face and shoulders. Music and dance were utilized for scene transitions. The actors wore black costumes with multicolored T-shirts. The main character, the artist, was dressed more elaborately. Audience members were arranged in a semicircle, with actors seated to the sides of the artist, who was center-stage. Scenes were presented proscenium-style, in open lines facing the audience. The play began and ended with actors mingling directly through the audience.

Finally, aesthetic evaluation refers to how an artwork is evaluated. The play was evaluated in several ways. First, postproduction rating surveys were obtained from the ninety audience members (fifteen were completed in part or in full). The majority of evaluation came in the form of verbal feedback from guests, staff, the older adult participants themselves, and my own ethnodrama field notes and those from the devising company. The final reminiscence theatre piece was aesthetically strong—smooth transitions between scenes, great use of relevant songs, light, movement, and text. The included older adult participants' story experiences were recognizable. The production was visually pleasing and emotionally moving. This was evidenced in evaluation surveys and direct comments from audience and participants alike.

Although aesthetics discourse is important to applied theatre, I feel it is more valuable here to comment on the aesthetics of experience in everyday life that, in my view, was immensely significant to this study. From observations as a healthcare provider, researcher, and artist, I assert that dementia individuals are not viewing theatre for idealistic aesthetic quality; they are, as I am too, most interested in the moment by moment experiences.

I turn to the dementia audience members, whose comments speak for themselves. The following citations, recorded in my ethnotheatre journal, exemplify their creative capabilities while dispelling stereotypical perceptions of loss and disability. As noted by Basting (2006), while memory in dementia dissipates, the ability to engage in imaginative activity remains.

A few notable preproduction comments stand out. One participant, during a life history interview, protested: "This is ridiculous. Can't we just have a conversation, please?" (Pauluth-Penner 2018: 821). Another participant requested: "Why not tell the story just as it was? Why not use my name as it is; my face too? It shows who I am and my story. Please do tell, for it is what matters most to me!" (837).

A number of postproduction comments were noteworthy. After the final musical dance number, a participant exclaimed while walking back to her room: "I love your love songs ... they felt like a massage" (Pauluth-Penner 2018: 357). Another participant stated that it was like watching a rainbow dance; she engulfed me with a huge hug and said: "I can't believe you all did this for us" (359). She then asked why, and I responded, "Because you are important to us" (359). And finally, a nurse commented about one of the participants: "Joe is back ... sparkling, interacting with others ... goes for walks now ... he awaits the arrival of the young people" (786).

Although aesthetically successful, the production was ethically remiss on participants' representation. A few family members expressed disappointment about the absence of their loved one's stories. In this interdisciplinary reminiscence theatre study, despite efforts to set the context for collaboration and equitable relations, the aesthetics discourse dominated over the aims and ethical intentions of the health research—paying tribute and honoring the lived experiences of all older adult participants. Representation for each participant was overshadowed by the desire to create quality theatre. An ethics of acceptance framework could be beneficial in navigating such conflicts in applied theatre endeavors.

Conclusion

While advocating an ethics of acceptance for applied theatre practice, it is important to stress that acceptance is not capitulation or surrender. Rather, it is a reciprocal negotiation process acknowledging contextual limitations, while facilitating deeper understanding that encourages connections between diverse practices. When we acknowledge the constraints beyond our control that implicitly or explicitly influence our work, we are more likely to successfully navigate systems with ethical integrity while at the same time discovering the through-line that equitably balances aesthetic and representational intentions.

This chapter closes with a poetic narrative representative of one older adult participant's story. As expressed by Jack (2018), poetry can reconnect us with an emotional experience, allowing us to articulate what we have not yet understood but have felt. Poetic inquiry as a form of social science research elicits emotional response to create a shared experience, reconfirming and reconstructing the lived experience of others. Prendergast (2009) points out that poetic inquiry aims to synthesize experience in a direct and affective manner. Poetic inquiry occurred intuitively for me when writing up the older adult participants' stories for the dissertation, as synthesized stories prefaced with found poems created out of my data.

Here is Damian's story, which exemplifies remarkable inspirational resilience, yet was notably absent from the reminiscence theatre performance of *The Artist and Her Daughter.*

To Dare
(Adapted from a case study transcript; in Pauluth-Penner 2018: 263–4)
 One, two, three …
I dare you
Dare you
stand on the x
Dare you
utter a sound
or
break a stick
with your
worn out
boot.

Dare you …
Come on,
I will if
you will
stand on the x.

Here, take my hand,
hold tight
on the count of 3
one …
 two …
three.

Jump,
one
Bullet
One

stomach
no longer.

Damien (pseudonym), aged 92, was born in a town in Ukraine in an area that was part of the former eastern Czechoslovakia. He had a very traumatic life during the Second World War; despite this, he had great adventures with his best friend as they joyfully out-dared each other.

One such adventure changed their lives forever. Damien and his friend, convinced that their citizenship in the Czechoslovakian Republic would shield them from any harm, ventured off to what they believed was the Polish border, between Finland and Russia. They had been enticed by rumors of "Xs" on the ground that marked the territory at the border. Although they knew that crossing the markers was strictly forbidden, they ventured off regardless, protected (so they thought) by their shield of armor with which they had so keenly become accustomed.

Tragically, these Xs did not mark the Polish border but the Russian one. Damien recalled armed guards marching along the border line. When the two guards had their backs turned, 200 yards away, they decided to play a game and cross the line, believing they would go unnoticed. Both took the leap, directly into a line of fire. Damien exclaimed: "They shot him … I watched him fall … Me? … no shot for me; because I was so small, the soldiers believed I was a child … too young … They felt sorry for me … Even the Russians have heart!" Consequently, Damien served three years in one camp, then several others, the last in a Russian camp close to the Finnish border. He described the deplorable conditions: "You live, sleep in the same clothes … outside 40 degrees below zero; then you work." Damian is a true hero of resilience as he bears no hatred—just an enthusiasm for life, an acceptance for what was, and a heartfelt appreciation for his life here. I leave you with his last words to me:

My Life Now: 'From Home to Home'

(Adapted from a case study transcript; in Pauluth-Penner 2018: 270)
I have come from the camps
To here; I live here now

At the sea's edge
A good place for me,
my friend's house,
my private place,
What more can I ask for?

Shelter, to sleep, food to eat
And the most beautiful beach in the world
That I now call home.

References

Afolabi, T. (2018), "Becoming ethical through relational interaction: an examination of a performance among internally displaced persons in Nigeria," *Performing Ethos*, 8 (1), 3–18. doi:10.1386/peet.8.3_1

Basting, A. D. (2006), "Arts in dementia care: 'this is not the end … it's the end of this chapter,'"*Generations*, 30 (1), 16–20.

Beck, J., Belliveau, G., Lea, G., and Wager, A. (2011), "Delineating a spectrum of research-based theatre," *Qualitative Inquiry*, 17 (8), 687–700.

Bishop, K. (2014), "Six perspectives in search of an ethical solution: utilising a moral imperative with a multiple ethics paradigm to guide research-based theatre/applied theatre," *Research in Drama Education: The Journal of Applied Theatre and Performance*, 19 (1), 64–75.

Bruce, A., Beuthin, R., Shields, L., Molzahn, A., and Schick-Makaroff, K. (2016), "Narrative research evolving: evolving through narrative research," *International Journal of Qualitative Methods*, 15 (1), 1–6. doi:10.1177/1609406916659292

Campbell, E. and Lassiter, L. E. (2015), *Doing Ethnography Today: Theories, Methods, Exercises*. Chichester, West Sussex: Wiley.

Cohen, C. E., Varea, R. G., and Walker, P. O. (eds) (2011), *Acting Together: Performance and the Creative Transformation of Violence: Vol. 1: Resistance and Reconciliation in Regions of Violence*. New York: New Village Press.

Dalrymple, L. (2006), "Has it made a difference? Understanding and measuring the impact of applied theatre with young people in the South African context," *Research in Drama Education: The Journal of Applied Theatre and Performance*, 11 (2), 201–18.

Dobson, W. and Goode, T. (2002), "Taking care of basics: a reminiscence theatre project," in B. Warren (ed.), *Creating a Theatre in Your Classroom and Community* (2nd ed.). North York, ON: Captus Press, pp. 179–92.

Eifert, G. H. and Forsyth, J. P. (2005), *Acceptance and Commitment Therapy for Anxiety Disorders*. Oakland, CA: New Harbinger Publications.

Gjaerum, R. G. (2013), "Applied theatre research: discourses in the field," *European Scientific Journal*, 9 (10), 347–61. https://doi.org/10.19044/esj.2013.v9n10p%25p

Hayes, S. C., Strosahl, K. D., Bunting, K., Twohig, M., and Wilson, K. G. (2004), "What is acceptance and commitment therapy?," in S. C. Hayes and K. D. Strosahl (eds), A *Practical Guide to Acceptance and Commitment Therapy*. New York: Springer, pp. 3–29.

Jack, B. (2018), "The art of medicine: poetry and emotion," *The Lancet*, 391, 732–3.

Kerr, D. (2009), "Ethics of applied theatre," *South African Theatre Journal*, 23 (1), 177–87.

Kontos, P. C. (2010), "Embodied selfhood: ethnographic reflections, performing ethnography, and humanizing dementia care," in J. E. Graham and P. H. Stephenson (eds), *Contesting Aging & Loss*. Toronto, ON: University of Toronto Press, pp. 125–52.

Neelands, J. (2007), "Taming the political: the struggle over recognition in the politics of applied theatre," *Research in Drama Education: The Journal of Applied Theatre and Performance*, 12 (3), 305–17.

Nicholson, H. (2005), "On ethics," *Research in Drama Education: The Journal of Applied Theatre and Performance*, 10 (2), 119–25.

Nicholson, H. (2011), "Making home work: theatre-making with older adults in residential care," *NJ: Drama Australia Journal*, 35 (1), 47–62.

Nuffield Council on Bioethics (2009), *Dementia: Ethical Issues*. Cambridge: Cambridge Publishers Ltd.

Oxford University Press (2018), *Oxford Dictionary of English*. Available online: www.softwareabyss.net/2014/10/oxford-dictionary-of-english-free.html (accessed April 30, 2021).

Pauluth-Penner, T. (2018), "Moving forwards backwards: exploring the impact of active engagement in reminiscence theatre with older adults in residential care with mild to moderate cognitive impairment," unpublished PhD dissertation. University of Victoria, Victoria, BC. Available online: https://dspace.library.uvic.ca//handle/1828/10130 (accessed April 30, 2021).

Prendergast, M. (2009), "'Poem is what?' Poetic inquiry in qualitative social science research," *International Review of Qualitative Research*, 1 (4), 541–68.

Sadeghi-Yekta, K. (2015), "Competing international players and their aesthetic initiatives: the future of internationalized applied theatre practice?," in G. White (ed.), *Applied Theatre: Aesthetics*. London: Bloomsbury, pp. 156–93.

Simons, H. (2006), "Ethics in evaluation," in I. F. Shaw, J. C. Greene, and M. M. Mark (eds), *The SAGE Handbook of Evaluation*. London: SAGE, pp. 243–65.

Stuart Fisher, A. (2005), "Developing an ethics of practice in applied theatre: Badiou and fidelity to the truth of the event," *Research in Drama Education: The Journal of Applied Theatre and Performance*, 10 (2), 257–62.

Tuokko, H. A. and Smart, C. M. (2018), *Neuropsychology of Cognitive Decline: A Developmental Approach to Assessment and Intervention*. New York: Guilford Press.

White, M. (2009), *Arts Development in Community Health: A Social Tonic*. Oxford: Radcliffe Publishing.

Wilkinson, S. and Kitzinger, C. (2009), "Representing the other," in T. Prentki and S. Preston (eds), *The Applied Theatre Reader*. New York: Routledge, pp. 86–93.

8

"Dark Night Ends": The Ethics of Vulnerability in Applied Theatre

Zoe Zontou

Question: Have you ever experienced the dark night of the soul? Your teachings have been so helpful through this difficult period. Can you address this subject?

Eckhart: The "dark night of the soul" is a term that goes back a long time. Yes, I have also experienced it. It is a term used to describe what one could call a collapse of a perceived meaning in life … an eruption into your life of a deep sense of meaninglessness. The inner state in some cases is very close to what is conventionally called depression. Nothing makes sense anymore, there's no purpose to anything. (Tolle 2020: n.p.)

Eckhart Tolle, a spiritual teacher and author renowned for his work on depression and spiritual awakening, exemplifies the experiences of depression and deep meaninglessness experienced by many people. He is using the metaphor of "dark night of the soul" as a medium to address and give meaning to emotions and inner states that at times are difficult to articulate in words. Tolle's quote was the entering point of the performance project "Creative Conversations," a verbatim dance theatre project with people in recovery from addiction to alcohol and other drugs that took place in Liverpool, UK, in 2017 and 2018. My involvement in the project was as a member of the creative team and project evaluator. For the first session, participants were asked to bring readings or texts that had inspired or helped their recovery process. "Dan,"[1] one of the participants, brought the above extract from Tolle's interview that stimulated really interesting conversations among the participants and the creative team. He explained that Tolle's quote resonates with his experiences of recovery from addiction to substances, and that the symbolism of dark night is a useful allegory to depict his experiences. Other members shared similar experiences of trauma, pain, chaos, and a sense of loss of control, accompanied by messages of hope for a positive future. Each story revealed the complexity, diversity, and ambiguity of what it means to be in recovery from addiction. A common ground among participants was established very quickly, emphasizing that personal accounts of addiction recovery are varied and too complex to fully articulate into words. Hence, borrowing from Tolle, *Dark Night Ends* was chosen as the theme to explore throughout the project and subsequently became the title of the final performance.

This initial sharing of ideas and personal experiences created a framework for the start of the creative process, but also raised some immediate ethical tensions and artistic dilemmas, in terms of how to represent personal experiences of "dark night of the soul" on stage in ways that avoid the risk of re-traumatization or victimization. It raised the following questions: What ethical guidelines and modes of ethical practice are appropriate in working artistically with lived experiences, particularly when the project is focusing on difficult and painful experiences? What are effective ways to handle the risks of reinforcing re-stigmatization and unequal power relations in the context of applied theatre that draw on the personal and collective experiences of participants? How does one deal with the complexities of vulnerability in co-creating artistic practice for the development of a performance?

The project has enabled a rethinking of the ethics in making performance based on personal experiences of addiction recovery. Extending from Rosi Braidotti's suggestion that we need to "invent a form of ethical relations, norms and values worthy of the complexity of our times" (Braidotti 2013: 86), this chapter traces how my thinking about ethics in applied theatre practice has shifted, particularly in terms of how we respond to the concept of vulnerability. This has been influenced by Fiona Bannon (2019), who in her book *Considering*

Ethics in Dance, Theatre and Performance explores the concept of relational ethics, in conjunction with Erinn Gilson's (2016) *The Ethics of Vulnerability: A Feminist Analysis of Social Life and Practice*, which questions current discourses on vulnerability and otherness. In doing so, I suggest that applied theatre needs to attend to the important ethical issues of power dynamics, duty of care, and relational practice when lived experiences are employed in performance creation.

Creative Conversations: Background to Project

The project "Creative Conversations" was led by Fallen Angels Dance Theatre (henceforth Fallen Angels), a charity working with people in recovery from addiction, and in collaboration with the multi-instrument composer Lee Affen and myself as an applied theatre practitioner-researcher and project evaluator. Supported by the Paul Hamlyn Foundation Access and Participation Fund Explore and Test, the project aimed to develop an innovative approach to creating fully inclusive performances with people in recovery from addiction, that initiate "creative conversations" with the wider public about addiction stigma and recovery. In particular, it aimed to address the possibilities and challenges of using spoken word, music, and dance to create a methodology of dramatizing and choreographing personal experiences of addiction and recovery. The project took place in Merseyside, UK, and engaged with three local addiction recovery groups. These comprised members of the Spider Project, a creative arts and well-being recovery community project based on the Wirral, Merseyside, members of Tom Harrison House: Military Veteran Addiction Recovery Center, which is a specialist facility providing an addiction recovery program exclusively for military veterans, and members of Fallen Angels Liverpool recovery dance group with a previous experience of working with dance and theatre.

The participants were in different stages of their recovery process, varying from one month to two years, and had a wide range of cultural and personal backgrounds in addiction and recovery. Moreover, a number of members were participating for the first time in a creative project of this scale. Fallen Angels' previous projects evidenced an increased participation of people with complex well-being and social needs. The artistic methodology deployed in this project explored alternative ways of gathering and telling stories of addiction recovery through movement. It emphasized the lived experiences of the participants' personal stories of addiction recovery, which frequently offer poignant insight into the often-unspoken stories and experiences of overcoming addiction.[2]

My role as a member of the creative team allowed an insider/ outsider status in the process of choreographing the piece and directing the final performance, while providing a framework for a contextual analysis of Fallen Angels' artistic approach. As a member of the creative team, I was responsible for the delivery of the project and worked in liaison with Fallen Angels' artistic director Paul Bayes Kitcher to create the final performance. As part of this, I acquired an insider's access to the artistic rationale behind the project, and intimate knowledge of the group's dynamics. In my secondary role as a project evaluator, I had to distance myself from the creative process in order to effectively monitor and gather evidence about the participants' experiences. Hence, in addition to documenting how the participants engaged with the project, I aimed to closely observe the creative methodologies deployed by Fallen Angels in translating personal stories into performance work. My analysis focuses on the conversations of the creative team and participants' responses.

Towards an Ethics of Vulnerability in Applied Theatre Practice

Applied theatre considers vulnerability in multiple ways. Thus, vulnerability plays a crucial part in the process of making performance in different contexts, and with different social groups. It is often targeted at participants who might already be classified as "vulnerable" or "at risk of being vulnerable" in social, political, and economic terms. Indeed, participation in the process of making performance invariably requires a subjective "disposition" drawn from the individual's own experiences. To this end, the process of making performances requires a degree of openness to *becoming* vulnerable and being exposed to and with others. Our subjective vulnerabilities are constantly shifting and changing as we learn to share our personal experiences, co-create with others, and shape the creative process. Vulnerability is relational in that sense, but also because our connectivity and collective moments of creativity with others are in themselves potentially both vulnerable and precarious.

In her book *Daring Greatly*, Brené Brown discusses the concept of vulnerability, which she connects with feelings of uncertainty, risk, and emotional exposure. She argues that vulnerability is "the birthplace of love, belonging, joy, courage, empathy, and creativity. It is the source of hope, empathy, accountability, and authenticity" (Brown 2012: 33). According to Brown (2012) the tendency to associate vulnerability only as weakness or with dark emotions that we do not want to discuss is a dangerous misconception. Her definition has been key in shifting my understanding of the role of vulnerability in applied theatre ethics, particularly when we consider how prevalent the concept of vulnerability as weakness is within the bounds of this field. Within applied theatre the term has been used to describe groups such as, for example, offenders, children, disadvantaged youth, or victims of domestic abuse as vulnerable populations, or as those at "vulnerable points in their lives" (Nicholson 2005: 119). Brown's position on vulnerability urges us to make a clearer distinction between vulnerability as a condition imposed upon the vulnerable others or as a necessary act of growing, maturing, and finding the courage to express ourselves.

In the context of applied theatre, being vulnerable means being exposed together both as artists/facilitators and participants and learning to *create together* without entering into paradigms of exploitation and re-traumatization, and in ways that value personal experience. As Helen Nicholson maintains, it helps develop creative spaces "in which people feel safe enough to take risks and to allow themselves and others to experience vulnerability" (Nicholson 2005: 129). Hence, the moments of creating applied theatre are as vulnerable as the people who engage in it. Applied theatre requires a certain degree of exposure and risk alongside a radical openness to other people's differences and creative imperatives. From an ethical perspective this would mean that the issues of power dynamics, agency, and duty of care heavily rely on the interpersonal understandings and multilayered levels of vulnerability that coexist in the workshop/rehearsal space. However, extending the definition of vulnerability becomes complicated when working with participants who are considered as vulnerable or at risk of being vulnerable in social, political, or economic terms. These issues can be amplified by the fact that in many cases participants in applied theatre projects might not have previous experience of participating in a creative project, let alone have used their personal lived experiences to create a performance. Hence, it might be difficult for participants to anticipate what comes next, what the outcomes may entail for them, and what the ramifications of the process might be. This raises fundamental concerns about how to work with lived experiences and vulnerabilities in an ethically sustainable manner.

Other scholars in the field share similar concerns. For instance, Salverson (1996) argues that a potential weakness of theatre that draws on the lived experiences of participants is the idealization of staging vulnerability as worthwhile or a notable achievement in itself. Baim makes this point more explicitly by stating that "by merely staging pain and suffering is not an answer in itself and runs the serious risk of voyeurism, collusion with oppression, and even re-abuse and re-traumatization of victims" (2017: 87). He moves on to assert that if we are to remain ethical, personal stories of vulnerability "should never be presented as an unexamined spectacle and never with the assumption that the theatre artist is rebalancing the scale of justice" (88). These scholars both recognize the complexity of working with vulnerabilities and highlight the significant need to constantly reflect upon and renegotiate our ethical models of practice. They call for caution in the use of lived experiences, which, although they have become a consolidated feature of applied theatre, may not be unproblematic. This is particularly the case in reference to issues related to exposing participants' vulnerabilities as personal failures, and in perpetuating existing misconceptions about, for example, recovery and addiction. Practitioners and performers in the field should be aware of such complexities and give priority to considering the ethics that underpin such acts. Hence, both Salverson and Baim propose that attention needs to be placed upon the development of an ethics of practice that avoids either trivialization or sensationalization of personal experiences. This, in turn, echoes the suggestion by Braidotti that ethics need to be concerned with a different level of accountability that allows us to find new ways to combine "self-interests with the well-being of an enlarged sense of community" (2006: 35). I am therefore advocating a re-theorization of vulnerability in relation to ethics in applied theatre. We must consider in more depth what we mean by vulnerability in the context of applied theatre practice, and by the same token, what it means to experience vulnerability in order to better explore ethical responses.

In *The Ethics of Vulnerability*, Gilson moves this argument further when exploring the implications of how different assertions on vulnerability led to its association with weakness, liabilities, incapability, and notions of powerlessness. Similarly to Brown (2012), Gilson argues that these negative connotations are reductive for two main reasons: firstly, they imply an implicit understanding of vulnerability as a sign of weakness; and secondly, they devalue vulnerability as something socially "bad," a sign of personal failure. She refuses to accept the normative frame of vulnerability as given but rather examines it as a possibility. For Gilson, vulnerability describes the very structure of subjectivity, and its "transcendental condition, pointing to an openness and plasticity that makes possible transformation" (2016: 10). She maintains that vulnerability can be viewed as an ethical resource that helps manifest virtues of empathy, compassion, and community. Hence, by treating vulnerability as politically productive, as a contingent performative process rather than as a stable categorical marker, we can better understand what it achieves.

In extending this argument, I examine Alice O'Grady's concept of "critical vulnerability," which she uses to examine "how the core characteristics of openness, uncertainty, and varying degrees of exposure contribute to an aesthetic paradigm where risk is deployed as an intentional tactic, a strategy of engagement" (O'Grady 2017: xi). In a similar vein to Brown (2012) and Gilson (2016), vulnerability for O'Grady offers itself as a possibility, in which openness, uncertainty, and exposure become a deliberate aesthetic choice and a critical tool for engagement. Applied theatre develops creative spaces in which participants and facilitators might experience moments of *critical* vulnerabilities together, and in so doing, ethical relations are informed by an ethos that embraces *being-with-others*. An ethics of vulnerability is framed as an adaptive practice of being and doing beyond any prefixed moral codes.

For instance, in the "Creative Conversations" project, each workshop began with open discussion (check-in) in which everyone had the chance to talk about their feelings in the present moment. This was an opportunity to talk to each other, share stories, news, or even just express feelings in the moment. These introductory discussions aimed to help participants express themselves in an open environment, connect with each other, and focus on the here and now of the workshop. It set up the foundations for the workshop, as often the participants were asked to reflect through movement on a specific area of their life story, or events and feelings that were shared at the start of the workshop. The same approach was utilized at the end of each workshop (check-out), when the participants had an opportunity to reflect and share their responses with each other. This ceremonial space allowed the participants to open up and relate to each other. It gave them the opportunity to discuss issues that mattered to them in the current moment and an agency to shape the creative process based on these sharing experiences. This mode of practice offers an appreciation of ethical work as relational in association with the others with whom we co-create and correspond.

Crucially, an ethics of vulnerability affords participants the agency to make their own choices and offers a paradigm within which to understand the complexities of working with embodied, difficult past and present experiences. The role of the artist/facilitator in the instance is to provide spaces for the participants' shared vulnerabilities to constitute the basis of ethical responsiveness. For example, in the second workshop one participant discussed how they often experience intense moments of racing thoughts which can be confusing and conflicting and cause anxiety and distress. That week they started going for long walks on the beach, which seemed to help them to calm down. Other participants discussed similar experiences and shared ideas on how breathing, meditation, and connecting with nature can be useful self-care practices for people in recovery. Following this disclosure, Bayes Kitcher invited the participants to create a sequence of movements that contrast racing, confused thoughts with calmness, tranquility, and serenity. He urged participants to use the beach as the starting point of their movement improvisation, recalling its smells, sounds, and colors. The participants created movements that reflected the transitions from distress to calmness. Wheeling and erratic movements were followed by stillness, breathing, and slow movements. This moment of shared vulnerability in participants' lives became the starting point of a new aesthetic paradigm, where a traumatic experience is collectively explored as a strategy of engagement, creativity, and empathetic connection. Hence, working with juxtaposed movements in solo or pairs, and exploring contrasting feelings and experiences, helped to generate the creative material, and placed relationality and critical vulnerability at the core of the creative process.

Over the years of working with people in recovery from addiction to stage their lived experiences, I have become anxious as to how personal stories, such as the moment discussed above, can be translated in ways that do not victimize or produce the stereotypes and stigma attached to addiction. In my role in the artistic team as an applied theatre facilitator and in order to fully comprehend Bayes Kitcher's methods of working, I have sought to explore creative approaches that put value on the embodied experience and participants' artistry, and at the same time demonstrate duty of care. One of the fundamental insights of my ongoing inquiry in this field is that, when people in recovery from addiction are presented with opportunities to work creatively with their lived experiences, it is often accompanied by a notion of "redemption," an openness and strong imperative to tell and share their experience (Zontou 2017; 2019).

This imperative to share, however, presents an ethical problem for two main reasons. Firstly, public attitudes towards people with a history of drug dependency remain rather negative. Reports on attitudes towards people with drug dependency problems or those in recovery indicate that a significant proportion of the population believes that people with drug addiction have a responsibility for their own situation, and that recovery from addiction is a matter of personal agency (Lloyd 2010; Scottish Government 2016). These categorical ideas of responsibility and agency undermine the complexity involved in the process of recovering from addiction. They also suggest that shifting the public attitude on addiction recovery through performance is a rather complex process. Secondly, even when individuals are not identified as vulnerable or at risk, the nature of the lived experience shared, the context in which one is working, the processes used, or the mode in which the lived experience is presented in the workshop or to an audience may in fact make participants vulnerable. This raises a crucial question. How we can remain faithful to the participants' imperative to tell, but at the same time avoid stigmatization or reproduction of stereotypes?

Cathy Sloan (2017), in her account of directing Simon Mason's autobiographical solo performance *Too High Too Far Too Soon*, describes the challenge of avoiding "aesthetizing" the experiences of addiction. She draws attention to the fact that if we are to remain faithful to the lived experiences of people in recovery from addiction, we must inevitably consider including scenes that represent rituals and behavior patterns related to past drug-taking. She highlights that one of the most important aspects of staging real narratives of addiction recovery is the intention of passing on the hope of recovery to those who might have been affected by it, while also challenging the social attitudes towards addicts in the wider public. Similarly to Sloan, I regard my responsibility as an artist-outsider who enters the group setting is to transform participants' lived experiences into a performance that is meaningful and owned by them. This echoes Bannon, who maintains: "What remains important (…) is a developing association with ethics as a rational and social process. In this way, the journey is, in effect, an exploration of social and creative encounters that occur between individuals when they operate as beings-in-common" (2019: 6). Throughout the "Creative Conversations" project, we were offering the workshops as an open space in which stories of addiction and recovery could be expressed and realized as artistic material, as well as a space to openly discuss the ethical concerns that arose in the process and finding ways to overcome them. Understanding together the challenges presented in working towards a performance based on their experiences was highly important. In this way ethics became the participants' and facilitators' shared responsibility. Bayes Kitcher's personal experience of being in recovery from addiction operated as a crucial starting point in opening up a dialogue with the participants about addiction and recovery, and introduced them to ways of working creatively with these experiences. This generated a sense of emotional attunement between Bayes Kitcher as the leading facilitator and the participants that was informed by a relational interpersonal connection with their stories. His ability to connect with the participants at a personal level had a strong impact on the way that they engaged and responded to the creative process.

Critical vulnerability was mobilized as a useful tool throughout the creative process and established spaces in which participants felt open to express themselves and relate to others. As I discussed in the earlier examples and go on to explore in the next section, each session opened with personal sharing, which was then translated into movement. Hence, the lived experiences that participants chose to discuss or bring into the workshop space were at the core of the process. In this way, the participants were co-creators and collaborators, responding and reflecting on the material produced at the moment, and helping them become attuned with each other. Hence, relationality became an important component of our artistic practice. It enabled us to build a deeper connection with the group's creative imperative and challenged us to reconsider how we work together and what we thought might be possible within this particular process.

"Life on highs to high on life"

A moment of critical vulnerability occurred in the fourth workshop. "Jenny" had written a poem in which she described her journey from initial drug consumption and getting "high" to finding recovery. The poem was entitled "Life on highs to high on life" and traced her journey from the highs and lows of addiction to the lows and highs of being in recovery. She recalled writing the poem when she was not in a good place, feeling isolated, alone, and suicidal, then returning to it later to add another section on the merits of recovery ("Jenny" 2017). The creative team's initial response was that from an ethical perspective it was perhaps too "risky" to work creatively with the past traumatic experience cited in the poem. We had to be mindful of the participant's recovery stages and avoid specific triggers that might cause relapse or reinforce revisiting traumatic experiences both for Jenny and the other members. For example, the poem's opening line, "Flying so high up in the sky, fooled by the way drugs lie, losing touch with what was real, I loved the way drugs made me feel," could have been a trigger for relapse. Triggers are social, environmental, or emotional situations that remind people in recovery of their past drug or alcohol use. These cues bring about urges that may lead to a relapse. While triggers do not force a person to use drugs, they increase the likelihood of drug use (Relapse Triggers 2012). However, it also felt unethical to shut down Jenny's imperative to share her experiences. We therefore decided to find a symbolic and abstract way of "telling" the poem using fragmented text, sounds, and movement. We did a group reading of the poem and participants were asked to pick words or phrases that resonated with them, which we then used as a stimulus to create a sequence of movements and a soundscape. There were two parts in Jenny's poem. The first part, which was quite harsh, describing her attachment to drugs, loss of self and control, and so on, and the second, more positive part, in which she talked about her recovery. When we asked participants to choose a phrase that resonated with them, they all selected words from the first part, such as: "Death is ringing its alarm bell, as I went round on a drunk carousel, but soon obsession began to linger, time after time I kept on falling." This was astounding, and I was unsure why it happened. Was it the poetic language that draws them into this? Or does this show that this is the part of the story that they want to tell? How can we move the creative process from here? (Research diary 2017).

The initial discomfort I experienced when the participants chose phrases that alluded to their past active drug consumption, accompanied by not knowing how to steer the process away from the phrases, made me realize how in fact it was my own vulnerability that was blocking the process. I was perhaps too preoccupied in thinking of my obligation to cause no harm and was stuck in a prefixed definition of vulnerability. I had taken for granted that the meaning of vulnerability is to be susceptible to harm. In reflection, I recognize that this reaction was inherent from the institutional prescriptive and protective ethical protocols I am used to following, in which a set of guidelines are offered as a mechanism to ensure duty of care. My vulnerability here emerged out of fear of not knowing how to both embrace the participants' creative impulse and remain ethical in terms of causing no harm (possible relapse or distress). Aside from this, my vulnerability was amplified as I recognized my status as an outsider practitioner-academic, and as the only person in the room without a direct experience of recovering from addiction. This has created a dilemma between openly expressing my vulnerability—by admitting that I was unsure on how to navigate this challenging situation—and at the same time maintaining my credibility. The tension between remaining ethical, experiencing vulnerability, and seeking credibility created a significant challenge which added a tension between ethical dilemmas, artistic excellence, and accountability. It was my responsibility to demonstrate duty of care and professionalism in handling challenging situations, in addition to successfully delivering the project. This moment of practice revealed the complexity, diversity, and ambiguity surrounding who should be vulnerable in the context of the creative process, and how these dynamics are constantly shifting.

Gilson asserts that one of the central challenges of vulnerability is the fact that it derives from a deep sense of discomfort with the unfamiliar, the unpredictable, and uncontrollable. Yet it is through engagements with these experiences that we learn how to change and "extend ourselves beyond our current limits" (2016: 127). Learning how to balance the tension between vulnerability and credibility was an important learning curve in this process. Reflecting back on this moment of practice reveals that it was of paramount importance to *distance* myself from the preselected set of conceptions on what constitutes an ethical way and, rather, to allow the participants to reflect upon their own "repertoire" of stories and lived experiences. This moment of critical vulnerability helped me to recognize that the stories that participants choose to tell are "something that they care about, something important for them" (Mankowski and Rappaport 2000: 481), and for this reason, I sought to trust the participants' imperative to share their experiences. The way to deal with ethics is to approach the creative process with the necessary sensitivity and duty of care but in a way that allows participants and facilitators alike to experience vulnerability.

In the case of the "Creative Conversations" project, the participants wanted to put emphasis on the highs and lows of addiction, patterns of behavior, and moments of "dark night ends." Our responsibility as facilitators was to find ways of accommodating their imperative to tell this specific lived experience, and to openly acknowledge that as part of relational ethics of vulnerability, "we seek to deal with the reality and practice of changing relationships with our […] participants over time" (Ellis 2007: 4). For this it was necessary for us as facilitators to be open and honest in expressing our worries and anxieties. As I mentioned earlier, the participants had already established an emotional attunement and strong relationship with Bayes Kitcher, who has made it part of his practice to openly discuss his thoughts and worries with the groups on a regular basis during the check-in and check-out. Hence, I was the one that needed to deal with my vulnerability and let go of my fears of failing and losing credibility. During the check-out at the end of the session, I openly expressed my concerns about the ethical issues that might arise, highlighting that aside from participants, the experiences and behaviors cited in the poem might be triggering for any audience members in recovery. I acknowledged that I was unsure about the best way forward and invited the participants to share their thoughts. Following this, we reflected together as a group on how to creatively depict the experiences mentioned in the poem without "aestheticizing experiences" (Sloan 2017) or triggering cues of past behaviors. We collectively, therefore, agreed that symbolism and an abstract approach for navigating this process was the best way forward. Following from this moment of practice, rehearsals, decisions, and discussions of the creative challenges of choreographing extracts of the poem were navigated through a mutually reflexive process, a continual negotiation of what we all felt would be acceptable to perform and how it would be performed, including how the performance should safeguard audiences that had similar experiences. From this position, we acknowledged that it is our varied abilities to reflect upon experiences and contexts that will help us to recognize the best way of dealing with the ethical apparatuses of our practice. In this particular example of practice, the unpredictable response of the participants became the genesis of a moment of relational vulnerability and forced me in particular, as an outsider to the group, to reconsider my own subjectivity:

> When we moved into movement improvisation it was really fascinating to watch how they completely shifted the literal meaning of these phrases from their negative associations into something so beautiful and hopeful. Sharp movements of connecting and disconnecting their bodies, giving us glimpses of their shared histories and collective vulnerabilities. The emotions and behaviors described in the poem

were once their own reality too and is perhaps our duty not to shy away from them. (Research diary 2017)

The experiences of addiction and recovery made the participants who they are and without them it would have been impossible to create such work. Therefore, it became important to approach ethics as resource and possibility. For the final choreographed material, we used a red rope from which the dancers were trying to untangle themselves to represent the fragility and uncontrollable sense of loss of control experienced in active addiction. The preselected phrases from the poem were recorded and presented as fragments looping through the soundscape that composer Lee Affen created. By incorporating visuals, kinesthetics, and voice-overs, we were able to symbolically portray the lived experiences depicted in the poem and represent them through performance. The participants' experiences of the harsh reality of addiction found a way to be articulated and revisited through the co-creation of a sequence of movements and images.

Developing a non-linear, highly symbolic way of exploring life experiences became fundamental to dealing with the ethical dilemmas presented in this project. The creative process was shaped around the understanding that recovery journeys are non-linear and complex. Participants were encouraged to explore through movement and sound their transitions from the betwixt and between gray areas of addiction and recovery and share moments of when the "dark night ended": "There was something quite intriguing about observing the particular movements that the participants created as a response to Jenny's poem. Frantic, fragile, reaching out and resisting, pushing and pulling. Simultaneous moments of connecting and disconnecting, togetherness and separation, hope and hopelessness. The poetics of fragility" (Research diary, 2018).

Nussbaum (2016) writes of the need for openness to life in coming to terms with vulnerability, fragility, anger, and social justice. She highlights the balance between the capacity for vulnerability and the ability to trust others in exploring the ethical dimensions of resentment, generosity, anger, and forgiveness. This has many resonances with the

"Creative Conversations" project as, throughout it, the relations and bonds that we formed with the participants required us to reconsider what an ethics of care might look like. Jenny's poem "Life on highs to high on life" expresses the poetics of fragility and urges us to consider how moments of vulnerability in our lives can be the birthplace of belonging, creativity, and empathy (Brown 2012). The poetics of fragility is a useful metaphor to further articulate the role that relational ethics should play in applied theatre. Any consideration of ethics should encompass the idea that we must explore and share the things that make us uncomfortable, our vulnerabilities. As facilitators, we must lean into the discomfort to make sense of the messy emotions that surround the process of making applied theatre with different groups. In order to build stronger relationships and deliver better applied theatre practice, we must embrace the poetics of fragility.

Concluding Remarks

In this chapter, I examined in detail the ethical, methodological, and practical implications of the ethics of vulnerability in my work with people in recovery from addiction. Although much of the discussion documented here takes an anecdotal form, it is my hope that some insights offered might propose various useful strategies of working towards an ethics of vulnerability in applied theatre. Throughout my analysis I argued that a political approach to vulnerability in applied theatre sheds new light on the power dynamics at stake in the process of co-creating performance with marginalized groups. The project "Creative Conversations" project demonstrated a mode of ethics that both challenges and extends our understanding of ethical practice in applied theatre, and how we think about vulnerability, lived experiences, and the power of relationality in performance.

Through its improvisational structure and choreography, the project disrupted the normative way of "telling" a story on stage regarding how personal accounts can be interrogated in the performance. Both of the aforementioned concepts draw attention to the issues of co-creating work about lived experiences and negotiating the ethical dilemmas that arose in the process with sensitivity and with an acknowledgment of the role of vulnerability.

Throughout this chapter, I have argued that repositioning vulnerability at the center of applied theatre research and practice offers a new way of understanding the politics and ethics of representation. In aligning with the ethics and collaborative processes in applied theatre, I therefore assert that what is needed is an adaptive framework of ethics, as a practice that emerges through those interpersonal bonds and is the outcome of our responsible, responsive, and affective engagement with participants and facilitators. In the context of the "Creative Conversations" project, the ethical tensions that arose in the creative process made me reconsider how relational practices of vulnerability connect with power dynamics. The project contributed to a reconsideration of our capacity to engage with variation, in terms of the circumstances in which we each find ways to facilitate a retelling of "The Dark Night Ends." To conclude, my ethical principle would insist on the need to dismantle and reject negative assertions on vulnerability, particularly those that dictate the power dynamics of the creative process. We need to learn to provide spaces for our shared vulnerabilities to constitute the basis of ethical responsiveness. A reconsideration of the type of exposure associated with the notion of vulnerability in applied theatre might mean to conceive it positively, namely as a way of being open to the world and to others.

Notes

1   The participants' names have been changed to protect their identities.
2   For a detailed analysis of Fallen Angels' creative practice, see Zontou (2017, 2019).

References

Baim, C. (2017), "The drama spiral: a decision-making model for safe, ethical, and flexible practice when incorporating personal stories in applied theatre and performance," in A. O'Grady (ed.), *Risk, Participation, and Performance Practice: Critical Vulnerabilities in a Precarious World*. Cham, Switzerland: Palgrave Macmillan, pp. 79–109.

Bannon, F. (2019), *Considering Ethics in Dance, Theatre and Performance*. London: Palgrave Macmillan.

Braidotti, R. (2006), *Transpositions on Nomadic Ethics*. Cambridge: Polity Press.

Braidotti, R. (2013), *The Posthuman*. Oxford: Polity Press.

Brown, B. (2012), *How the Courage to be Vulnerable Transforms the Way We Live, Love, Parent and Lead*. New York: Gotham Books.

Ellis, C. (2007), "Telling secrets, revealing lives," *Qualitative Inquiry*, 13 (1), 3–29.

Gilson, E. C. (2016), *The Ethics of Vulnerability: A Feminist Analysis of Social Life and Practice*. London and New York: Routledge.

Lloyd, C. (2010), *Sinning and Sinned Against: The Stigmatisation of Problem Drug Users*. London: UK Drug Policy Commission.

Mankowski, E. S. and Rappaport, J. (2000), "Narrative concepts and analysis in spirituallybased communities," *Journal of Community Psychology*, 28 (5), 479–93.

Nicholson, H. (2005), *Applied Drama: The Gift of Theatre*. Houndmills, Basingstoke: Palgrave Macmillan.

Nussbaum, M. (2016), *Anger and Forgiveness: Resentment, Generosity, Justice*. New York: Oxford University Press.

O'Grady, A. ed. (2017), *Risk, participation, and performance practice: critical vulnerabilities in a precarious world*. Cham, Switzerland: Palgrave Macmillan.

Relapse Triggers (2012), "What are triggers and how do you identify them?" Drug Rehab. Available online: https://www.drugrehab.com/recovery/triggers/ (accessed June 23, 2020).

Salverson, J. (1996), "Performing emergency: witnessing, popular theatre, and the lie of the literal," *Theatre Topics*, 6 (2), 181–91.

Scottish Government (2016), *Public Attitudes towards People with Drug Dependency and People in Recovery*. Available online: http://www.gov.scot/Resource/0050/00501301.pdf (accessed March 20, 2020).

Sloan, C. (2017), "Aestheticizing addiction to generate change," *Performance Research*, 22 (6), 68–72.

Tolle, E. (2020), "Eckhart on the Dark Night of the Soul." Eckhart Tolle | Official Site—Spiritual Teachings and Tools for Personal Growth and Happiness. Available online: https://www.eckharttolle.com/eckhart-on-the-dark-night-of-the-soul (accessed June 5, 2020).

Zontou, Z. (2017), "Under the influence of … affective performance," *Performance Research*, 22 (6), 93–102.

Zontou, Z. (2019), "Performance, dislocation and spirituality," in M. Galea and M. Musca (eds), *Redefining Theatre Communities: International Perspectives in Community-Conscious Theatre-Making*. Bristol: Intellect, pp. 48–64.

9

Responsibility for the Other: An Ethic of Care in Applied Theatre Practice in Greek Refugee Camps

Anita Hallewas

Introduction

Refugee theatre falls under the applied theatre umbrella and yet Michael Balfour (2012) explains that it is not a term or style of theatre that was meant to exist as "no-one chooses to be a refugee and certainly it is a tag that new settlers seek to transcend as swiftly as possible" (xxi). For the purposes of this chapter, refugee theatre encompasses theatre created with and about refugees, as well as theatre created with former refugees who have found resettlement. Unfortunately, with global displacement growing by the millions annually, this subgenre of applied theatre is not going away. This chapter documents aspects of my doctoral research, which consisted of observational fieldwork in Greek island refugee camps in 2019 involving five theatre practitioners whose practice I share throughout this chapter. Italian Michele Senici taught drama workshops at Mazi, a school based at the foot of the Samos refugee camp. UK-based retired drama teacher Chris Walters taught drama at Gekko Kids, a school that supports unaccompanied minors on Lesvos, with his classes culminating in an English-Farsi adaptation of Brecht's *Caucasian Chalk Circle*. Kelly Buxton offers daily yoga classes at the women's only We Are One center on Samos, with her classes more closely aligning to drama and dance therapy. Two touring companies, Changing Stories from the Netherlands and The Flying Seagull Project from the UK, offer daily participatory programming for children and youth in and around the perimeter of the Samos and Lesvos camps. Both companies visit the islands with teams of actor-practitioners to offer a variety of programming including music, circus, clowning, crafting, face-painting, and participatory performance. I write this chapter through my lens as a drama teacher and community applied theatre practitioner and the experience that comes in addressing the many ethical challenges that working in these contexts present.

The Ethics of Refugee Theatre: A Brief Literature Review

Applied theatre often has strong foci for creating social change and yet this focus can also lead to excruciating ethical dilemmas (Kerr 2011). James Thompson (2006) explains that creating ethical practice is not as simple as finding the right balance, as imbalance can occur "with the slightest experiential push" (185). Practitioners intend to create safe spaces to carry out applied theatre, often in private environments (Nicholson 2005), yet practitioner intention and motivation can create ambiguity about the safety of a space. Perhaps more relevant, what if creating a safe space within the confines of a refugee camp makes this proposition challenging or impossible?

Caroline Wake (2013b) points out that verbatim theatre is the fastest-growing subgenre of refugee theatre, describing the practice as "an ethically risky proposition, rife with potential for pain and exploitation" (117). Its popularity likely stems from the ease with which verbatim theatre can be used to explore social issues with groups inexperienced in creating theatre; yet, as David Kerr (2011) argues, "a play or technique that is quite acceptable in one place or context may create severe moral problems in another" (180). Chris Baim (2020) warns that the "rapid expansion of personal stories on the stage, in their myriad sub-genres and hybrids, has meant that practice has raced ahead of theory" (28), leaving practitioners unsure of what an ethics of practice might look like. Finally, Thompson (2005a) argues that "without extreme care theatre projects that dig up narratives, experiences, and remembrances can blame, enact revenge, and foster animosity as much as they can develop dialogue, respect, or comfort" (151). Stella Barnes (2009) developed an ethical framework that assesses risks when creating theatre from personal stories in which she outlines how theatre created and performed by the survivors of trauma, particularly when the stories are not fictionalized, occupies the position of highest risk. Dwight Conquergood (1985) mapped an ethical framework for refugee theatre with four models of what he describes as ethically suspect performance practice. I wish to focus on just one of the four, The Curator's Exhibitionism, described as a style of performance that incites "sensationalism" and the "tourist's stare," where there is a danger of making the culturally different exotic, of romanticizing the other in order to astonish the audience; and, as a result, the sensationalism "dehumanizes the Other" (6). This idea of sensationalizing the other is something I expected to see on observing applied theatre projects during my fieldwork to Greek island refugee camps.

Methodology

In 2019 I traveled to five Greek islands to observe theatre projects conducted within refugee camps. I spent forty-three days on the islands, observing twenty-eight theatre and arts-based interventions, including theatre, music, dance, art, crafting, circus, clowning, podcasting, and jewelry-making. My initial plan had been to observe projects to discover if applied theatre practice in this context was a replica of the many verbatim-style projects I had encountered in my desktop research relating to theatre with resettled refugees in Western nations. My research questions would probe the ethics of refugee theatre in the camp context, but on arriving I observed how diverse and also complicated the field of practice was and I abandoned my preconceptions to employ a grounded theory approach. For instance, instead of attempting to compare or confirm an ethics of practice, I adjusted my outlook and spent time observing and in conversation with theatre practitioners, as well as other NGO workers and volunteers, in an attempt to understand the situation on the ground and to get a better sense of what the data was telling me rather than imposing my own ideas on the data (Schreiber 2001).

The sampling process involved selecting companies conducting projects in English and I made a point of demonstrating the variety of practice occurring on the islands. I conducted audio-recorded intensive interviews (Charmaz 2006) with research participants, discussing motivation for practice and the challenges encountered in the field. In a grounded theory style, I kept detailed memos of the research process, and in the spirit of Glaser's (2001) dictum "all is data" (145), memos became part of the analyzed data. Interviews and observational notes were transcribed and coded in NVivo. Initial coding produced 195 open codes which were sorted into eight parent codes, labeled as: challenges; the practitioner; benefits; safety; camp life; space and place; form and process; and trauma. The coding, and constant comparative and memoing processes "contributed to the robustness of the findings" (Birks and Mills 2015: 66) and resulted in the development of a central theme of a responsibility for the other—ethic of care, which I outline below.

Ethics as a Guiding Practice, but Not in Those Words

Writing memos is an integral part of the grounded theory process and when I began memoing I noted that the data did not appear to have anything to do with ethics. Yet, I was superimposing my own belief of what ethics (or lack thereof) looked like. What had been difficult to see up close was that although the word ethics was not in the vocabulary of the practitioners, this did not mean ethics were not their guiding principles. During this analysis process I attempted to uncover what grounded theorists refer to as the "shared basic social problem from the participant's perspective" (Schreiber 2001: 62) by answering the question, "what is happening here?" (Charmaz 2006: 20). Grounded in the data were three shared elements:

- The practitioner must adapt to the unpredictable and precarious aspects of camp life.
- In adapting, there is a focus on an ethic of care within either an intentioned or intuitive approach.
- Aesthetics of practice and practitioner agenda are secondary to supporting the needs of participants.

From here, I argue that theatre practitioners feel an innate responsibility for the other and put the needs and safety of the refugee participants—implementing an ethic of care—ahead of any personal or donor agenda, or even the aesthetic needs of their artistic practice.

Responsibility for the Other: An Ethic of Care

Emmanuel Levinas (1999) explains that in seeing the face of the other we are compelled to be of service to this face, with a fundamental urgency to help, to be generous, and without any expectation of reciprocity. It has been noted that many volunteer-humanitarians were triggered into action in 2015 on seeing the graphic images of 3-year-old Syrian Alan Kurdi lying drowned face down in the sand on a Turkish beach. This kind of action is Levinas's explanation of an infinite responsibility to act, marking "a non-indifference for me in my relation to the Other, in which I am never done with him" (105). Levinas describes this is an obligation of which we are never discharged, "the infinite, an inexhaustible, concrete responsibility. The impossibility of saying no" (105).

James Thompson (2015) interprets an ethic of care in applied theatre practice as "real attachments between individuals and groups, where there is a felt responsibility for the other and concomitant commitment to aid that other" (434). Anne Smith (2014) adds that an ethic of care is fostered through agency instead of dependency, with care both given and received, which allows refugee participants to experience empowerment. However, Levinas (1999) argues against this notion of reciprocity, explaining, "the moment one is generous in hopes of reciprocity, that relation no longer involves generosity but the commercial relation, the exchange of good behavior" (101).

Here I explore two aspects of a responsibility for the other through an ethic of care as observed in Greek refugee camps: intuition and generosity. Intuition in this context was viewed as a responsiveness, flexibility, and empathy enacted by the practitioner. Generosity appears as an innate offering and was present through the giving of time, physical and emotional energy, resources and creativity.

Intuition

In the three days I spent with Changing Stories I attended several of their presentations at Moria camp on Lesvos. On one occasion the team had planned on performing a short pantomime for the children in the camp; the same play had been well received the day before and the weather was good for an outdoor performance. Yet, on our arrival, we were greeted by lines of coaches and hundreds of camp residents waiting to board, readied with their life belongings in black garbage bags. For those who had witnessed this before, we knew the image meant that today was transfer day. Transfers to the mainland were time-consuming, exhausting—both emotionally and physically—anxiety-inducing, and took the best part of a day. The Changing Stories team returned their props to their van and instead grabbed their oversized bubble-blowing equipment. They explained that today it would be better to distract the children with big, wonderful bubbles.

I observed practitioners act responsively, flexibly, and empathetically in a reflexive nature, which allowed for intuitive change at a moment's notice. Italian drama teacher Michele Senici regularly uses music in his workshops, with his focus on a song's beats-per-minute that can enhance the mood. Senici intuitively reads the emotions and energy in the room and then carefully selects music that best supports both the workshop and the children in the room. UK-based drama teacher Chris Walters mentioned the phrase "shaking it out of my sleeve," meaning making it up as one goes along, and he joked that it wouldn't be long before his sleeve was empty. Walters often intuitively adapted to his teaching environment, cautiously making production choices and games to play in the classroom. He adapted to the students' language needs by creating a simple translation of the *Caucasian Chalk Circle* from English into Farsi. Often decisions were made very quickly by necessity; others allowed time for contemplation and thoughtful adjustment. Walters explained that on his arrival at Gekko Kids, the school administration presumed he would explore the students' feelings in his drama classes. But, as he explained,

> that would be a very dangerous thing to do, especially for somebody without very intense and psychological training and experience. In some ways, I am almost there to help them forget their feelings, in a way, to give them something to start building up some positive memories in their lives. They must have loads of awful memories, they must have dreadful things which have happened to them and to their family. In fact, I know one particular family who had three kids involved in the play, that they had a mother shot in front of them, and things of that kind.

Walters explained that with no psychological training, he allowed his intuition to guide his decisions. Intuition can be a useful tool for practitioners and keep things in check, allowing the heart and gut to guide important decisions in being ethical in the moment and to avoid the projection of one's own needs or desires on marginalized participants. It should be noted that although practitioners' decisions appear innately based on intuition, the Changing Stories team explain how they spend considerable time discussing ethical choices prior to embarking on their tours.

Generosity

In November 2019, I was sitting in the We Are One yoga studio chatting with Kelly Buxton. The night before, it had rained ferociously and kept me awake most of the night; I imagined how noisy, wet, and stressful it must have been for the thousands sleeping in tents only hundreds of meters away. Kelly knew her day would be busy; many of the women and their young children would want to dry out and rest in the warmth of their center. While we chatted, a message arrived for Kelly explaining that a volunteer English teacher was not coming; Kelly quickly resolved the problem by offering another yoga session in place of the English class. Kelly's classes are not yoga in the conventional sense, but are labeled so as a way to attract participants and as a pushback to resistance from participants' husbands who refused to allow their wives to attend dance classes. The yoga label was a more comfortable fit; Kelly described the classes as a dance and drama therapy fusion. Having participated in the classes, I observed Kelly invest mental, physical, and emotional energy. She would run three classes that day as an act of generosity to the women who visited the center.

Walters was required to recast many of the play's lead roles several times—including that of Azdak three days before the performance—because students stopped coming or had opportunities to leave the island. Within his responsibility for his students, he did not expect a reciprocated generosity; there was an acknowledged realization that an opportunity to leave Lesvos, even if it meant missing performing, was the better choice. Walters explained there were times when he needed to acquire costumes and invested his own money, looked for donations, and sought crowdfunding from UK friends rather than use the thinly stretched resources offered by the school. I witnessed other forms of generosity: for instance, on preparing his students for a performance, Senici realized performing for their peers would be detrimental to their mental health and progress. Senici sacrificed his own artistic (and academic) plans for the students' safety. There was also generosity of time. The Changing Stories team were limited by how long they could stay on the islands based on their paid work schedules and family obligations back in the Netherlands. In a kind of compromise, and sensing an incredible obligation to the camp residents and their Dutch donors back home, the team did not take any days off while in the field and instead devoted all their energy and time towards offering several workshops daily.

The Flying Seagulls explain "we are positivity," and each day I witnessed this in their non-stop play, expending physical and emotional energy in entertaining children. The Seagulls erected a big-top circus tent at the entrance of the Samos camp in October 2019 and utilized this for their daily activities. As the children became comfortable in the space, they began climbing to the top of the tent, arousing safety concerns that a child might fall off or through the plastic and injure themselves. Stationing volunteer security guards proved unsuccessful, and after exploring various options The Seagulls agreed the safest option was to pull the tent down. This was devastating for the team, who had invested so much time and resources in acquiring the tent for the benefit of the children, and equally devastating for the children who came daily to play in this unlikely space. The physical safety of the children was put ahead of the aesthetics and artistic integrity of the team.

Seven Ethical Principles in Applied Theatre with Refugees

Within my literature review process, my research uncovered seven recurring ethical concerns when practitioners create refugee theatre or refugee arts:

1. The retelling of trauma can re-traumatize survivors and, instead of being therapeutic, can work against the pain (see Cox 2015; Jeffers 2008; Nigh 2011; Salverson 1999; Thompson 2005a; Wake 2013a, b).

2. The repetition of a narrative perpetuating refugees as victims in need of saving. This victimization and savior mentality is often represented on stage "to elicit the audience's pity, shame, outrage and solidarity" (Cox 2015: 32), which can further homogenize the refugee experience while presenting cultural ignorance and insensitivity (see also Edmondson, 2005; Jackson 2002; Snyder-Young 2013; Thompson 2005a).

3. Complicated power differentials between practitioners and marginalized and vulnerable communities may result in the sharing of stories or information through a disempowered status, not knowing what and with whom to share sensitive information (Dennis 2007; Jeffers 2012; Wake 2013a).

4. The sensationalizing of stories by digging for "meaty material" (Conquergood 1985: 6) for the benefit of the audience.

5. The positioning of audiences as witness can cause (re) traumatization and create secondary witnesses, further distancing the audience from the story-sharers (Cohen-Cruz and Schutzman 2006; Gallagher 2011; Prendergast and Saxton 2015; Salverson 1999).

6. The acknowledgment that suppression may be a preferred form of healing and perhaps culturally or personally more appropriate for survivors (see Goodman 2004; Jacobs 2018).

7. The acknowledgment that (former) refugees may prefer to work with others who have also experienced life as a refugee (Jackson 2002; Loizos 1981).

The recurrence of these key issues is likely linked to an incorrect assumption that survivors want or need their stories heard, and a presumption by humanitarian interventionists that a well-intentioned offer of help is implicitly good and somehow above ethical scrutiny. Yet, Nicholson (2005) and Thompson (2005b) remind applied theatre practitioners that their work cannot be presumed good by virtue alone. This white savior mentality is a replication of what Edmondson (2005) "identifies [as] a consistent narrative that recurs in the stories of intervention, in which a disruption of (third world) order calls upon (first world) 'knights in white armour' to rescue the victims, who are uniformly cast as symbols of helplessness" (459). Knott (2018) observed how volunteers in Greek camps viewed themselves as "'saviours', in stark opposition to refugees, who were 'victims' to be 'helped'" (p. 360). When humanitarian intervention is seen as overwhelmingly urgent, ethical considerations can slip away. Yet, what I discovered in the field was practitioners deliberately avoided asking for or utilizing trauma stories in their applied theatre practice. For instance, Michele Senici explained that he did not solicit trauma stories from his students, and when these themes emerged, he repositioned the conversation; and Chris Walters stated he felt he was there to help them forget their trauma rather than revisit it.

Conclusion

James Thompson (2005b) states, "we must challenge the ease with which the act of telling is championed, yet detached from the difficult contexts in which it occurs" (40). In the camps I expected to see a similar curator's exhibitionism, yet my observations refuted this theory and this discovery allowed for the development of a grounded theory that derived from the data (Birks and Mills 2015). Responsibility for the other through an ethic of care translates into how theatre practitioners attempt to manage unpredictability in the liminal and precarious spaces of refugee camps, responding with intuition and generosity. Yet, it must be acknowledged that humanitarian intervention comes with its own ethical burdens. Projects I observed on the Greek islands offer participants very little autonomy in deciding what interventions are offered or how sourced funds are spent on the residents' welfare. Dwight Conquergood's (1985) ethical mapping, mentioned previously in this chapter, describes his preferred model of ethical practice as dialogical performance, yet this ideal was not achieved in any of the projects discussed here. Without autonomy, what are the risks of an ongoing savior and white-knight mentality in the humanitarian industry? Anne Smith (2014) explains that through reciprocity and shared ownership, relationships can be developed and empowerment can occur. Yet, for refugees, without experiencing empowerment in their own welfare, how do these projects perpetuate the refugee stereotype of a victim needing saving? And, importantly, what is the impact on the mental health of refugee participants when these theatre companies go home?

A Guiding Principle: Responsibility for the Other through an Ethic of Care

This research explores the many facets of attempting to conduct ethical applied theatre with marginalized and vulnerable populations, and often in very precarious and quickly changing locations. When there is an incredible sense of urgency to help, humanitarian interventionists and theatre practitioners must still take the time to pause and assess through a responsibility for the other in an ethic of care. In these precarious spaces shifts might occur on a daily, hourly, or even momentary basis and therefore are not predictable and cannot be planned. Thus, an applied theatre practitioner in the refugee camp context must carefully assess, observe, listen, and utilize intuition and generosity through responsiveness, flexibility, and empathy to ensure that the best interests of their vulnerable participants are being heard, even when no words are being used. Yet, I urge practitioners first examine the seven principles for ethical practice, shared earlier, to assess their own motivations for practice: as Hughes, Thompson, and Balfour (2009) explain, there is an ingrained idea that in times of crisis, "if we want to respond as theatre artists, we need to go 'over there' to do something" (284). I propose that the types of practice detailed here may not always be the most ethical choice, with other options, such as supporting refugee-led initiatives, being a more ethical approach. Finally, I propose that a responsibility for the other through an ethic of care become the foundation of theatre practice with resettled refugees to avoid potentially harmful practice that sensationalizes the other and risks re-traumatization.

References

Baim, C. (2020), *Staging the Personal: A Guide to Safe and Ethical Practice.* Basingstoke: Palgrave Macmillan.

Balfour, M. (2012), "Refugee performance: encounters with alterity," *Journal of Arts and Communities*, 2(3), 177–95. Available online: https://doi.org/10.1386/jaac.2.3.177_1

Barnes, S. (2009), "Drawing a Line: A discussion of ethics in participatory arts with young refugees," In S. Barnes (Ed.), *Participatory Arts with Young Refugees* (pp. 34–40). Oval House.

Birks, M. and Mills, J. (2015), *Grounded Theory: A Practical Guide*. London: SAGE.

Charmaz, K. (2006), *Constructing Grounded Theory: A Practical Guide through Qualitative Analysis*. London: SAGE.

Cohen-Cruz, J. and Schutzman, M. (2006), *A Boal Companion: Dialogues on Theatre and Cultural Politics*. New York: Routledge.

Conquergood, D. (1985), "Performing as a moral act: ethical dimensions of the ethnography of performance," *Literature in Performance: A Journal of Literary and Performing Art*, 5(2), 1.

Cox, E. (2015), *Performing Noncitizenship: Asylum Seekers in Australian Theatre, Film and Activism* (1st ed.). London: Anthem Press.

Dennis, R. (2007), "Inclusive democracy: a consideration of playback theatre with refugee and asylum seekers in Australia," *Research in Drama Education: The Journal of Applied Theatre and Performance*, 12(3), 355–70. Available online: https://doi.org/10.1080/13569780701560636

Edmondson, L. (2005), "Marketing trauma and the theatre of war in northern Uganda," *Theatre Journal*, 57 (3), 451–74. Available online: https://doi.org/10.1353/tj.2005.0098

Gallagher, K. (2011), "Roma refugee youth and applied theatre: imagining a future vernacular," *Niederdeutsches Jahrbuch: Jahrbuch des Vereins für Niederdeutsche Sprachforschung*, 35(1), 63. Available online: https://doi.org/10.1080/14452294.2011.11649542

Glaser, B. G. (2001), *The Grounded Theory Perspective: Conceptualization Contrasted with Description*. Mill Valley, CA: Sociology Press.

Goodman, J. H. (2004), "Coping with trauma and hardship among unaccompanied refugee youths from Sudan," *Qualitative Health Research*, 14(9), 1177–96. Available online: https://doi.org/10.1177/1049732304265923

Jackson, M. (2002), *Politics of Storytelling: Violence, Transgression and Intersubjectivity*. Copenhagen: Museum Tusculanum Press.

Jacobs, S. F. M. (2018), "Collective narrative practice with unaccompanied refugee minors: 'The Tree of Life' as a response to hardship," *Clinical Child Psychology and Psychiatry*, 23(2), 279–93.

Jeffers, A. (2008), "Dirty truth: personal narrative, victimhood and participatory theatre work with people seeking asylum," *Research in Drama Education: The Journal of Applied Theatre and Performance*, 13(2), 217–21. Available online: https://doi.org/10.1080/13569780802054919

Jeffers, A. (2012), *Refugees, Theatre and Crisis: Performing Global Identities*. Basingstoke: Palgrave Macmillan. Available online: https://doi.org/10.1057/9780230354821

Kerr, D. (2011), "Ethics of Applied Theatre," *South African Theatre Journal*, 23(1), 177–87. Available online: https://doi.org/10.1080/10137548.2009.9687908

Knott, A. (2018), "Guests on the Aegean: interactions between migrants and volunteers at Europe's southern border," *Mobilities*, 13(3), 349–66. Available online: https://doi.org/10.1080/17450101.2017.1368896

Levinas, E. (1999), *Alterity and Transcendence*. New York: Columbia University Press.

Loizos, P. (1981), *The Heart Grown Bitter: A Chronicle of Cypriot War Refugees*. London: Cambridge University Press.

Nicholson, H. (2005), *Applied Drama: The Gift of Theatre*. Basingstoke: Palgrave Macmillan.

Nigh, K. J. (2011), *Performing Nation, Performing Trauma: Theatre and Performance after September 11th, Hurricane Katrina and the Peruvian Dirty War*, PhD dissertation, Arizona State University.

Prendergast, M. and Saxton, J. (2015), "Seduction of the real: the significance of fiction in applied theatre," *Research in Drama Education: The Journal of Applied Theatre and Performance*, 20(3), 280–4. Available online: https://doi.org/10.1080/13569783.2015.1059747

Salverson, J. (1999), "Transgressive storytelling or an aesthetic of injury: performance, pedagogy and ethics," *Theatre Research in Canada*, 20(1), 35–51.

Schreiber, R. S. (2001), "How to of Grounded Theory: avoiding the pitfalls," in R. S. Schreiber and P. Noerager Stern (eds), *Using Grounded Theory in Nursing*. New York: Springer.

Smith, A. (2014), "Maximizing empowerment in applied theatre with refugees and migrants in the United Kingdom: facilitation shaped by an ethic of care," *Journal of Arts and Communities*, 6(2/3), 177–88. Available online: https://doi.org/10.1386/jaac.6.2-3.177_1

Snyder-Young, D. (2013), *Theatre of Good Intentions*. Basingstoke: Palgrave Macmillan. Available online: https://doi.org/10.1057/9781137293039

Thompson, J. (2005a), "Digging up stories: an archaeology of theatre in war," *TDR/The Drama Review*, 48(3), 150–64. Available online: https://doi.org/ https://doi.org/10.1162/1054204041667749

Thompson, J. (2005b), *Digging up Stories: Applied Theatre, Performance and War*. Manchester: Manchester University Press.

Thompson, J. (2006). *Applied Theatre: Bewilderment and Beyond*. Oxford: Peter Lang.

Thompson, J. (2015), "Towards an aesthetics of care," *Research in Drama Education: The Journal of Applied Theatre and Performance*, 20(4), 430–41.

Wake, C. (2013a), "Between repetition and oblivion: performance, testimony, and ontology in the refugee determination process," *Text and Performance Quarterly*, 33(4), 326–43. Available online: https://doi.org/10.1080/104629 37.2013.818164

Wake, C. (2013b), "To witness mimesis: the politics, ethics, and aesthetics of testimonial theatre in *Through the Wire*," *Modern Drama*, 56(1), 102–25. Available online: https://doi.org/10.3138/md.2012-0465

10

"Standing in the Trouble": Tensions and Ethics of Engagement in Utilizing Applied Theatre in the Context of Police Training

Yasmine Kandil

The work of understanding the ethics of a given project often involves confronting the tensions that emerge from initiatives aimed at creating a shift in perspectives—a shift in how people, policies, and entrenched practices have cemented themselves in different contexts. The project I discuss here, on the use of applied theatre in the training of police officers, has brought to the forefront the "tensions of engagement" like no other project I have worked on. For that reason, I have had to examine what was not clear to me at the outset of my work with police, and in the process, I too experienced a shift in perspective, one that enabled me to adjust my goals and approaches when using applied theatre techniques in police training contexts. This chapter is a reflection-on-practice that brings together issues of internalized bias and learning to "stand in the trouble" (Haraway 2016) when working within contexts where a facilitator's outsider status is sometimes perceived as a threat to those with whom we are collaborating. Taking time to listen, engage authentically, and to keep in mind the stakes for all those involved proved to be a useful way to forge new pathways with those whose world is so very different from mine.

Collisions of Personal History

I began writing this chapter in January 2020 before our world was forever changed by Covid-19, before the George Floyd murder by a Minneapolis police officer, and before the second wave of the Black Lives Matter movement, which, in Canada, gave birth to serious renewed initiatives to defund the police (Maynard 2017; Cole 2020). As readers make themselves familiar with the world of policing as I describe it here, I am sure they may ask themselves about the ethical tensions of advocating for the police. What does it mean to work with police officers as participants when many in our left-leaning academic milieu, artists, and activist practitioners have been vocal about initiatives to defund the police?

My relationship with the police was formed based on my upbringing in my native country, Egypt, where they (in close alliance with the Egyptian government) were known for their corruption, brutality, and their senseless flaunting of power over the largely powerless citizens who constitute the majority of the country's population. That power could not have been made more stark than with the mass arrests that took place in the 1990s of young men and women of my age and from my social circles, in what became known as the effort to clean Cairo of "Satan worshippers" (Masoud 1999). I was in my late teens at the time and knew individuals who were arrested in these police raids; some spent months in jail before being released to face a very surreal and twisted world. The lesson and message was clear: you behave yourself and act the way you're supposed to, or you'll end up in jail in the grips of men who know no mercy. Those incidents had a profound impact on my relationship with authority and men in power.

A few years later, in my mid-twenties, there was another incident— the "Queen Boat" arrests: fifty-two young men, their faces plastered all over the news, were thrown in jail and sentenced for the crime of "debauchery," or what we knew on the ground to mean "homosexuality" (Long 2004). Eighteen years later, I am in this country we call Canada, in a respectable university job, working with police officers on shifting their training to make space for the experiences of those in mental health crises. While police in Canada are not the same as police in Egypt, the scars of trauma still mark my psyche.

I offer my reader this background so that you may understand the tensions I bring with me to this encounter, and so that you may appreciate that if we are truly honest about our practice, we will admit that no path of advocacy is ever straightforward or easy. What is surprising to me, and what I will try to track here, is how my allegiance and partnership with police has shifted as a result of my work with them. The more I learned about their world, the more I began to understand their predicament. I began to see how difficult it is for some of them to exist in this culture that is shaped by generations of officers who are their seniors. As such, ethics and advocacy take on new meaning as we all begin to make sense of the colliding worlds of policing and advocacy for people in mental health crises. For me in particular, my own personal history rears its head from time to time, reminding me of my past and its effect on me. But first, let me begin with how I came upon this project.

Context

In the summer of 2016 theatre/performance scholar Dr. Natalie Alvarez invited me (an applied theatre practitioner/scholar) to collaborate with her on putting together a federal Social Sciences and Humanities Research Council (SSHRC) Insight Grant to look into the impacts and efficacy of scenario-based training for police officers in Ontario. This came just as the Ontario Ombudsman published his investigation titled *A Matter of Life and Death* (Dubé 2016) that looked at the training of police officers to respond to conflict situations with civilians in mental health distress. The investigation was a direct response to the public outcry over Constable James Forcillo's shooting and killing of 18-year-old Sammy Yatim on a streetcar in Toronto (Loriggio 2020). When videos of this shooting surfaced, the public was aghast that the young man, who was brandishing a knife and clearly in a state of emotional distress, was shot eight times by Forcillo. Forcillo fired five of those shots after Yatim had fallen to the ground (the young man had already been shot by the same officer). What was later revealed was that Yatim was standing alone inside an empty streetcar while six or more police officers were in position outside the car, two of them pointing their guns straight at the young man.

Sadly, it was not an isolated incident. Across Canada, the number of similar fatal shootings of people in mental health crises have prompted inquests, reports, and recommendations (Iacobucci 2014; Cotton and Coleman 2014). Many accounts point to a gap in police training: "[o]ver and over, dating back nearly three decades, these reports and recommendations have emphasized the importance of police using de-escalation techniques when dealing with people in crisis" (Dubé 2016: 6). Two main points from the Dubé report, supported by the Iacobucci and Coleman and Cotton reports, pertain to the design of our research study: first, that police training is largely focused on "use-of-force" tactics and not enough on communication skills for de-escalating people in mental health crisis; and second, that the police culture unfortunately "perpetuates the notion that fatal shootings of persons with mental illness are simply inevitable" (Dubé 2016: 7). These reports point to an absence of: (a) opportunities for trainees to work on scenarios that are designed in consultation with a variety of different stakeholders, including people with lived experience of mental health illness; and (b) an evaluation of the efficacy of these scenarios, and a way to track the impact on officers as they apply their skills in action.

We received the SSHRC grant in March 2017. Our team included myself, Dr. Alvarez (lead researcher), and Dr. Jennifer Lavoie (co-lead), as well as forensic psychologists, criminologists, mental health response nurses, people with lived experience of mental health illness, cultural competence trainers, and police officers. We began to formulate a drama-based method of training and assessment that tests the efficacy of using scenarios and role-play to educate officers in de-escalation techniques. The use of scenarios is not new in police training, but ours was positioned to make a significant shift in design and implementation, in that *theatre* scholars were involved in writing and training these live scenario-based interactions. Another difference was that the interdisciplinary team of experts from a variety of relevant fields not only contributed to the design of the proposed training curriculum, but were also available to offer on-the-spot responses to trainees as they variously attempted de-escalation strategies. By replicating as closely as possible the high-intensity encounters that officers confront in these high-stakes situations, we sought throughout the simulation experiences to open up a safe space for officers to try out their interventions and to experience *in the moment* what might trigger a person in crisis and what might help de-escalate their actions. Part of the process involved helping officers to realize that their presence alone could be a major factor in escalating the actions of the person in crisis. Our program offers police trainees opportunities to test out how their body language, tone of voice, and what they say and do can impact the behavior and response of the person in crisis. Our goal is to foster a method of practice in which officers can effectively reflect-in-action, monitor, and adjust their responses to people in mental health crises, and at the same time manage the stress of such encounters.

In the process of using applied theatre techniques to launch our training package, I was acutely aware that our study was bringing together two very different worlds: the world of policing, in which training is largely based on use-of-force tactics, and the world of applied theatre as a tool for social justice, where the voices of the oppressed and marginalized lie at the heart of our project designs and facilitation plans. What drove this study was the team's commitment to advocacy for people in mental health crises. We wanted to open a channel of communication where the police could better understand this group's suffering in their moment of distress. The team's challenge was to marry the world of policing with that of drama-based social justice training without compromising the integrity of either, and to take into account the complex ethical considerations that are at play at any given point in this research process. These considerations shifted and changed as I began to comprehend, through my close encounters with each stakeholder group, the various factors that complicate the role of police officers when they respond to calls involving people in mental health crisis.

Developing a Training and Assessment Model

In a previous job, I was tasked with hiring and teaching people to be Standardized Patients (Wallace 2007) for scenario training in medical education. This gave me experience in how to introduce gently the functions of drama into contexts where such practices can sometimes be dismissed because of their affiliation with the "arts." This resistance to using the arts for training in non-arts-based contexts is not uncommon. As Lina de Guevara (2017) notes in her own work with police officers in British Columbia,

> Using arts-based methods to achieve results of any kind is unusual in [policing] environments; they are deemed inappropriate because theatre is usually considered entertainment. It isn't uncommon for theatre practitioners to encounter skepticism and negativity when trying to work with the police. The police, moreover, have more urgent preoccupations and it often seems impossible for them to include these activities in their busy, complicated schedules. (11)

Understanding the challenge ahead of us, the team went about developing a number of goals for creating scenarios that might help offset some of that skepticism:

1. The scenarios should be authentic, replicating as closely as possible the real-life encounters officers experience on the job.
2. The narrative has to draw our participants in, so the first few moments were crucial in "arresting their attention" (Heathcote 1971, as quoted in *Three Looms Waiting*).

3. The encounter could not lead to a dead-end, resulting in unavoidable use-of-force, so the scenario has to be balanced out to offer opportunities for the officer to engage with the person in crisis, and effectively de-escalate the situation.

The team was also aware of the importance of testing the efficacy of this model, and created an evaluation tool that could be used to measure a trainee's skills and abilities at de-escalation before and after the training concluded.

Boal's Methodology and Police Training

Forum Theatre, a key ingredient of Boal's Theatre of the Oppressed (1979), is a practice that plays out the dynamic of oppression as experienced by the protagonist (the oppressed), with the goal of creating a space for audiences (whom Boal terms "spect-actors") to try out different interventions to "put right injustice" (Jackson 2009: 43). Key to Forum Theatre is the encounter between the protagonist and the oppressor, which is deliberately staged to "agitate" those observing (the audience). We use this basic understanding of what Jackson calls "seduction" to draw our participants into the narrative so that they too may feel a compelling need to try out the encounter with the person in crisis to attempt to change the outcome.

We begin with what we have called the "Springboard," which is a short version of the scenario, the narrative of which is loosely based on an inquest report. In the Springboard an experienced police officer (one of our team members, who has rehearsed this with us prior to the training day) goes through the encounter of responding to a call regarding a person in crisis, and which purposely results in the officer using lethal force. The trainees, having observed the scene, discuss the choices that the officer had in responding to the encounter. This important step in the training sets up the premise for active, engaged, problem-based learning to take place.

Through this initial activity, we can either draw our trainees/ participant observers (audience) into the narrative and subsequently into the training we have set up for them, or we can lose them. The latter may occur if the scene is too sensationalized, unrealistic, or focuses on the victimization of the person in crisis; hence, effectively alienating the very target group whose trust we hope to win. The scene has to be set up in such a way that those observing identify with the officer and the choices made to protect self and public from harm. As such, the use-of-force option our Springboard officer chooses must appear to be warranted. The craft here is to open a small window of opportunity, where the participant observer can see another approach to de-escalate the situation without having to use force. For example, the trainees might note that the officer in the Springboard was standing too close to the person in crisis, and hence did not leave enough time and distance to effectively de-escalate the situation. The discussion that follows the Springboard is often moderated in smaller groups by our expert team, who are present during the session to offer feedback and deliver important content on mental health and de-escalation tactics.

After the discussion our trainees, as in Forum Theatre, take turns to trying out different interventions to de-escalate the situation, each time receiving valuable feedback from their peers and our expert team. The tension in the encounter between trainee and person in crisis is maintained through careful observation and on-the-spot feedback by the use-of-force officer, whose job is to alert trainees if they endanger themselves or the public by letting their guard down, getting too close to the person in crisis, or not being alert enough to manage the situation if it gets out of hand. The feedback offered by the rest of the expert team is focused on how to build rapport with the person in crisis. References to body language, verbal cues, and facial expressions of the person in crisis serve as a way to remind trainees to look and read these cues to aid them in their engagement with this individual.

"Man in a mess"

In this context I realize that by focusing on the officer trainee as the protagonist, we are turning Boal's methodology upside down. To be true to Boal, this scene would be about the person in crisis. As such, the interventions would provide opportunities for us to unpack the relationship between the person in crisis and the police, essentially giving the person in distress the tools to "speak back to oppression." But we are not doing that. Here, we are intervening to explore the different approaches the officer trainee could employ to prevent a much more serious incident occurring, one which is *centered on* the person in crisis. We are in essence dissecting the role of the police officer and providing the tools to change the methods used to respond to the person in crisis. What the team hopes is that the trainee will begin to empathize with this person, to listen, to troubleshoot, to problem-solve, and essentially to begin to work *in collaboration* with the person in crisis.

If, as Dorothy Heathcote suggests in *Three Looms Waiting*, drama is about "a man in a mess!" we are subverting the traditional Forum Theatre structure by implying that both the officer *and* the person in mental health distress are "in a mess." There is no "magic solution." I argue that by working *with* the officer through the delicate functions of Forum Theatre, we are working on creating a shift in policing. This shift is one that enables officers to better understand the implications of their presence in a situation when someone is in crisis. Such an awareness can begin to alter officers' perceptions of their role in relation to the person in crisis, and they begin to question the very culture that condemns the encounter to a fatal shooting as an inevitability (Dubé 2016).

Warren Linds (2006) writes, "The space of dramatic metaxis occurs in the moments questions arise, when we ask, what if things could be different? The space is informed by, and respectful of, a complex world, and it helps those who occupy it discover different, unknown, and unrecognized spaces within their world, selves, or community" (122).

Given that officers "function in a paramilitary culture that promotes physical and mental strength" (Dubé 2012: 14), and that "their use-of-force training is largely focused on the use of weapons, with very little training on the verbal tools for de-escalation" (Dubé 2016: 6–7), the methodology I am describing disrupts and dismantles hidden assumptions about the role of police in relation to persons in crises. By encouraging different observation and communication skills, ones that are shaped to help an officer better respond to a person in crisis, we are creating a shift in police training culture.

Standing in the Trouble

Taking inspiration from David Kerr's essay "Ethics of applied theatre" (2009), I examine the ethics of undertaking work with communities whose world is so different from my own. The research that began as a form of activism and advocacy for people in mental health crises has evolved to integrate the complex web of pressures placed on police officers when they respond to a given call. As the project evolved, I realized that police officers, and the systems that govern their ethos around use-of-force, stand to benefit greatly from what we are undertaking here. My "moral sensibilities and activist commitments" (Kerr 2009: 177). have evolved too, shifting my responsibility and advocacy role to include police officers and the struggles they face when presented with a situation for which they have received very little training.

The main lesson I have learned has come from understanding how I began to shift my location within this context—as a woman of color, a researcher, and an activist with mostly left-leaning political views. There are so many contradictions just in reckoning with my origins and how that connects to who I am and what I stand for, and in reconciling with my past and allowing my present to inform my approach with these officers. For years, my research has centered on advocacy for autonomy and ethical representation of the communities with whom we work. My focus has mostly been on making visible those whose voices and images are not always factored into decisions that impact them. Unexpectedly, I found the same ethos informs my work with police. Their fear of working with outsiders, like me and my team, is shaped by continuously being villainized in the media due to the fatal overreactions of the few (officer James Forcillo, for example). In order to create this scenario-based training, I had to understand the world that police officers inhabit in an effort to represent the challenges and tensions that surround them in their daily interactions, particularly in encounters with people in mental health crisis. I co-created a world within which officers began to reimagine a new way of engaging with vulnerable people. Donna Haraway (2016) describes our human desire to create imagined futures that are free from pain as a means of coping with our present suffering. She advocates for us to "stay with the trouble." She writes that "staying with the trouble requires learning to be truly present, not as vanishing pivot between awful or edenic pasts and apocalyptic or salvific futures, but as moral critters entwined in myriad unfinished configurations of places, times, matters, meanings" (1). My history is entwined with my present, and the present is a space I occupy with my policing partners and mental health advocates, who also bring with them their own history and baggage. Our ability to stand in the trouble might be our way through this tangled "myriad [of] unfinished configurations."

As I spent more time in this world of policing, I began to appreciate James Thompson's (1998) advocacy of understanding the landscape of the world that communities inhabit so that, through theatre and drama, we can create situations where they are able to reimagine new ways of living in that world (125). And to do so, I had to stand in the trouble and be truly present. Standing in the trouble took on new meaning as I comprehended how difficult this task was, to navigate the terrain of advocacy for those in mental health crises and for the police, who are also "in the mess." I stood in the trouble as I watched officers explain why they had to shoot someone who was wielding a knife with the intention of clearly harming only himself. They explained to me how quickly the situation could turn on the officer and any bystander, if the person in crisis decides to harm others. With a limited distance between the person in crisis and those around him or her, the officer is unable to help and instead is compelled to use force to protect self and others on the scene. I had to exercise patience and foresight as I held back and adjusted my designs to make room for the officers' reservations about the scenarios. In a scene involving an international student in crisis, for example, an officer interrupted to warn me that having any perceived weapon in the dorm room would prompt the officer to draw his firearm, an outcome that would invariably result in retriggering a person already in distress. I replaced the knife with a blunt pair of scissors of the kind clearly used for simple crafts-making and not intended to do harm. This simple shift allowed the officer to enter the room and *engage* with the person in crisis to assist them in this moment, thus putting the focus on teaching the trainees important communication skills tactics. Once these skills had been honed, the scenario could be heightened, adding the knife in the room, so that the officer could now practice what they had learned as well as choose whether or not to draw their firearm. The point was to begin to see the person in crisis as someone needing help, and not as a threat.

A Paradigm Shift

In a recent chapter I co-authored with my colleagues Joe Norris and Lynn Fels (2019), we looked at how surrendering to the ambiguity of our creative work is necessary in arts-based, applied theatre methods of practice and research. I believe it is this surrender and embrace of ambiguity that has allowed me to see police officers and the landscape of the world they inhabit in a different light. The back and forth, the adjusting and tweaking of scenarios, the discussions and multiple perspectives from people with varying agendas and backgrounds, all informed by the ethics of advocacy, helped us navigate this difficult terrain of finding common ground where both police officers and people in mental health crises could be represented fairly in the training model.

What is surprising is not only the shift in how I began to perceive police officers in their work, but how they too began to shift their perspectives on policing as a result of their work with my colleagues and me. At a later point in developing our scenarios, the officer in the encounter I describe above walked into a scene where a teenage transgender youth was engaged in self-harm, reduced to a sense of hopelessness in a world that does not accept people like him. Within minutes in this role-played encounter, the officer managed to get the youth to drop the scissors, effectively disarming him. During the feedback, the actor expressed that as the youth he felt humiliated, exposed, disempowered, and invisible in those few minutes. Our officer felt proud that he had done his job, that his intervention had prevented this youth from harming himself today. During reflection, I asked the officer if he thought this person in crisis would ever trust another member of the police force again. He paused for a moment, and I could hear the penny drop. He said it was in that moment he realized that it was not just about this encounter, today; it was about the future as well. What he did *today* to de-escalate the person in crisis would impact how this person engaged with another officer *in the future*. He later admitted to me that, in his opinion, this training could be making a paradigm shift in policing possible.

Conclusion

The most gratifying part of this work is feeling that this training model is making a difference, both for police officers and those living with mental illness. While some participants may still remain skeptical of our model due to its person in crisis-centered approach, many make a point of thanking the team at the end of the training. Some have said that it has given them one more tool to add to their toolbelt, and to me, that means this tool could easily be accessed before or even instead of a firearm. In that moment, my sense of fulfillment and satisfaction comes with the feeling that I am doing work that is aligned with my social-justice values.

But that sense of fulfillment is not always guaranteed. In the summer of 2020, I was working on revisions for this chapter when news broke that another fatal shooting had occurred in Ontario. This time it was a man from the Middle East who could not speak English, and was out on his balcony in distress. His family had called the police to seek their help; instead the man ended up being shot (Wilson and Aguilar 2020). As I read the news report I envisioned the scene in my mind's eye, and I went through all the policing safety protocols that would have compelled the responding officers to shoot him. The entrapment of this man on his balcony, the number of officers who responded to the scene, the time it took to shoot him, in my opinion did not match the type of threat this man was posing.

When I hear of incidents like this, my heart aches. I ache for the man who was struggling with mental illness, trying to make sense of a world foreign to him. I ache for his family, who are likely feeling betrayed and robbed of their ability to trust police. Reflecting on the incident with my colleagues and partners in this research, I recall regretting that this situation might have had a different outcome had these officers taken our training.

After hearing of this incident, my instinct is not to turn away from the police but rather to walk towards them, and to engage with them even more. My ethics as an applied theatre practitioner tell me that I can only make a difference if I stand in the trouble, if I am present, and if I go towards that which disturbs and frightens me. Some do so with banners and fists held in the air, a valid form of protest; others, like myself, can use our art and our experience to stand with others in the trouble and, together, find our way through.

References

Boal, A. (1979), *Theatre of the Oppressed*, trans. C. A. and M. Leal MacBride and E. Fryer. London: Pluto Press.

Cole, D. (2020), *The Skin We're In: A Year of Black Resistance and Power*. Toronto, ON: Doubleday Canada.

Cotton, D. and Coleman, T. (2014), *Tempo: Police Interactions. A Report Towards Improving Interactions between Police and People Living with Mental Health Problems.* Ottawa, ON: Mental Health Commission of Canada.

De Guevara, L. (2017), "Where policing and community meet," *Alt Theatre: Cultural Diversity and the Stage*, 14 (1), 10–16.

Dubé, P. (2012), *In the Line of Duty: Investigation into how the Ontario Provincial Police and the Ministry of Community Safety and Correctional Services Have Addressed Operational Stress Injuries Affecting Police Officers.* Ontario Ombudsman. Available online: https://www.ombudsman.on.ca/ resources/reports-and-case-summaries/reports-on-investigations/2012/in-the-line-of-duty (accessed April 29, 2021).

Dubé, P. (2016), *A Matter of Life and Death: Investigation into the Direction Provided by the Ministry of Community Safety and Correctional Services to Ontario's Police Services for De-escalation of Conflict Situations.* Ontario Ombudsman. Available online: https://www.ombudsman.on.ca/resources/ reports-and-case-summaries/reports-on-investigations/2016/a-matter-of-life-and-death (accessed April 29, 2021).

Haraway, D. (2016), *Staying with the Trouble: Making Kin in the Chthulucene.* Durham, NC, and London: Duke University Press.

Heathcote, D. (1971), *Three Looms Waiting* (dir. R. Smedley). BBC Omnibus.

Iacobucci, F. (2014), *Police Encounters with People in Crisis.* Toronto, ON: Ontario Police Service.

Jackson, A. (2009), "Provoking intervention," in T. Prentki and S. Preston (eds), *The Applied Theatre Reader.* New York: Routledge, pp. 41–6.

Kerr, D. (2009), "Ethics of applied theatre," *South African Theatre Journal*, 23 (1), 177–87.

Linds, W. (2006), "Metaxis: dancing (in) the in-between," in J. Cohen-Cruz and M.Schutzman (eds), *A Boal Companion: Dialogues on Theatre and Cultural Politics.* New York: Routledge, pp. 114–24.

Long, S. (2004), "The trials of culture: sex and security in Egypt," *Middle East Report*, 34 (230), 12–20.

Loriggio, P. (2020), *The Globe and Mail.* Available online: https://www. theglobeandmail.com/canada/toronto/article-toronto-officer-convicted-in-shooting-of-sammy-yatim-granted-full/ (accessed April 29, 2021).

Masoud, T. E. (1999), "The Arabs and Islam: the troubled search for legitimacy," *Daedalus*, 128 (2), 127–45.

Maynard, R. (2017), *Policing Black Lives: State Violence in Canada from Slavery to the Present.* Winnipeg, MB: Fernwood Publishing.

Norris, J., Fels, L., and Kandil, Y. (2019), "Surrender, pedagogy ambiguity, research and impossibility: cats @ play," in P. Duffy, C. Hatton, and R. Sallis (eds), *Drama Research Methods: Provocations of Practice*. Leiden and Boston, MA: Brill Sense, pp. 97–115.

Thompson, J. (ed.) (1998), *Prison Theatre Perspectives and Practices*. London: Jessica Kingsley.

Wallace, P. (2007), *Coaching Standardized Patients: For Use in the Assessment of Clinical Competence*. New York: Springer.

Wilson, C. and Aguilar, B. (2020) "Family of 62-year-old man fatally shot by police in Mississauga, Ont. calls for public inquiry," CTV News. Available online: https://toronto.ctvnews.ca/family-of-62-year-old-man-fatally-shot-by-police-in-mississauga-ont-calls-for-public-inquiry-1.4993369 (accessed April 29, 2021).

11

Ethics of Precarity in Applied Theatre: A Case Study from Nigeria

Taiwo Afolabi

Vignette I

Phone rings and the receiver picks up on the other end.

Voice I: Hey man, do you still plan to come here?

Voice II: Yes.

Voice I: Are you interested in my thoughts?

Voice II: Of course, you know you can be open with me, man.

Voice I: Here's the thing ... You are not needed here ... do not bother to come ...

Voice II: Really?

Voice I: What we need is not drama ... What we need is not your presence but your presents ...

Voice II: But ... we have been planning my coming for a while now ... hello ...

Voice I: I understand man, but what can we do when we are faced with guns and our lives are in danger again here in Plateau State? I don't think that's the condition we need drama ... (Silence)

Voice II: Hello ... hello ... [network interruption, eventually the call ends.]

A phone conversation between the author/researcher and contact in Nigeria.

Vignette II

I was scheduled to conduct two interviews with important informants—a journalist and the community chief. However, prior to the interview, the journalist requested a meeting with my contact, a resident of Ile-Ife, Osun State, Nigeria. The journalist did not want me to come, only to be disappointed, so he refused to participate in the interview because it was too dangerous for him. My contact met with the community chief, who also declined to participate in the interview. He agreed initially but later decided to check with his community members first. According to the community chief, he could not speak about the crisis because the entire community had been ordered not to discuss the incident that took place over a year ago. He could not disobey the order. My contact left with no scheduled interview or any information about the Yoruba and the Hausa crisis that occurred in March 2017 in Ile-Ife.

Introduction

As an artist-researcher of Nigerian descent who has experienced displacement and created performances with/for people in conflict zones, I recognize the fragile nature, the unsaid daily realities of displaced people, and the working conditions of artists and organizations in war zones. In this chapter, I explore the ethics of precarity when working in war or post-conflict zones. Through a series of conversations, interviews, and discussions during my field research among a displaced population in Nigeria, I argue that precarity becomes a determining factor in framing the ethics of practice when working in underserved communities. That is, the precariousness of the living conditions and vulnerability of the population involved (in this context, internally displaced persons) need to be considered ethically and aesthetically when undertaking theatre interventions. I investigate the *ethics of precarity* and how it can affect theatre practitioners working among displaced populations in post-conflict zones. For ethical reasons, apart from myself, all other parties cited in this chapter preferred to remain anonymous. I employ narrative inquiry, specifically reflective practitioner research, to recount my stories and experiences.

Scholars have articulated the importance of theatre in war zones, and refugee and concentration camps (see Dinesh 2016; Colleran 2012; Balfour et al. 2009; Balfour 2001). The focus has been on the changes and impact theatre has made and can make in such extreme conditions. Although these changes may be small, they make theatre matter. For example, Michael Balfour in his book titled *Theatre and War, 1933–1945: Performance in Extremis* (2001), historicizes different forms theatre took during the extreme political and social turmoil of the Second World War. He builds a case for how and why theatre thrived and survived amid mass killing, starvation, degradation, disease, and continual fear. And he reiterates the thesis that human nature seeks ways to play and create psychological and emotional escape from horrible physical conditions and psychological spaces such as concentration camps. In fact, testimonies and diaries of actors like Jonas Turkow (cited in Balfour 2001) show the extent performers and audiences went to mount a theatre or musical production. Balfour raises an important question that his collected essays attempt to unpack: "given the risks, why did artists and audiences risk their lives for these performances?" (3). The creativity to devise performances under such extreme conditions enabled participants to exercise some control in their work and ultimately in their lives. Because the act and art of creating performances can give the artist a sense of agency, artists were able to create dramatic spaces in which they "commanded power denied them in reality" and "evade[d] the painful reality of prison camp life" (4). Balfour reinforces the idea of control, the ability to enact power and authority, and at least a momentary sense of dignity and self-worth because both artists and audience create a space where they can envision a better world.

James Thompson and his colleagues, in *Performance in Places of War* (2009), offer scholarly contributions on the importance of theatre in different parts of the world, especially in post-conflict/war zones that are mostly in developing countries. The authors reiterate that "theatre and performances have also long been used to support war efforts, and performance artists in places of conflict seek to intervene in contexts that are already highly theatricalized" (Thompson, Hughes and Balfour 2009: 4). Artists' interventions become channels to produce aesthetics and address postwar issues of justice, reconciliation, history, and peace-building. Although authors articulate a case for theatre in such uncommon places, settings, and contexts, the reality of the precarious conditions of the communities requires critical and ethical reasoning. For example, Nandita Dinesh (2016), in her autobiographical monograph based on her field experience in Rwanda and northern Uganda, inquires: "Why do I make theatre in places of war? Where will I intervene? Who am I creating work with/for? What are the aesthetic strategies that I will use? And when might it be time to leave?" (2). How can we, or even *should* we, ethically create theatre with populations in precarious conditions? These questions have ethical implications. It is the ethics of engaging with internally displaced communities that I focus on in this chapter. I reflect on precarity as an ethical reality, and how the notion of precarity guided me in addressing the ethical dilemmas I encountered in my research in Nigeria.

Unpacking Precarity

The word *precarious*, from which *precarity* is derived, has its root in the Latin word *precari* meaning "to pray," "to ask, entreat" (*Online Etymology Dictionary*). As it describes a state of insecurity and vulnerability, it means one is in a position of dependence on something or someone (Buchanan 2018). Also, as Jenny Hughes (2019) notes in her research on precarity in the contexts of applied and socially engaged theatre, precariousness is used in the context of employment and welfare. The definition assumes that there are two groups—the group that *asks, entreats, or seeks help,* and the other group that *gives or helps.* It underscores the fact that one group is privileged over the other, even if this is temporary. There is a recognition of a condition that has resulted in dire need and instability, whether in material or immaterial realities (Gallagher and Rodricks 2017). And it is the unstable condition that warrants a plea for mercy from one group to the other. For example, using the word "precarious" within the context of mental health service users, these people are often considered as objects "upon which interventions are enacted upon rather than the subject" of their own experience and journey through mental health (Stannage 2017: 154). The use of the word "precarity" is becoming more visible in theatre and performance (see Costa and Field 2021; Fragkou 2018).

Apart from material precarity, the word precarity (also precariousness) evokes a sense of danger. It is a feeling that unsettles and destabilizes. To be in a precarious situation means to be in an insecure position; dangerously likely to fall or collapse. It is a state of instability, unsettledness, unpredictability, vulnerability, and quagmire. Inspired by and premised on the September 11, 2001 attack in the United States, Judith Butler's 2004 collection of essays *Precarious Life* critiques the politics of war, violence, and mourning that produces precarious life. Precarious life often refers to life conditions that are unsteady and uncertain. It reflects individuals' vulnerabilities in these conditions. The broad definition of precarity recognizes that uncertainties can be present in all forms of life. Life is Janus-faced, double-sided, with precarity as a constant possibility in human existence. For instance, the celebration of a child's birth could not be possible without going through the mother's precarious moments of life and death in giving birth, with all of its pain, uncertainty, and vulnerability. Beyond the sociological and existential aspects, precarity "designates that politically-induced condition in which certain populations suffer from failing economic and social networks of support, and become differentially exposed to injury" (Butler 2004: 25).

Describing the condition of artists in postcolonial Africa, the renowned Nigerian playwright Femi Osofisan introduced the idea of "playing dangerously" (1998: 1). According to Osofisan, to play dangerously as an artist is to understand the sociopolitical conditions of the state and the implications of these conditions on both the masses and the artist. Such conditions are precarious because they recognize terror and violence as features of the current political landscape in the sub-Sahara, which has resulted in political instability, inequality, undemocratic so-called democracies, and military regimes (Osofisan 1998). Thus, a society with such attributes is creating for its citizens a condition of and for precarity. According to Osofisan, the artist living in such terror and violence needs to challenge authority in creative ways. The connection between precarity and playing dangerously is that both recognize the prevailing unpleasant sociopolitical conditions, the effect of terror and violence on society, and the process of finding solutions to such situations from, with, and by the affected communities.

Socially engaged arts—and by extension applied theatre— thrive on the emotional currency of a community. And in many cases, the ecology of this practice focuses on addressing social issues as experienced by people and in different places. A community's experience that is a result of dominant interests and powers may create the systemic formation of vulnerability. This systemic design needs to be considered when engaging and interacting with any community. Ethical practice is not a given; rather, it requires a deliberate process of choosing, defending, recommending, and at times systematizing values and concepts of right or wrong behavior (*Online Encyclopedia of Philosophy*). Ethics focuses on a moral code or ethical principles to serve as guiding values when relating and engaging with the other. In this context, ethics of precarity refers to the *sensibility* and *sensitivity* of working with vulnerable populations. The critical mindset and generous mindfulness I refer to is not in the sense of fragility or the overexploitation of care, because to some people, *care* is not only an act or an art, it is a lifestyle; a life that many have been called to that gives them a sense of purpose in society. Rather, by recognizing the realities of a community, I suggest that thinking ethically about precarity in applied theatre practice can offer us both critical and pragmatic insights when working with vulnerable communities. This is because precarity evokes a certain stance: an inside and an outside position. It is assumed that the "inside" group is in a dire condition, or has had an experience worth exploring through theatre, while the "outside" group can attend to these needs. This divide already creates a power imbalance; therefore, ethics is fundamental to our practice. This sensibility and sensitivity can impact pedagogy, methodologies, and other research activities in our field because it can enable researchers and practitioners to think of how they frame participation, and how they work with their chosen communities.

In discussing the ethics of precarity, I propose an ethical code around precarity as a principle in understanding ethics and participation (considered as a form of labor) in applied theatre. Precarity as an ethical code recognizes a holistic consideration of people's conditions and those of the systems in which such people exist. It also acknowledges the nature of the art form involved. Like many arts-based initiatives, applied theatre is an affect-driven, cognitive and creative exchange, and often requires emotional labor. As an affect-driven practice, applied theatre requires an emotional connection (i.e., feelings), and it is creative because it involves the imagination of participants and an artistic process or product. These attributes are achieved many times through immaterial labor, "affective and cognitive commodities produced by work that exist outside the traditional wage-based considering of labour as a material-commodity-producing activity" (Dowling, Nunes and Trott 2007).

Therefore, precarity as an ethical code considers both the material and immaterial realities of people's living conditions and the systems in which they exist. It also aligns with the notion that paying attention to the realities of the community participants fosters a healthy relational interaction rather than a transactional one. The consideration of precarity as part of ethics of practice does not only show commitment to ethical practice, it offers the potential for our work to critique the system in which such conditions exist, and to create a space that amplifies precarious voices. Precarity as an ethical code can provide theoretical insights into and empirical evidence of the way in which the process of participating in an applied theatre project (a form of labor) is organized and deployed, and the uncertainty of the conditions of participants involved in such projects. These key considerations are highlighted through my fieldwork experience in the remainder of this chapter.

Ethics of Precarity: Story of the Making

In 2017, I contacted potential organizations in Plateau State, Nigeria, for my doctoral field research. I intentionally chose Plateau State because of my personal connection to the state. First, I lived in the capital city, Jos, for six years (2005–2011) as an undergraduate student at the University of Jos. As students, we were attacked by the Hausa ethnic group, which resulted in our displacement and interruptions in the school calendar. We experienced loss of belongings, we mourned, and we buried both students and residents of Plateau State. My experience of displacement and the overwhelming number of displaced persons internationally who have crossed international state-recognized borders (refugees), together with the politics of resettlement, led me to focus my research on internally displaced persons (IDPs) within the state border and outside the nation-state border. Years after I left Jos, I was preparing to return to Plateau State for my field research.

The causes of the incessant Jos crisis are complex as they range from political to religious, economic, ethnic, and ideological differences (Higazi 2011). Considering my personal connection to Jos, I wanted to conduct my research among IDPs—both in IDP camps/communities and in schools. It is interesting that in the discourse about IDPs in Nigeria, those displaced by ethnic cleansing, tribal clashes, climate change, and religious crises in other states are rarely mentioned, except for the case of Boko Haram, which has produced the highest number of IDPs in the country (Owolade 2014). Boko Haram is a religious Islamic sect who are in resistance to Western education, while the ongoing Jos crisis is around settler claims, and religious and political issues (Danfulani 2005; Segun 2013). For instance, it seems the focus is on Maiduguri, Adamawa State, while little attention is paid to other places in the region. This leads me to consider the politicization of Boko Haram especially by international communities. There are other similar situations in the country that have led to displacement: for example, the Fulani herdsmen killing in southwest and eastern Nigeria, and the Yoruba and the Hausa clash in Ile-Ife.[1] As someone who has experienced displacement, I am interested in creating awareness of some of the hidden realities of precarity and providing spaces through artistic expression for unheard voices, unseen faces, and unknown stories.

I secured permission to conduct research at the IDP camp in Bukuru and in a secondary school in Plateau State. However, less than eight months after I received approval, the situation changed. The camp in Bukuru and the school were closed, a fact which reinforces the volatility and instability of protracted displacement and the precariousness of the people's circumstances. The government closed these camps, and IDPs were at the mercy of other agencies and humanitarian groups for help.

Fast-forward to August 2018; I was ready for my field research, but before I embarked on a 38-hour journey to Nigeria from Canada, I needed to make my last check-in calls. The phone conversations were with my three contacts and they almost brought my research to a halt. My contacts were born in Plateau State. They grew up there and we attended the University of Jos together. They all studied theatre and one of them has a Master's degree in media and conflict resolution, while the other two are both stage and screen actors. This team of three were passionate about my project and they were generous with their resources. In fact, they risked their lives to ensure that I secured permission from appropriate authorities. They believe that theatre can facilitate an atmosphere for the peaceful dialogue essential to conflict resolution. However, the phone conversations I had with two of my contacts at different times shocked me. Both of them responded in the same way (and here I paraphrase and summarize):

> To be honest with you, Taiwo, the situation on ground now does not need theatre. We need resources for those in need, we need relief

materials for those that are dying, and we need shelter for those stranded to find a place to rest their heads … As beautiful as the idea of theatre is, it is time we drop it because it is not just what we need. We need you to mobilize resources, get into your contacts and help in whatever capacity you can … We also need you alive because we do not want you to be killed in the name of research. (Phone conversations, September 5, 2018, 10:55–11:27 a.m.)

Later, when I talked to others about the phone conversation, I was told to thank my contacts for their honesty, because they saved my life. 'Some would have asked you to come … even tell you to bring all your money and they will collect it from you … because people are desperate in this country right now … and desperate times call for desperate moves (Conversation with passengers, Lagos stopover, October 6, 2018, 04:56–6:15 p.m.). I have worked in countries such as Sudan, Burkina Faso, China, and Iran, so I understand what it means when an honest gatekeeper or an unbiased contact gives you a situational assessment and offers advice. In many cases, such advice can be a lifesaver. I also know what happens when such advice is not heeded. One reason that has kept me from being mobbed in conflict zones is that I yield to the advice of my contacts because they know the region better than me.

My contacts explored different avenues to make my research possible. First, it was not safe to take theatre to the people or engage theatre with the people due to the current political instability and economic scarcity. Time was of the essence in this context. Second, politically, there had been severe unrest in the state, and the economic situation in the wider country was tough, which meant that participants expected to be remunerated. According to my contacts, nobody would attend to me or my project without incentive and I did not have the resources to compensate research participants. Also, I was coming from a developed country, Canada. This third reason itself brought an additional economic burden because there is an assumption in Nigeria that those living abroad are economically affluent. Finally, I did not want to compromise the ethics of my practice. I have critiqued some unethical theatre for development practices as "parachute theatre"—a practice whereby an expert comes into a community for a short time to deliver a message-laden performance to the people and then disappears forever (Afolabi 2019; Hallewas 2019). That was why I had proposed to live in the camp for three months. In fact, I had made all the necessary contacts and figured out my plans, but from both political and economic standpoints, that plan was no longer feasible.

Now that my contacts had told me not to come, I had to consider how to solve this challenge and still uphold appropriate ethical practice. First, we explored the possibility of taking the project to Abuja, but this would have proved ethically challenging for the same reasons I explained above. For ethical reasons, I did not want to put on the expert hat and facilitate a workshop that was not co-created with these students, because they understand their experiences better than I do. Although I have lived in a similarly volatile environment, I cannot impose my experience on others or assume my experience is the same. It was also seven years ago, and the situation was different. Ethical considerations were important to me and I was not interested in jeopardizing my ethical standards.

I resolved to conduct my research in Ile-Ife, Osun State, Nigeria. Ile-Ife is considered the cradle of the Yoruba race (Akinjogbin 1992). Apart from the fact that it is my hometown, Ile-Ife has become a meeting point for many tribes in the country. It has three higher education institutions: Obafemi Awolowo University, Oduduwa University, and the Polytechnic, Ife. It has several private hospitals and one federal hospital, Obafemi Awolowo Teaching Hospital. Ile-Ife has experienced two major ethnic clashes within the past ten years. The most recent happened in March 2017. The earlier ethnic crisis was between Ife and Modakeke, while the most recent was between the Yoruba and the Hausa. Like many cities in the southwest region of Nigeria, the Hausa people have their own area called Sabo. They are also scattered around the city, selling commodities like vegetables and wristwatches, and exchanging foreign currencies. I designed and facilitated a series of drama workshops in a school based on major themes from the

UN *Guiding Principles on Internal Displacement* (Deng 1998) and the Kampala Convention on Refugees (2009) which could be useful in the civic education curriculum.

I focus on taking theatre to forgotten corridors, unveiling unheard stories, and perhaps engaging theatre to amplify citizens' realities. With this ambitious mission, there is always the need to consider the situation of the community involved. On arriving in Ile-Ife, I faced a challenge, as there was no one who was interested in talking about the crisis. In fact, the leader of the Hausa tribe (Seriki) said they had been instructed not to talk about the crisis. Journalists who had reported on the crisis refused to participate in any interview because of the sensitivity of the issue. Those who agreed to be interviewed preferred to talk casually about the incident and wanted to remain anonymous. Interestingly, none of them gave me permission to write anything down, and I was told to use the information I could remember after our talk without connecting it to them. How could I engage theatre in a situation when literally no one was ready to be involved?

Precarity as an Ethical Code: An Ethical Solution to a Changing Situation

As a holistic ethical code, precarity takes into account human conditions and the system in which such conditions exist. Both material and immaterial conditions are two sides of the same coin. For example, in the context of my work, the precarity in conflict/post-conflict zones affects the living conditions of the population, and I did not shy away from discussing these conditions as long as people were interested in talking about them. The conditions of heightened vulnerability and aggression that often characterize places of war are undeniable and often result in the use of violence as a response to loss. Beyond the conditions that produce suffering and destruction, "geographies of power" are unstable (Olaoluwa 2019). The precarity of populations in conflict/post-conflict zones in this context refers to the quality of life of the people and the political-economic realities of the state involved. It considers the instability of the political situation and the resultant effect of such politics on people's living conditions. It strongly underscores the violence, vulnerability, and loss that are evident in dislocated places and displaced populations, and the implication for those whose life is grievable (Butler 2004). In *Frames of War* (2009), Butler considers how some lives become grief-worthy, while others are perceived as undeserving of grief or even incomprehensible as lives. It is important to see how geographies of power are frequently responsible for the cause of grief, which on many occasions have provoked a violent response. In the cases of the Ife–Modakeke, Yoruba–Hausa, and Jos crises, violence was in response to people's grief caused by land disputes, politics, and tribalism (Elugbaju 2018; Asiyanbola 2010; Ogundipe 1996). Thus, Butler argues for the dislocation of first-world privilege and offers instead a chance to imagine a world in which violence might be minimized and in which interdependency is acknowledged as the basis for a global political community.

In this project, I identified and critiqued systems of oppression because precarious conditions and experiences can create opportunities to unsettle geographies of power and envision new realities. I positioned myself within this complex system and reflected on how I navigated daily realities while in Nigeria. This is important because it helped me talk about the occasionally transactional nature of research and the transfer of knowledge (and power) that occurs during the research process. Precarious conditions can provide leverage for my participants to challenge geographies of power. However, it is only after the need to understand the situation and resolve conflict non-violently (if and when necessary) that the possibility of engaging the creative and theatrical comes into play. The reality remains that the vast majority considers precarity as negative because of the connotations and experiences that surround it. There is precarity in forced migration, along with a social stigma attached to such experience, especially as a refugee or an IDP. When engaging with and making research choices in such communities, there is a need for a profound sense of recognition of both past and present realities, such as the condition of the people and the timing of the incident. Ethics of precarity involves recognizing these realities and acting in the best interest of the people involved, because it is about relational interaction that is accountable, responsible, and answerable.

Conclusion: Preparing for Ethics of Precarity

The ethics of *being* should align with the ethics of *doing*. An intellectual knowledge about ethical practice is different from an experiential knowledge. In other words, *writing* about ethics is different from *doing* ethics (Afolabi 2021). Both processes cannot be mutually exclusive. As an applied theatre practitioner living in Canada who has had the opportunity to work in different social contexts internationally, I knew my research was going to raise some serious ethical concerns: (1) It was due to take place in an international jurisdiction (in another country); (2) in a post-conflict zone; (3) among vulnerable populations (internally displaced people, including women and children); and (4) it was happening in a country in the Global South. To some extent, I understood the ethics of working in a precarious situation. Apart from the fact that I have experienced displacement myself, I have worked in tense, unstable, and dangerous geopolitical sites. I was not only considering the ethics of *doing* research, I was well aware of the ethics of *being* in a precarious condition such as displacement and its implications on different aspects of life. The ethics of precarity starts from recognizing the realities of being at the mercy of the other, in a position of uncertainty, and how this affects whatever the practitioner is doing and the people impacted by those conditions.

In my case, I was fully aware of the material and immaterial realities as part of my lived experience. However, what happens when such reality is not part of a researcher's knowledge or background? Research stories of people who have experienced or who are still experiencing the reality in question. For me, rather than focusing on existing literature alone, I connected with and listened to individuals with lived experiences. The two vignettes at the beginning of this chapter were real-life conversations that led to the change in the direction of my research. As I noted earlier, paying attention to the reality of the displaced population was more important than my research study. Ultimately, my choice affected the research, including my methodology and aesthetics. For example, instead of staying in an IDP camp as planned, I moved my research location to a school, and designed and facilitated a series of drama workshops that could be useful for civic education. There was no public performance as I originally planned. Rather than focusing on my research, the maxim of my action was about the community and building ethical relationships with them on their terms. Although I have to admit that my research took place in a familiar territory, in every sense of the word, I still had to consider my responsibilities as a researcher, practitioner, and as a son of the soil.

Finally, ethics of precarity is about relational responsibility towards the past and the future. Although the quality of life of displaced populations can provide an opportunity for dialogue or a space for non-violent means of conflict resolution, mindfulness is important. Mindfulness means being present or absent when necessary, listening and caring for others, and being cared for (Segal, Williams and Teasdale 2013). To engage the ethics of precarity, it is worth asking questions such as: what are the limits of the arts? In what ways are practitioners creating a false impression of what socially engaged arts such as applied theatre can achieve?

Note

1   https://www.vanguardngr.com/2017/03/46-killed-96-wounded-ile-ife-yoruba-hausa-clash-police/https://www.sunnewsonline.com/ile-ife-crisis-untold-story-of-yorubahausa-clash/https://www.baptistpress.com/resource-library/news/fulani-herdsmen-kill-300-nigerian-christians/

References

Afolabi, T. (2019), "Performing arts-based interventions in post-conflict zones: critical and ethical question," *NJ: Journal of Drama Australia*, 43 (1), 51–66.

Afolabi, T. (2021), "From *writing* ethics to *doing* ethics: ethical questioning of a practitioner," *Research in Drama Education: The Journal of Applied Theatre and Performance*, 26 (2), 352–7.

Akinjogbin, I. A. (1992), *The Cradle of a Race: Ife from the Beginning to 1980*. Port Harcourt, Nigeria: Sunray Publishers.

Asiyanbola, R. A. (2010), "Ethnic conflicts in Nigeria: a case of Ife-Modakeke in historical perspective," *Journal of Humanities, Social Sciences and Creative Arts*, 5 (1), 61–78.

Balfour, M. (2001), *Theatre and War 1933–1945: Performances in Extremis*. Oxford: Berghahn Books.

Balfour, M., Bundy, P., Burton, B., Dunn, J., and Woodrow, N. (2015), *Applied Theatre Resettlement: Drama, Refugee and Resilience*. London: Bloomsbury Methuen Drama.

Buchanan, I. (2018). *A Dictionary of Critical Theory* (2nd ed.). Oxford: Oxford University Press. doi:10.1093/acref/9780198794790.001.0001

Butler, J. (2004), *Precarious Life: The Power of Mourning and Violence*. London: Verso.

Butler, J. (2009), *Frames of War: When is Life Grievable?* London and New York: Verso.

Colleran, J. (2012), *Theatre and War: Theatrical Responses since 1991*. New York: Palgrave Macmillan.

Costa, M. and Field, A. (2021), *Performance in an Age of Precarity: 40 Reflections*. London: Bloomsbury.

Danfulani, U. H. D. (2005), *The Jos Peace Conference and the Indigene/Settler Question in Nigerian Politics*. Leiden and Nigeria: African Studies Centre/ University of Jos. Available online: http://www.ascleiden.nl/pdf/paper-danfulani.pdf (accessed November 25, 2020).

Deng, F. (1998), *The Guiding Principles on Internal Displacement*, E/ CN.4/1998/53. New York: United Nations.

Dinesh, N. (2016), *Theatre and War: Notes from the Field*. Cambridge, UK: Open Book Publishers.

Dowling, E., Nunes, R., and Trott, B. (2007), "Immaterial and affective labour: explored," *Ephemera: Theory & Politics in Organization*, 7 (1), 1–7.

Elugbaju, A. (2018), "Ife-Modakeke crisis (1849–2000): re-thinking the conflict and the methods of resolution," *Journal of Science, Humanities, and Arts*, 5 (8), 483–98.

Fragkou, M. (2018), *Ecologies of Precarity in Twenty-First Century Theatre: Politics, Affect, Responsibility*. London: Bloomsbury.

Gallagher, K. and Rodricks, D. J. (2017), "Hope despite hopelessness: race, gender, and the pedagogies of drama/applied theatre as a relational ethic in neoliberal times," *Youth Theatre Journal*, 31 (2), 114–28.

Hallewas, A. (2019), "Researching and devising youth theatre: loss of voice and agency through parachute theatre," *Youth Theatre Journal*, 33 (2), 153–62.

Higazi, A. (2011), "The Jos crisis: the recurrent Nigerian tragedy," Discussion Paper No. 2, *Friedrich-Ebert-Stiftung*. Available online: http://library.fes.de/pdf-files/bueros/nigeria/07812.pdf (accessed November 25, 2020).

Hughes, J. (2019). *Precariousness and the Performances of Welfare*. New York: Routledge.

Internet Encyclopedia of Philosophy ("ethics"), https://www.iep.utm.edu/ethics/

Kampala Declaration on Refugees, Returnees and Internally Displaced Persons in Africa. Adopted by the Special Summit of the African Union held in Kampala, Uganda, October 22–23, 2009.

Ogundipe, B. (1996), *Modakeke History in Ile-Ife: The Facts and the Falsehood. A Great Ife Movement Publication*. Ife, Nigeria: OPN LIFE.

Olaoluwa, S. (2019), "Beyond backpacking: solo 'guerrilla' border crossing and the penetration of geographies of power in Olabisi Ajala's *An African Abroad*," *Journal of Borderlands Studies*, 36 (3), 487–501. doi:10.1080/0886 5655.2019.1571431

Online Etymology Dictionary ("precarity"), https://www.etymonline.com/search?q=precarity

Osofisan, F. (1998), *Playing Dangerously: Drama at the Frontiers of Terror in a "Postcolonial" State*. Ibadan, Nigeria: University of Ibadan.

Owolade, F. (2014), "Boko Haram: how a militant Islamist group emerged in Nigeria," Gatestone Institute. Available online: http://www.gatestoneinstitute.org/4232/boko-haram-nigeria (accessed November 20, 2014).

Segal, Z. V., Williams, J. M. G., and Teasdale, J. D. (2013), *Mindfulness Based Cognitive Therapy for Depression* (2nd ed.). New York: Guilford Press.

Segun, J. (2013), "Ethnicisation of violent conflicts in Jos?," *Global Journal of Human Social Science*, 13 (7), 37–42.

Stannage, E. (2017), "Precariousness and groundedness in arts in mental health," *Research in Drama Education: The Journal of Applied Theatre and Performance*, 22 (1), 153–6.

Thompson, J., Hughes, J., and Balfour, M. (2009), *Performance in Place of War*. London: Seagull Books.

12

Research Ethics as Censorship in Applied Theatre

Sheila Christie

Applied theatre relies on participants' willingness to take risks. For this reason, applied theatre in university contexts runs counter to the ethics policies defined by governmental, arm's-length, research-funding organizations; in Canada, these function collectively as the Tri-Council funding agencies. While this paper focuses on the Canadian context, my observations apply to research ethics policies more generally. The *Tri-Council Policy Statement: Ethical Conduct for Research Involving Humans* (TCPS2 2018) (Canadian Institutes 2018) directs researchers to "eliminate or minimize" risk (Panel on Research Ethics 2010: Module 1) under the core principle of "Concern for Welfare"; the goal is to help researchers avoid causing participants unnecessary risk. However, the assumption that risk is inherently negative limits applied theatre research, encouraging self-censorship and skewing projects by framing risk as something participants should avoid. The TCPS2 does not account for the ethics of applied theatre, and its interpretation by university Research Ethics Boards (REBs) in Canada can further undermine applied theatre research. Researchers must collectively define a code of ethics and use academic associations to represent applied theatre within larger debates around ethical research. In this chapter, I discuss the existing ethics of applied theatre practice, identify

Thanks to attendees of the 2019 Canadian Association of Theatre Research conference and to Cape Breton University's Humanities and Social Sciences Working Group for feedback, and to Anita Hallewas and Taiwo Afolabi for insight on student experiences of the Canadian ethics process.

the limitations of the TCPS2, and provide a foundation for an applied theatre code of ethics to guide practice and support ethics board negotiations.

Risky Business

Risk has always been a component of applied theatre. In *Theatre of the Oppressed*, Augusto Boal describes his approach as "a rehearsal for the revolution" (1979: 122). In 1974 Brazil, Boal was not referring vaguely to "a" revolution; he meant *the* revolution: specific, targeted resistance against identifiable oppressors who retaliated with imprisonment, torture, and exile. His theatre risked real consequences. In European and North American contexts where the line between oppressed and oppressor can be less defined, Theatre of the Oppressed became gentler, more flexible, less revolutionary. For example, David Diamond's (2007) Theatre for Living, developed in Vancouver, Canada, uses Boal's techniques to dismantle systemic oppressions on an individual level. Risk, however, remains a component because participants share personal narratives as part of the process: participation requires radical vulnerability (a concept explored in Richa Nagar's work, most recently in *Hungry Translations* 2019: 38). Some modes of applied theatre, including verbatim and playback theatre, devise performances using non-actors' intimate stories, gathered through interviews and during performances. Other approaches, such as popular theatre, may eschew personal narratives but take risks by critiquing oppressive political or social structures, or by disrupting aesthetic expectations and risking negative audience reactions (see Balme 2008: 180–1; Kerr 2009: 180–2; Prendergast and Saxon 2016: 45–9; O'Grady 2017: 16–21). Applied theatre practitioners often engage with populations who experience risk, asking participants to explore their own vulnerabilities and personal narratives. Risk is "a core aesthetic" (O'Grady 2017: 4) of applied theatre.

Because risk is central to applied theatre, practitioners think carefully about ethics. Introductory textbooks, such as Monica Prendergast and Juliana Saxton's *Applied Theatre* (2016) and Tim Prentki and Nicola Abraham's *The Applied Theatre Reader* (2021), raise ethics directly, and journals like *Research in Drama Education: The Journal of Applied Theatre and Performance* and *Applied Theatre Research* regularly publish on ethical practice. Asking participants and audiences to be vulnerable carries an obligation of care, both out of human decency and to protect our practice.[1] Manipulative, self-serving, or exploitative practices (e.g., coerced participation, misrepresentation, prioritizing funders' agendas) threaten practitioners' abilities to do meaningful work and undermine the efforts of other applied theatre facilitators.

Non-academic practitioners use various techniques to address risk, largely by emphasizing participants' autonomy. In choosing to attend a performance or workshop, participants tacitly accept responsibility for their own actions and reactions. Paid and volunteer performers are assumed to have agency to engage and disengage as needed. Practitioners highlight participants' autonomy by committing to mutually negotiated ground rules, voluntary participation, and active listening. Diamond, for example, requires all workshop participants to attend voluntarily; he urges participants to trust in the process, but also to know themselves and care for their emotional needs.[2] Marc Weinblatt, from the Port Townsend Mandala Center for Change, focuses on being present and attentive without judging or attempting to control responses, allowing participants to raise concerns and seek solutions consensually.[3] Many practitioners use opening and closing circles, where each participant speaks without interruption, to develop rapport and empower participants. While there are many guides for applied theatre practitioners that address ethical practice (e.g., Rohd 1998: 5–6, 130–1; Baim, Brookes and Mountford 2002: 23–9; Nicholson 2005a: 155–67; Taylor 2003: 76–101), they primarily urge clarity about a project's aims and participants' roles. A few texts go further: Teresa Fisher and Leslie Smith (2010) discuss informed consent (although in an academic journal, which limits circulation), and Clark Baim's *Staging the Personal: A Guide to Safe and Ethical Practice* (2020) articulates an ethical-decision-making model (the drama spiral). In practice, however, applied theatre ethics relies on agency, trusting participants to negotiate their own levels of risk.

Problematic Policies

Applied theatre conducted within a Canadian university context is held to the rigorous, formalized standard of the TCPS2, which reflects neither applied theatre's critical relationship with risk nor its emphasis on participant autonomy. The policy relies on three core principles – respect for persons, concern for welfare, and justice – but the implementation of these principles creates problems for applied theatre research. The policy requires researchers to "assess risks and potential benefits" (7) and "attempt to minimize the risks" (8), making risk mitigation central to ethics approval. Directly contrasted with benefit, risk is "the possibility of the occurrence of harm" (201), and harm is "anything that has a negative effect on participants' welfare, broadly construed" (195). The policy thus frames risk as inherently negative, failing to allow for the potential of productive risk that is imbedded in applied theatre practice. As Astrid Breel argues, "The ethics of participation is more complicated ... than simply ensuring that the risk of harm to participants is minimised; in fact, effective participation may mean putting participants in a challenging situation" (2015: 46). Applied theatre's conception of risk is nuanced, but the TCPS2's definition of risk allows REBs to define the "challenging situation[s]" of applied theatre as requiring mitigation.

Applied theatre is not alone in embracing a positive conception of risk. Psychology identifies some risks as "constructive for development" (Duell and Steinberg 2019: 48); risk helps people "develop a sense of purpose ... and identity" (51). In other words, risk can foster personal growth. Similarly, Brian Arao and Kirsti Clemens (2013) distinguish between "safe" and "brave" pedagogical spaces, asserting that "authentic learning about social justice often requires the very qualities of risk, difficulty, and controversy that are defined as incompatible with safety" (139). Applied theatre is not a safe practice, but it is a brave one, providing opportunities to learn "a new way of seeing things" (R. Boostrom, quoted in Arao and Clemens 2013: 141). In contrast, "avoidance of risk stunts our development and leads to inactivity, inertia, and apathy in the world at large" (O'Grady 2017: 15). For Alice O'Grady and other applied theatre practitioners, "the theatre [is] a place that allows us to rehearse action ... where risk is deployed as a tactic by which we learn to act and take action in our lives" (15). Risk is not only positive; it is necessary.

The TCPS2's emphasis on negative risk undermines the policy's commitment to participant autonomy, the principle of "respect for persons" which is critical for applied theatre. As contributors to *Ethics Rupture* (Van den Hoonaard and Hamilton 2016) frequently attest, university research ethics policies are informed by biological research, which must address knowledge gaps between researchers and subjects. Clarifying complex ideas and protecting participants who lack disciplinary knowledge is appropriate in biomedical contexts, but can result in the "infantilization of human beings" (Van den Hoonaard and Hamilton 2016: 8) when applied indiscriminately to the social sciences, humanities, and arts. Disciplines that engage participants as collaborators or co-researchers eschew the knowledge gap of biomedical research; they understand that researchers and participants alike contribute expertise. Unlike a model that identifies and mitigates risk prior to interaction with research participants, applied theatre relies on participant autonomy as a component of agency and the ability to negotiate risk.

Applied theatre most closely aligns with the TCPS2 adaptations for Qualitative Research (Chapter 10), but inconsistencies and ambiguities within this section of the policy reveal a limited understanding of qualitative disciplines. This chapter acknowledges that some research relies on "emergent design" (134), "may include 'giving voice' to a particular population, [or] engaging in research that is critical of settings and systems or the power of those being studied" (135), and that "sometimes the researcher cannot ascertain the process [of consent] in advance of the research" (ibid.). Nevertheless, REBs may retreat to the clarity of the policy's core principles when faced with the contradictions in this chapter. For example, despite acknowledging that "It is sometimes difficult to ascertain the beginning and end of a qualitative research project" (137), Article 10.1 requires researchers to submit "research proposals ... prior to the start of recruitment of participants, data collection or access to data" (136). Elsewhere, the policy permits researchers to engage in preliminary work prior to the start of a project, but defines such work as "preced[ing] the formal data collection involving participants" (137). Given that access to research funding is generally dependent on ethics approval, researchers are bureaucratically and financially deterred from preliminary work with participants to collaboratively establish project scope, ethics, and research questions. Anita Hallewas (2021) describes this limitation in her article "Applied theatre as research: Devising social theatre across the whole community." Although Hallewas envisioned a fully collaborative project with her community partners, the ethics approval process required research questions in advance. The discussion for Article 10.1 states: "if researchers later wish to use material from this [preliminary] phase, they shall say so in their research proposal and include any plan to seek consent from those interviewed" (137). This statement ignores the evolving nature of "qualitative research" and expects researchers to predict relevance, but applied theatre relies on a critical "indeterminacy" that allows "what might be to emerge in the creative process" (Sloan 2018: 586); we frequently do not know what is relevant until after the fact. Requiring us to pretend we can suggests a focus on liability, rather than good practice.

Further limitations of the policy's qualitative research contingencies are evidenced in Article 10.5, which acknowledges that "emergent design involves data collection and analysis that can evolve over the course of a research project" and that "specific questions ... may be difficult to anticipate, identify and articulate fully in the research proposal in advance of the project's implementation" (141). While acknowledging emergent design is promising, the discussion focuses on definable research tools such as surveys and interview questions, providing no guidance on the emergent processes relevant to applied theatre.

Beyond the problems the TCPS2 presents in justifying research practices to REBs, the policy's prioritization of written consent threatens the collaborative relationships that applied theatre researchers seek to establish with participants. In my experience, participants often view consent forms with indifference or suspicion. They tune out verbal discussion of consent, sign forms without reading them, or demonstrate through body language and humor their discomfort with legalistic formalities. Applied theatre scholars working in development settings find written consent especially problematic: participants can be "illiterate and may write a cross ... without any understanding of the form" or may "have lost family members and loved ones after signing forms" (Sadeghi-Yekta 2021). Formalized written consent also frames risk as negative, fueling participants' reluctance to negotiate risk within a project. REB-mandated efforts to mitigate risk, such as providing on-site counseling or listing support services, can also elevate perceptions of negative risk. REBs often require that researchers highlight these mitigation efforts in written consent forms or as part of the consent process, which further disrupts efforts to build collaborative relationships.

While the policy acknowledges that under some circumstances "written consent is not appropriate" and that participants may see "attempts to legalize or formalize the process as a violation of ... trust" (137), the criteria for altering consent procedures (Article 3.7A) are restrictive. Researchers must argue for any deviation from the standard model, and permission depends on REB interpretation. REBs unfamiliar with community-engaged, emergent, or arts-based research may resort to clearer aspects of the TCPS2 and be unwilling to consider alternatives to written consent.

The disjunct between applied theatre ethics and the TCPS2 most directly affects the policy's third principle, justice, which includes "distributing the benefits and burdens of research participation in such a way that no segment of the population is unduly burdened by the harms of research or denied the benefits of the knowledge generated from it" (8). Both practitioners and participants may self-censor because the ethics process frames risk as undesirable. Applied theatre researchers are less likely to work with vulnerable populations if ethics clearance is seen as difficult to obtain. Anxiety over the tensions between applied theatre practice and the TCPS2 may lead scholars to choose less risky projects and participants, denying some populations the benefits of research. These problems are amplified in the case of student researchers, where institutional power dynamics can prevent students from defending ethically valid approaches to supervisors and REBs.

Creating a Code

It is easy to critique research ethics policies and raise concerns over their interpretation. These policies attempt to advise ethics in a wide range of disciplines, and ethics boards are staffed by colleagues from equally diverse backgrounds. While policies should evolve to better reflect collaborative research, another solution is to define our own code of ethics. Ethics boards will give more consideration to accepted disciplinary standards than to individual researchers' arguments, and subscribing to a standard will support students and junior colleagues who struggle to negotiate with ethics boards. Rather than independently battling ethics boards over the interpretation of research ethics policies, we need a collective articulation of the values that inform our work. As the editors of this book argue, we need a code of ethics for applied theatre research.

Our code should articulate the principles we value, and describe how we ensure that participants are treated ethically while respecting agency and autonomy. The four principles below have arisen consistently in my own work and in other scholars' published considerations of applied theatre ethics. Other principles should arise from further conversation around ethical challenges not well served by ethics policies, such as questions of compensation, incentive, equity, and diversity. The principles below provide a basis for conversations around formulating a code for applied theatre research.

1. Participants are autonomous collaborators whose participation is voluntary

Whether participants supply material for devising, engage in exploratory exercises, or perform for private or public audiences, we consider them research collaborators with their own autonomy. Even in instances where autonomy is legally or medically limited, researchers must seek assent throughout the process and respect participants as collaborators.

Theatre that aims to shift power dynamics, whether within the development of a project or between performers and audience, cannot succeed through coercion. Whether developing exercises or performances, researchers must ensure voluntary participation, which includes considering the power dynamics and incentives that bring participants to the work. Underprivileged individuals, for example, may attend to access food and shelter, while incarcerated individuals may be mandated to participate. Research funding privileges partnerships with organizations (e.g., youth groups, schools, and social services) that may not guarantee the voluntary participation of their charges or clients. When attendance may be involuntary or influenced by incentives unrelated to the work, applied theatre researchers must ensure voluntary participation and accommodate participants' expectations. This may be as simple as modifying an activity or as difficult as halting a project entirely.

Theatre in contexts of incarceration demonstrates the ethical challenges of voluntary, autonomous participation. The Theatre in Prisons Project (TiPP) works with prisons in the Manchester region (UK), providing weekly drama and music sessions that also serve as learning spaces for university students. Participation is voluntary but nonetheless reflects on inmates' records of behavior. When I shadowed the TiPP facilitators, sessions were modified to prioritize voluntary participation so that inmates could benefit from the session and get credit within the prison system. The first session was underattended, with one of the three participants leaving almost immediately. The TiPP facilitator directly addressed the mood in the room, revising the agenda to discuss what had occurred. The facilitator drew on preexisting rapport to acknowledge participants' concerns outside of the session. In turn, the participants relaxed, spoke more freely, and elected to continue with the planned activities. The conversation reaffirmed the participants' humanity and agency, emphasizing their larger concerns and their right to participate voluntarily. Active listening and constructing a safe space enabled voluntary participation. In another session, the TiPP facilitator introduced light-hearted games to rebuild a rapport that had been disrupted by a participant the week prior. In both cases, TiPP facilitators shifted the agenda to accommodate the participants and ensure voluntary participation. They acknowledged participants' mindsets when entering the workspace, and adapted accordingly. Prioritizing autonomy means being mindful of where participants are at and adapting accordingly.

2. Consent is ongoing and signaled, depending on the level of risk and capacity of participants, by attendance, participation, verbal consent, and if necessary, written consent

Research ethics policies emphasizing up-front, written consent imply that consent is addressed once and presumed thereafter. Jenny Hughes argues against one-time consent practices, prioritizing "active, participatory, dialogic and negotiated" ethics as "an ongoing interaction of values in shifting contexts and relationships ... [not] something delivered by a signed consent form" (2005: 231). Similarly, Helen Nicholson, citing Tim May's critique of standardized ethics, states that rigid application of any ethical code or policy "takes insufficient account of contextuality" by "fail[ing] to address how changing circumstances and local factors ... might affect the work" (2005b: 121). Because "in relation to risk, context is everything" (O'Grady 2017: 5), we must incorporate a respect for contextuality directly into our code of ethics. Ongoing consent, signaled in multiple ways throughout the process, better ensures respect for voluntary participation. Risk levels often cannot be approved in advance because the narratives and their attendant risks come from participants. When consent is sought throughout the process in varying degrees of formality, participants trust that their concerns and decisions will be respected. Applied theatre practitioners seek consent through participants' attendance and participation, conversation and direct request for commitment or permission, or written consent as appropriate. For example, I ask permission before demonstrating an exercise that involves physical contact, something that prior written consent cannot replace. I also address risk differently depending on the stage of the process: early in a process I discuss confidentiality, emotional challenges, and the need for self-care; closer to performance, I emphasize de-roling and have participants consider how to handle audience and community reactions.

Prioritizing ongoing consent with a sliding scale of formality (i.e., from presence to written consent) honors autonomy and demonstrates respect. While consent should be informed and articulated from the start, formal records of verbal or written consent become necessary only if participants insist on engaging in higher levels of risk, or if participants are of diminished mental or legal capacity. Written consent is appropriate when parental or guardian approval is necessary, as when working with children or seniors who may lack mental capacity, although researchers should also obtain participant assent in addition to legal consent.

3. Risk is mutually negotiated and agreed upon consensually

This principle deviates the most from policies like the TCPS2. Whereas research ethics policies aim to mitigate risk, applied theatre relies on taking acceptable risks in order to foster growth and change. Paul Spicker and David Byrne believe "the ethical objective is not to minimize avoidable harm [but] to ensure that any adverse consequences will be legitimate and defensible" (in Schrag 2016: 323). Researchers and participants must separately and collectively identify risks and benefits, working together to negotiate plans for managing these risks. Engaging in collaborative risk assessment before a project begins can ensure all perspectives are considered in the project's design.

One reason risk must be negotiated collaboratively is that participants often have a more informed understanding of risks and benefits within the context of their own lives. David Kerr (2009) describes several examples where participants were better suited to assess their ability and willingness to face the risks of their projects; his facilitation team helped participants identify and articulate risk, but the decision to engage in that risk lay with the participants. He asserts, "the only authentic and ethically sound initiatives of theatre radicalism, particularly those with overt political implications come from those who are inextricably part of the struggle, not outsiders 'parachuted' in for short term action there" (182). We must consider risk in project design and throughout projects, including our own risks (such as blurred boundaries and the risk of burnout), but participants know best what risks are supportable within their own lives and communities.

4. Communication must be open, transparent, and clear throughout a project's development

As researchers, we must articulate for ourselves and our participants what motivates a project, what we stand to gain or achieve, and what we expect of others. We must also make space to hear our participant-collaborators' expectations, desires, and needs. In Kathy Bishop's "Six perspectives in search of an ethical solution" (2014), Tim Prentki stresses the need "to be transparent about your intentions in pursuing an ethnodrama project" (72). For Bishop, this call for transparency "speaks to the deeper level needed for theatre-based researchers to engage in self-reflection and inquiry ... to clarify their own positions and ensure that 'right choices' are made" (72). In the same article, Johnny Saldaña recommends ongoing communication and clarity among both participants and audience members (69–70). Failure to communicate causes the kind of harm that ethics policies aim to prevent. In her experiences with a refugee theatre project, Yasmine Kandil (2016) encountered ethical pitfalls when the intended use of participants' narratives was neither articulated in advance, nor negotiated in process. The "ambiguity of [the call for participants], and its lack of clear explanation of the steps involved in the creative process" (205) resulted in Kandil reliving a difficult personal narrative repeatedly through the performance. Kandil urges consultation with participants and contributors throughout the process (211), and clarity "about the goals of the project, the steps involved in each stage, and the parameters of the work" (210). Kandil's experience demonstrates the critical need for researchers and practitioners alike to articulate expectations and address participants' concerns.

Just as we should clarify our intentions and evolving plans, we must also communicate boundaries and limitations. Discussing the challenges of working as a community outsider, Kirsten Sadeghi-Yekta (2016) advocates for transparent entrance and exit plans, clarifying where our involvement starts and ends, as well as who will be responsible for the outcomes and consequences of a project after we depart. Prendergast and Saxton (2016) reiterate that exit plans are "one of the least-addressed" (240) yet ethically necessary aspects of applied theatre, when research often takes place within a limited time frame, restricting our ability to address long-term consequences. A related limitation is our inability to predict outcomes. Prendergast and Saxton (242) warn against making unsupported claims for the utility of applied theatre. Michael Balfour (2009) specifically critiques "the tautologies of transformation" (350), the tendency of practitioners to make grand claims for the transformative potential of our work. He urges us to resist "the bait of social change, rehabilitation, behavioural objectives and outcomes," and instead to acknowledge that applied theatre is "more often messy, incomplete, complex and tentative" (357). Articulating what we can do means clarifying what we cannot.

We must also maintain communication with participants when plans go awry. For example, we cannot control who answers a call to participate; nor can we prepare in advance for the impact of participants leaving a project. I experienced both challenges during a 2017 project in the Cape Breton Regional Municipality. I initially planned to use participants' experiences of a local flood to investigate social trust; a few participants responded specifically with "flood stories," but most joined the project to learn about applied theatre more generally. I handled this disconnect between the call and participants' expectations by sharing my curiosity about social trust, which allowed us to choose a new project focus collaboratively. Open, transparent, and clear communication resulted in a more rewarding process and a more effective performance. Similarly, when two participants withdrew from the project during the performance development phase, I acknowledged the distress this caused for the team, and I reaffirmed our mutual commitment to confidentiality. In the end, the participants used forum to show how technology and busy schedules impede social trust, and to help audiences address these barriers. Ongoing communication was critical not only to allow the project to proceed but also to honor participants as co-researchers and reaffirm autonomy in the face of risk.

Concluding Thoughts

Creating a code of ethics requires extensive conversation among applied theatre researchers, but its development will facilitate our research and our students' work. Through its application, we will more thoroughly examine and enact the ethics of our work. A code will enrich our students' education and clarify our intentions for community partners and participants. It will also facilitate negotiations with ethics boards, helping to shape future iterations of research ethics policies so that participants are better represented as collaborators and co-researchers.

Rather than each scholar reinventing applied theatre's core ethical principles in isolation, and instead of disdaining university ethics procedures as a bureaucratic hoop, let us collaborate on a code that represents the values that make our work possible.

Notes

1   Applied theatre's "ethics of care" features in Anne Smith's 2014 article on theatre with refugees and migrants, and more recently in Amanda Stuart Fisher and James Thompson's *Performing Care* (2020).
2   Diamond articulated these expectations during workshops I attended in 2014, 2016, and 2020.
3   I observed Weinblatt's approach during a workshop in 2016.

References

Arao, B. and Clemens, K. (2013), "From safe spaces to brave spaces: a new way to frame dialogue around diversity and social justice," in L. Landreman (ed.), *The Art of Effective Facilitation: Reflections from Social Justice Educators*. Sterling, VA: Stylus Publishing, pp. 135–50. Available online: https://tlss.uottawa.ca/site/perspective-autochtone/1d-_From-Safe-Spaces-to-Brave-Spaces.pdf (accessed May 2, 2021).

Baim, C. (2020), *Staging the Personal: A Guide to Safe and Ethical Practice*. Cham, Switzerland: Palgrave Macmillan.

Baim, C., Brookes, S., and Mountford, A. (eds) (2002), *The Geese Theatre Handbook: Drama with Offenders and People at Risk*. Sherfield-on-Loddon, Hants: Waterside Press.

Balfour, M. (2009), "The politics of intention: looking for a theatre of little changes," *Research and Drama Education: The Journal of Applied Theatre and Performance*, 14 (3), 347–59, doi:10.1080/13569780903072125.

Balme, C. B. (2008), *The Cambridge Introduction to Theatre Studies*. Cambridge: Cambridge University Press.

Bishop, K. (2014), "Six perspectives in search of an ethical solution: utilising a moral imperative with a multiple ethics paradigm to guide research-based theatre/applied theatre," *Research and Drama Education: The Journal of Applied Theatre and Performance*, 19 (1), 64–75, doi:10.1080/13569783.2013.872426

Boal, A. (1979), *Theatre of the Oppressed*, trans. C. A. McBride and M. Leal McBride. New York: Theatre Communications Group; reprint.

Breel, A. (2015), "Aesthetic relationships and ethics in the oh fuck moment," *Research and Drama Education: The Journal of Applied Theatre and Performance*, 20 (1), 39–49. doi:10.1080/13569783.2014.985643.

Canadian Institutes of Health Research, Natural Sciences and Engineering Research Council of Canada, and Social Sciences and Humanities Research Council (2018), *Tri-Council Policy Statement: Ethical Conduct for Research Involving Humans*. Ottawa: Government of Canada. Available online: https://ethics.gc.ca/eng/documents/tcps2-2018-en-interactive-final.pdf (accessed May 2, 2021).

Diamond, D. (2007), *Theatre for Living: The Art and Science of Community-Based Dialogue*. Victoria, BC: Trafford.

Duell, N. and Steinberg, L. (2019), "Positive risk taking in adolescence," *Child Development Perspectives*, 13 (1), 48–52.

Fisher, T. and Smith, L. (2010), "First do no harm: informed consent principles for trust and understanding in applied theatre practice," *Journal of Applied Arts and Health*, 1 (2), 157–64.

Hallewas, A. (2021), "Applied theatre as research: devising social theatre across the whole community," in H. Fitzsimmons-Frey and J. McKinnon (eds), *Why Devise?* Bristol: Intellect, pp. 281–96.

Hughes, J. (2005), "Ethical cleansing? The process of gaining 'ethical approval' for a new research project exploring performance in place of war," *Research and Drama Education: The Journal of Applied Theatre and Performance*, 10 (2), 229–32. doi:10.1080/13569780500103968

Kandil, Y. (2016), "Personal stories in applied theatre contexts: redefining the blurred lines," *Research and Drama Education: The Journal of Applied Theatre and Performance*, 21 (2), 201–13, doi:10.1080/13569783.2016.1155408

Kerr, D. (2009), "Ethics of applied theatre," *South African Theatre Journal*, 23 (1), 177–87, doi:10.1080/10137548.2009.9687908

Nagar, R. (2019), *Hungry Translations: Relearning the World through Radical Vulnerability*. Urbana: University of Illinois Press.

Nicholson, H. (2005a), *Applied Drama: The Gift of Theatre*. New York: Palgrave Macmillan.

Nicholson, H. (2005b), "On ethics," *Research and Drama Education: The Journal of Applied Theatre and Performance*, 10 (2), 119–25, doi:10.1080/13569780500103414

O'Grady, A. (ed.) (2017), *Risk, Participation, and Performance Practice: Critical Vulnerabilities in a Precarious World*. New York: Palgrave Macmillan.

Panel on Research Ethics (2010), *TCPS 2: CORE — Tutorial*. Government of Canada. Available online: https://tcps2core.ca/welcome (accessed May 2, 2021).

Prendergast, M. and Saxton, J. (eds) (2016), *Applied Theatre: International Case Studies and Challenges for Practice* (2nd ed.). Bristol: Intellect.

Prentki, T. and Abraham, N. (2021), *The Applied Theatre Reader* (2nd ed.). New York: Routledge.

Rohd, M. (1998), *Theatre for Community, Conflict & Dialogue: The Hope is Vital Training Manual*. Portsmouth, Hants: Heinemann.

Sadeghi-Yekta, K. (2016), Conversation with the author, August 5.

Sadeghi-Yekta, K. (2021), Personal correspondence, January 14.

Schrag, Z. M. (2016), "Ethical pluralism: scholarly societies and regulation," in W. C. Van den Hoonaard and A. Hamilton (eds), *Ethics Rupture: Exploring Alternatives to Formal Research Ethics Review*. Toronto, ON: University of Toronto Press, pp. 317–34.

Sloan, C. (2018), "Understanding spaces of potentiality in applied theatre," *Research and Drama Education: The Journal of Applied Theatre and Performance*, 23 (4), 582–97.

Smith, A. (2014), "Maximizing empowerment in applied theatre with refugees and migrants in the United Kingdom: facilitation shaped by an ethic of care," *Journal of Arts and Communities*, 6 (3), 177–88, doi:10.1386/jaac.6.2-3.177_1

Stuart Fisher, A. and Thompson, J. (eds) (2020), *Performing Care: New Perspectives on Socially-Engaged Performance*. Manchester: Manchester University Press.

Taylor, P. (2003), *Applied Theatre: Creating Transformative Encounters in the Community*. Portsmouth, Hants: Heinemann.

Van den Hoonaard, W. C. and Hamilton, A. (eds) (2016), *Ethics Rupture: Exploring Alternatives to Formal Research Ethics Review*. Toronto, ON: University of Toronto Press.

13

Colonial Adventurism in Applied Theatre: An Ethical Self-Critique

Dennis D. Gupa

Aboard a passenger vessel going to an island community in Western Samar, the Philippines, I wrote some of my thoughts about my initial experiences in conducting field research. Passenger boats in island communities in the Philippines come up against threats of tempests, volatile weather, and unforeseen accidents. Without fear, I fashioned this academic adventurism[1] with my summer look, complete with Columbia blue ball cap, sports wristwatch, and waterproof knapsack. This passenger boat ferries the local community from the island to the city and back. I wore a T-shirt that identified my academic affiliation. For many of the passengers, this university did not exist until my presence had showcased it. The text on my T-shirt appeared impressive but I suppose it could also have been threatening for the passengers. I had one week to spend on the island to meet the *tambalan* (traditional healer/shaman) and to "test the waters" if the village that I was about to visit was the "right" site for my dissertation project. For someone who was born and raised in the Philippines, I was confident that doing a field research outside Manila would be a manageable process for me. But I was wrong. This was my first trip to the island where I aimed to conduct my field research, and I wanted to find out if there were any ritualists who would be willing to collaborate with me for my doctoral dissertation's applied theatre performance. I envisioned how their rituals of healing could be part of the aesthetics of the performance that I would be creating. Behind me was a miscellany of products to be sold on our island destination. From time to time, I would cover my nose to avoid inhaling the powdery lime dust floating out from the sacks of cement that enveloped the boat. My academic and artistic adventurism, characterized by an affinity towards the exotic objectification of the *tambalan* and his magical practices, was a misaligned orientation that misunderstood the *tambalan* as a "subject" that could be examined. How does one become critically aware of the potential exploitation of people, their lives, and their stories in conducting practice-based research? This question is important to me as I attempt to theorize the ambivalences that an applied theatre researcher experiences in field research. While I am turning to narrative inquiry as a strategic gesture towards critical positionality to answer this question, it will also guide me in shaping this essay that sketches the limits of my own experience in cross-cultural engagement with (the stories) of the *tambalan* and in unpacking a postcolonial reading of this experience. This essay will also examine *Abat*, which is the Waray[2] concept of affective relationality.

A (Mis)encounter and the Affective Processes of *Abat*

This chapter is a narrative inquiry of my (mis)encounter with the *tambalan* of Samar Province and the ethical procedures I had to consider during my field research. I argue that this (mis)encounter in cross-cultural communication fosters self-reflexivity informed by the Waray concept of affect, *Abat*. For my Waray collaborator, Mrs. Erlinda Abuyen, *Abat* is an affective self-referentiality (Abuyen 2018). In the early phase of my research, I was interested in examining the rituals of the shamans in Samar Province that could be used as a topic for my doctoral touring performance as a way to bring about greater awareness of Indigenous knowledge on environmental stewardship by these local healers. Through self-reflexivity that stemmed from my own (mis) encounter, I learned that my tendencies to theorize and examine these ritual performances exposed my underlying colonial interests. What uncovered this coloniality was a kind of an affective subjectivity inherent in the logic of *Abat* that results in the processes of self-interrogation and self-knowing. The introspective dialogue I was having during the time that I was talking with the *tambalan* was a (mis)encounter of my own benign colonial tendencies. To create a clear understanding of the word "(mis)encounter," I provide below a three-pronged definition of the term supported by a graph and two tables that describe the event that was happening during my encounter with the *tambalan* and my thoughts that illustrate this (mis)encounter. (Mis)encounter is:

1. a temporal interrogation of an encounter with the possible collaborator that manifests various feelings like awkwardness, apprehensions, and anxiety;
2. it is a process of self-dialoguing (of the researcher) within a cross-cultural conversation in settings with implicit asymmetry powers;
3. and an approach of inquiry that engages the sense of "outsiderness" where interpersonal and social relationality may occur.

And from these tensions of self-dialoguing and the sense of "outsiderness" comes the construction of an ethical obligation in relationship-building with the community members. I contend that this is a significant juncture of self-reflexivity, auto-critique, and auto-ethnography[3] (Docot 2018: 6). The unidentified sensation in this encounter brings about a self-referential acknowledgment of the politics of locatedness and privileges. By incorporating a phenomenological reading of *Abat* within cross-cultural communication, I aim to foreground ethical and decolonizing applied theatre research through self-reflexivity buttressed by the concepts of (mis)encounter and *Abat* as ethical processes of decolonizing research. I think of *Abat* as an affective process of sensing people's emotions. Through the process of *Abat*, one perceives certain emotions that arise from different situations and circumstances. The confluences of the non-verbal and verbal significations foster a subjective experience. I wish to argue that *Abat* is a consequence of an affective self-reflexivity—within oneself and between entities—that can inform the ethical obligation of a decolonizing approach in applied theatre research.

Figure 2 An "S" graph illustrating the affective process of self-reflexivity that involves *Abat*. The ecliptic representation of self-reflexivity renders the process of intrapersonal dynamics that combines personal subjectivity and Waray's local concept of affective social and relationality experience.

The subliminal logic of *Abat* within the experience of (mis) encounter results in an introspection that can provide more meaningful interpersonal and social relational interactions in an applied theatre research site. To support this argument, this essay will narrate my internal negotiations. I have scaffolded the conversations I had with the *tambalan* in two tables to demonstrate the "affective discomfort" (Gallagher, Rodricks, and Jacobson 2018: 319) that I experienced. What are the ethics of the *dayo* (outsider) who navigates the pathways of inquiry in communities considered precarious? And in answering this question, I bring the affective processes of *Abat* into the discussion of ethical research in our field by:

1. foregrounding my auto-ethnographic encounters with the local *tambalan* that juxtapose critical reflections with the sociohistorical disaster in Samar Province;

2. excavating the subtextual or internal negotiations through Linda
   Finlay's (2002) "meta-reflexive voice" (209) and Peter E. Jones's
   (2009) "inner forms of language" (167) in synchronicity with
   spoken lines that occurred within interpersonal communication;
   and

3. lastly, to conclude with *Kapwa*, a Filipino relational concept
   of social interaction that intersects with the underpinning
   epistemology of *Abat* towards an ethical practice of conducting
   applied theatre research with the goal of co-community-based
   theatre performances with community members.

In this essay, Kenneth J. Gergen and Mary M. Gergen's (2018: 273)
evocative ethnography affords me a rendering of my personal narrative
to underscore the ethics of cross-cultural encounter via *Abat*. You will
read the story of the *tambalan* from my point of view, which can, I hope
"offer the reader a complex and multihued adventure in understanding"
(276). To further clarify the intrapersonal (mis)encounter that I wish
to illustrate here, I provide an inner dialogue that delineates the inner
processes that transpire between the *tambalan* and me. This apertural
exposure of the interiority of these (mis)encounters presents itself as a
narrative inquiry of my personal stories of encountering the *tambalan*
in one of the island communities in Samar Province. I have included
two tables that present my *Abat* self-dialogues to render the nuanced
counterpoints of discourse from what is uttered and imparted both
implicitly and explicitly. Again, I approach this by referencing Linda
Finlay's (2002) "meta-reflexive voice" (209). I am borrowing her concept
of self-reflexivity to show clues of my "intersubjective reflection" (215)
coinciding with the interpersonal mis(encounter) between me and
the *tambalan*. My "meta-reflexive voice" is presented in the two tables
inserted in this essay. The texts in these tables were taken from the
memories of my cross-cultural encounters with the *tambalan*. These
lines present my ethical negotiations and criticality that underpin
my *Abat*. They are presented parallel to each other like musical
fugues, allowing an unfolding of a counternarrative discourse and

interrogation of a potential ethical obligation in the field site. In these tables, the first column comprises lines spoken by the *tambalan* and the community members, while the second column contains my own thoughts. They are rendered in the form of dramatic texts as a way to scaffold the concurrent realities that occur in converging temporalities within cross-cultural (mis)encounters. I hope I can also identify the inner *Abat* of the *tambalan*. But there are sites of unknowability that are difficult to decode, since I can only operate from the limits of my own experience.

Meeting the *Tambalan* in Western Samar

My collaborator[4] and I entered an old shack made of bamboo with a galvanized iron roof. This was the house of the oldest *tambalan*[5] in one of the furthermost island villages in Western Samar. I visited this island on the last day of February 2018 on the recommendation of a theatre colleague. She suggested that I consider this island as my field site. We arrived late in the afternoon and waited for the following day to meet with the *tambalan*. I was accompanied by my artist-collaborator and two schoolteachers whom we had met on the *banka* (passenger boat) and a *kagawad* (village councilor) of the *barangay* (village). Before going to the house of the *tambalan*, we had to inform the *barangay* captain of our presence and eventually seek his permission to conduct research in the area. We took the *habal-habal* (motorbike taxi) going to the village where the *tambalan* lived.

When we entered his house, we found ourselves in a small room with a picture of a young man hanging on the bamboo wall his house. For many years his house had become the center of *hilot* (traditional massage) and other traditional healing practices. No one knew his actual age, but the timbre of his voice and weather-beaten face made me suspect that he was around 70 years of age. He could not speak Tagalog. Both the *kagawad* and the schoolteachers agreed to serve as our interpreters. I noticed that this kindness towards a visitor was customary, to the point

Table 1 Borrowing Finlay's meta-reflexive voice, I created this table to present the inner processes of my *Abat*. While the conventional dialogues in a dramatic text are written one after another, in this chapter, the parenthetical lines that describe the response of the *tambalan* are positioned parallel to each other. The right column/row is my own *Abat*. The table presents the characters (the *tambalan* and me), the (mis)encounter that transpired between me and the *tambalan* that resulted in my intra-communicational processing. These tables show the *tambalan* who encounters me and me who (mis)encounters my inner emotionality.

His encounter to me	My (mis)encounter to myself	My *Abat*
Tambalan: (Explains the challenges of being a *tambalan*.)	Me to myself: *Baka sya na yung pwede kong pag-aralan. Parang pwede itong site kasi may kahirapan ang buhay. Pero gusto kaya nya na ma-interview? Papaano ko ipapaliwanag ang aking dissertation sa kanya. Papaano ko kaya siya matutulungan napaka-hirap ng buhay ng tambalan ng ito.* (Maybe he's the right person to study. This seems like the right site; there is poverty here. But does the *tambalan* want to be interviewed? How will I explain to him my dissertation? Maybe he cannot understand it.)	Excitement to uncertainty

that the community members would drop their work to accommodate the requests of their guests. I asked the *tambalan* if I could possibly conduct research on his ritual. He is known to have a special healing procedure for his clients, who mostly come from his village. During our conversation, I tried to concentrate on what the *tambalan* was saying. But I noticed that while I was listening to him, I was also having an internal dialogue.

My translator explained to him that I was not intending to be a *tambalan* and that I would only document his practice for the purposes of my doctoral research. His long silences turned into deafening ones that bespoke of the problem and complexity of subject–object expectation.

Table 2 In this table, my *Abat* that formed into an emotion of confusion would later develop into fear and anxiety when he narrated to us the process of acquiring his herbal medicines.

His encounter to me	My (mis)encounter to myself	My *Abat*
Tambalan: (Continues to explain the challenges that a *tambalan* experiences before the ritual healing is performed.)	Me to myself: *Ayaw bang mag pa-interview ng tambalan? Saan ako hahanap ng iba pang pag-aaralan?* (Doesn't he want to be interviewed? Where will I look for another one that I can study?)	Confusion Anxiety

While I was at the field site, I found that one must learn how to navigate nuanced conversations that appear benign and indirect. The silences were punctuated with utterances of short lines of precautions.

The *tambalans* in the Philippines are known to obtain their medicinal herbs in the cemetery or caves, and spirit possessions may occur if they are not spiritually ready.[6] My relatives in Balangkayan, Eastern Samar, have shared with me the stories of my great-great-grandfather, Cesnero Contado, about how he wanted to transfer his shamanistic skills to his daughter. But the daughter was scared to engage in such practice due to the unknown spiritual realms she may enter. Prayers and rituals for the *bisa* (potency) of medicinal herbs are performed for unseen beings like the *digkosanon*[7] who inhabit the cemeteries and caves and may stop the *tambalan* from getting their herbal medicines.[8] It is a test of courage and challenge—this spiritual determination of the *tambalan* and his/her protégé or assistant. The *tambalan* shared with us his stories about the confrontation he experienced with the *digkosanon* on his way to the cemetery. As I listened to him, he would repeat these experiences, and I relive, here, the uncanny, strange, and alienating feeling that caused me discomfort at the time. Then, I began to sense fear from the stories of the invisible beings and the adversarial events that a *tambalan* goes through. The eeriness of the moment was punctuated with his resolute words that being a *tambalan* is a calling. He told us that it is hard to be a *tambalan*, a line that kept on ringing in my head as we returned home. I found myself leaving with an unpleasant sensation that came from my solar plexus and intoxicated me with unwelcome thoughts of fear. Teresa Brennan (2004) defines affect as "physiological shift accompanying a judgement" (5). She continues, "What does need to be borne in mind is that all affects, including even 'flat affects,' are material and physiological things" (6). Her words give meaning to that inexplicable vibrational sensation inside my body—an affective subjectivity that I mentioned above. The fear I felt was also telling of my sudden reluctance towards studying his practice. The precautionary words—that it was hard to undertake the task of a *tambalan*—forced me to reflect on how my research commits me to ethical procedures and obligations.

By the time we finished the conversation, his family members had congregated outside the house with several very young kids observing me, the *dayo*. The Theravada Buddhist monk Ajahn Munindo (2018) mentions "a feeling investigation" (81) that develops from contemplative practice. He affirms that "we are able to pay attention in a more feeling way—a feeling investigation … When we develop the ability to investigate without the persistent interruption of mental verbiage, we will have access to a different quality of discernment, where discriminative intelligence and intuition can work creatively together as partners, untangling our confusion" (81). I suture this "feeling investigation" in my elucidation of *Abat* as a process of intuitional judgments that can be relevant in the interpersonal communications within the researcher's field site.

The unexpected and emergent moments of (mis)encounters can induce feelings of ambiguity because the original plans and schedules are not working.[9] But these moments can also be a significant time of self-reflexivity. My encounter with the *tambalan* is a (mis)encounter that exposed my colonial adventurism and tendency for exoticization. These experiential (mis)encounters with the *tambalan* expose the implicit colonial interests that stem from self-reflexivity. Here, I use *Abat* as affective discourse as an ethics of inquiry to decolonize my practice of applied theatre. Dorinne K. Kondo (1990) asserts that embodied experiences cannot be delineated from theory:

> Consequently, experience, and the *specificity* of my experience—a particular human being who encounters particular others at a particular historical moment and has particular stakes in that interaction—is not opposed to theory; it *enacts* and *embodies* theory. That is to say, the so-called personal details of the encounters, and of the concrete processes through which research problems emerged, are constitutive of theory; one cannot be separated from the other. (24, emphasis in original)

Kondo asserts that these private and personal experiences are inherently theoretical. This contention is an invigorative argument that puts forward affective experiences as sources of critical subjectivities. From this assertion, I foreground the Waray's *Abat* as an embodied knowing from affective process that can lead to respect and a better estimation of people's subjectivity. Ultimately, when shared between entities, *Abat* as an interpersonal negotiation becomes an intersubjective ethic of relationality towards the pursuit of artistic co-creation and knowledge production.

Conclusion

Field research is an interplay of encounters with people, their natural environment, and (mis)encounters with affective subjectivities within oneself. My affective (mis)encounters resulted in my internal examination of my colonial tendencies as a *dayo*[10] or outsider intent on examining the culture and people within that culture for my own academic and artistic interests. At the beginning of my field research, I was excited to look for a collaborator in precarious communities perceived to be a good subject of inquiry for my project. But through the process of cross-cultural encounters, I faced implicit resistance which engendered apprehensions and other affects. My "self-conscious introspection" (Anderson 2006: 383), which I have presented here in the form of meta-narrative conversations, exposed my colonial tendencies manifested in the desire for discovery and adventurism. This "self-conscious introspection" (383) is antithetical to colonial gazing and exotification. Leon Anderson's "analytic ethnographic paradigm" (374) is a worthwhile idea to quote here as a guide in examining one's actions and perceptions in reference to and in dialogue with those of others (383). He deploys ethnography not just as a method of inquiry but also as a process of self-reflexivity and critical introspection. From Anderson, I pivot to Virgilio Enriquez's (1977) *Pakikipagkapwa*, a relational concept of interrelationality in research. The father of Filipino social psychology, Enriquez explains *Pakikipagkapwa* as a "human concern and inter-action as one with others" (4). It is from this ethic that I aimed to re-root my practice of inquiry as an antidote to potential acts of extractive research. And through our *Pakikipagkapwa*, we take the pathways of knowledge production and sharing towards the transformation of our blinkered dispositions and narrowed ideas of the world for our own enlightened becoming.

Notes

1   I use the term "adventurism" in this essay to characterize the thematics of taking risks in an unknown place and the acts of improvising from the encounters with conditions or circumstances that arise from these adventurous acts of unknowability, curiosity, and wonderment. I bring this into the discussion of colonialism, in which I rely on the work of David Narrett's *Adventurism and Empire: The Struggle for Mastery in the Louisiana-Florida Borderlands, 1762–1980* (2018).

2   The people who are originally from Samar Province and speak the Waray-Waray language.

3   The concepts of "auto-critique" and "self-reflexivity" in this essay is drawn from the dissertation of the Filipina anthropologist Dada Docot on *Anthropology of the Hometown: The Workings of Migration and Intimacy in the Town of Dollars, Philippines.*

4   Francis Mateau, my artistic collaborator, joined me in this initial field trip.

5   I will keep the name of this *tambalan* anonymous, since I did opt not to engage him as my collaborator. This is to protect his identity.

6   See the work of Richard Arens, *Folk Practices and Beliefs of Leyte and Samar* (1978).

7   Tacloban-based writer and University of the Philippines Professor Emeritus Merlie Alunan says that *Digkosanon* is a contraction of the Waray words "Diri sugad ha aton" (Those beings that are not the same as us) (Alunan 2019). In preparation for the medicinal plants that will be used for healing procedures, the *tambalan* goes to the cave or cemetery during the Holy Week or *Semana Santa*, which is a week-long commemoration of the death and resurrection of Christ. It is celebrated with various rituals during summer. For the *tambalans*, this particular period of the year is a sacred time to reinvigorate their healing powers.

8   I first heard about this spiritual initiation from my father, who told me the story of his grandmother Isabel Baris, who was chosen by Cesnero Contado to continue his divinatory practice of healing. I later learned that my great-great-grandfather felt that Isabel, of all his children, was the one most capable of protecting the island of Minasangay in Balangkayan, Eastern Samar, that Contado is believed to have inherited from the spiritual world. Baris, according to my father and confirmed by my relatives, possessed an intelligence and managerial skills admired by many. And most importantly, she was intuitive, a character fit to handle the function as a community healer. My father told me that on his deathbed, Contado instructed Baris to go to the cemetery at midnight after his body was buried. In his instruction, Contado revealed to Baris that an amulet must be recovered from the area of his tomb, and that only she knew about this. Fear began to creep in to my great-grandmother, and she could not follow his instructions. Thus, the healing tradition in our family stopped.

9   An important work to refer to in this context is Dada Docot's (2017) "Negative productions during fieldwork in the hometown," along with Chaya Ocampo Go's (2017), "I go home to do the work: a Filipina's practice of activist scholarship in the wake of super typhoon Yolanda."

10 Nick Deocampo (2018) translates the word *dayo* as "foreigner" in his article "New perspectives: Philippine cinema at the crossroads."

References

Abuyen, E. (2018), Interview with the author, April 1.

"Adventurism." (2020), Merriam-Webster.com. https://www.merriam-webster. com (accessed June 13, 2020).

Alunan, M. (2019), Interview with the author, June 22.

Anderson, L. (2006), "Analytic autoethnography," *Journal of Contemporary Ethnography*, 35 (4), 373–95. doi:10.1177/0891241605280449

Arens, R. (1978), *Folk Practices and Beliefs of Leyte and Samar*. Edited by G. C. Luangco. Tacloban City, Philippines: Divine Word University Publications.

Brennan, T. (2004), *The Transmission of Affect*. Ithaca, NY: Cornell University Press.

Deocampo, N. (2019), "New perspectives: Philippine cinema at the crossroads," in *Art Archive 02: A Collection of Essays on Philippine Contemporary Literature & Film*. Manila: Japan Foundation. Available online: https://jfmo.org.ph/wp-content/uploads/2019/10/Art-Archive-2_ Original-Size-LowRes.pdf (accessed April 29, 2021).

Docot, D. (2017), "Negative productions during fieldwork in the hometown," *GeoHumanities*, 3 (2), 307–27. doi:10.1080/2373566x.2017.1370385

Docot, D. (2018), *Anthropology of the Hometown: The Workings of Migration and Intimacy in the Town of Dollars, Philippines*, PhD dissertation, University of British Columbia, Vancouver. Available online: https:// open.library.ubc.ca/soa/cIRcle/collections/ubctheses/24/items/1.0371908 (accessed August 30, 2021).

Enriquez, V. G. (1977), "Filipino psychology in the Third World," *Philippine Journal of Psychology*, 10 (1), 3–18.

Finlay, L. (2002), "Negotiating the swamp: the opportunity and challenge of reflexivity in research practice," *Qualitative Research*, 2 (2), 209–30. doi:10.1177/146879410200200205

Gallagher, K., Rodricks, D. J., and K. Jacobson (2018), "Introduction: A situated, ethical, imaginative doing and being in the encounter of research," in K. Gallagher, D. J. Rodricks, and K. Jacobson (eds), *Global Youth Citizenry and Radical Hope: Perspectives on Children and Young People*. New York: Springer, pp. 1–20. doi:10.1007/978-981-15-1282-7_1

Gergen, K. J. and Gergen, M. M. (2018), "Doing things with words: toward evocative ethnography," *Qualitative Research in Psychology*, 15 (2/3), 272–86. doi:10.1080/14780887.2018.1430004

Go, C. O. (2017), "I go home to do the work: a Filipina's practice of activist scholarship in the wake of super typhoon Yolanda," *Critical Asian Studies*, 49 (3), 448–50. doi:10.1080/14672715.2017.1339453

Jones, P. E. (2009), "From 'external speech' to 'inner speech' in Vygotsky: a critical appraisal and fresh perspectives," *Language and Communication*, 29 (2), 166–81. doi:10.1016/j.langcom.2008.12.003

Kondo, D. K. (1990), *Crafting Selves: Power, Gender, and Discourses of Identity in a Japanese Workplace*. Chicago: University of Chicago Press.

Munindo, A. (2018), *Servant of Reality*. Chennai: Aruno Publications.

Narrett, D. (2017), *Adventurism and Empire: The Struggle for Mastery in the Louisiana-Florida Borderlands, 1762–1980* (The David J. Weber Series in the New Borderlands History). Chapel Hill: University of North Carolina Press.

14

Locked down with *Ikigai*: Initial Thoughts on the Essential Void

Ruwanthie de Chickera

Ten months into lockdown[1] *I sit, folded small, facing my well-known, much-loved, doctor. I take up as little space as possible. Do not touch any surfaces. The tightness in my body reflects the emptiness I feel within. My world has both shrunk to the walls of my small flat and exploded into unending "screen time" clashes with my two teenage daughters.*

I am spent.

My doctor tells me about Ikigai—*the Japanese philosophy of the space that draws one forward; the vacuum you are compelled to fill, also called the "essential void." Apparently, once the shape of that void is clear, stepping into it is a blissful act of coming into one's own.*

I cycle home slowly. Lockdown has gifted Colombo city[2] *with breathing space. Instead of lines of stagnant vehicles and exhaust fumes, one encounters new skies and ancient trees.*

But I struggle on my bike. It's old and the roads have long been broken by the pound of relentless traffic. I push on stoically.

I contemplate Ikigai—*that "essential void" which is supposed to pull one forward. Instinctively I focus my gaze two meters ahead of my moving bike, willing into existence a vacuum, a void. Imperceptibly a shift occurs and I find that I am no longer pushing myself forward, instead, I am being pulled. Is this possible? I wobble as I lose confidence and concentration. Immediately the energy in my body falls behind me. Once again I am pushing on, straining.*

I gather my focus and visualize the void again. I concentrate my breath and gaze on that point just two meters ahead—and again, the bike is drawn forward into the moving vacuum, the essential void. This time I manage to keep my focus steady and the ride from this point on is almost effortless.

Later that night I reflect on Ikigai in relation to my own theatre practice.[3] Can Ikigai be useful in identifying and understanding some of the challenges of applied theatre? Could it, perhaps, provide us with a moral compass? How does a group of people, searching for an emerging play, collectively identify an essential void? Is there any way I could consistently recreate that dynamic I felt on the bike—of being drawn forward effortlessly into the inevitable—in a rehearsal room? And what would alter in my practice if I insisted on maintaining a commitment to Ikigai?

Ikigai, oneself and the artwork

The next morning, I am slightly more enthusiastic to pick up my flagging yoga practice. I now have a technique I want to test.

I sit for a minute and visualize the pose I am about to make with my body. I wait till I see the shape clearly before me; till I feel its pull. Then, I stand up and step into the shape.

The difference? Again, imperceptible and unforgettable at the same time.

Instead of straining from inside to achieve the pose, the space, the essential shape of what I am meant to be, holds me together, binds me tight. I feel collected and but a small, definite part of something much bigger.

What would change
if we submit to the principles of the essential void
when determining the shape of new work
and the shape of ourselves
within that work?

It seems that
the better and busier we get at our game,
the more confidence we gain in our approach,
the less diligently we search
for those unique and essential shapes
that we know
can emerge
only once.

I have made the mistake of being too lazy,
too rushed;
of transplanting familiar formulas, roles,
working methods
unthinkingly into new situations;
juggling vague and shifting silhouettes
of myself and the artwork.

And I have had to then push through,
gritted teeth,
propelled by determination, ego, discipline, and
perhaps a memory of something that worked before;
rather than being pulled forward
into that inevitable and distinct shape
that binds the work together
and holds me within it.

Ikigai and others

Lockdown drained my words of their weight. My daughters no longer hear what I say. I have used my words in all the combinations I can think of, to tell them the same few things over and over again.

Depleted (and a little injured), I decide, instead, to spend a day in complete silence. The girls were intrigued and excited. Is it possible that I would actually say nothing to them? No matter what?

I retreat wordlessly from the battlefield.

In the space that opens up, one child uses the time to play the piano, paint, read and write. At the end of the day we have a lot to talk about. My other daughter spends the entire day in front of a screen. At the end of the day she is exhausted, fraught, and can't string a sentence together.

I keep my promise and say nothing, but my mind is spinning.

I realize that though I see my daughter's potential and keep pushing her to fill that shape in life, until she sees that shape herself, it will not be an essential void and she would not be able to fill it in any enduring manner.

My job, then, is not to force her to fill this shape, but help her see it.

A central task in leading a group in a journey of applied theatre
is creating those dynamic spaces
that draw people in
and fill them with the need to express themselves.

In the collective creative journey,
these spaces link together to create the shape of the artwork.

Submitting to the principle of the essential void,
one has to be careful that the vision of these shapes is,
indeed,
a shared essential one.

I now see that however convinced one could be of the validity of a space,
unless others recognize it as essential for themselves,
it runs the risk of not being lastingly dynamic.

The challenge, then,
is to keep honing these spaces,
turning them from appealing, interesting, challenging,
to essential.
Spaces that pull others in, inevitably, effortlessly.

Of course, having the restraint and humility to not rush forward and
fill the spaces
that others leave empty ...

Well, that's another challenge ...

Ikigai in absence

There was little our theatre group could do in 2020. So we decided to write critical reflections on seventeen plays we had devised over the past decade.

I was in charge of steering the artists in their writing. I was looking forward to reading their reflections on the beloved plays we had devised together. I knew the artists had an intricate knowledge of the creative journey.

However, I found myself initially surprised and then shocked at the reflections that came in. Much of what was said I found quite lacking in understanding. Not immediately picking up on the lesson, I asked for rewrites and engaged them in long conversations on the plays. But subsequent drafts returned much the same.

I was struggling. How could these artists who I worked so closely with, who had created so much of this content themselves, not really understand what we had portrayed? Hadn't they been *listening* in rehearsals? Weren't they right by my side through it all? How was it possible that a shared journey was not a shared perspective?

I remember my father's advice to me,
grounded in his own experience of leadership and community service ...
"Show the way and then get out of the way."

In the world of applied theatre
I imagine this means,
once we lead a group in creating something collective,
we need to remove ourselves from it.

Now this is difficult, because we love and believe in the work,
and sometimes we love and believe in the potential of the work more.

And so we carry it to audiences,
to the world,
rushing to interpret, write reports, give talks,
compensating reality with the strength of our dreams,
filling empty spaces with the fierceness of our convictions.

If we, instead,
had the strength
to remove ourselves
from what we created,
we would allow it to assume
its essential shape in the world.

Emptiness is not *Ikigai*

I talk on the phone with a close friend from Europe. She is upset she can't travel to continue her work in theatre. She has worked for years in the Global South on conflict issues. She is a sensitive and clever artist. I choose my words carefully. "Why don't you start working over there? There are many real problems there; and they affect us all."

"Its cold here. It's not that interesting here. I miss travelling. The grant has to be spent in the Global South."

All of us have improvised creative spaces outside
in order to fill emptiness within.

This kind of space is not an essential space.

Because the need for it is not located within the work itself.
It is born elsewhere,
within a career of an individual artist,
within the mandates of funding bodies.

If we are not very careful of this pitfall,
we begin to clutter our artworks and our practice,
our vocabulary and imaginations
with noisy spaces
that are only
empty
in their generic loudness.

However, there is no space in our conversation for me to say this to my friend.

So I don't.

Ikigai within *Ikigai*

As practitioners of applied theatre,
called upon to lead different groups in collective creative journeys,
we often play the role of sole rulers of tiny isolated kingdoms.

We draw out boundaries, we guide our subjects, we defend our worlds,
but, how much do we really know of what is happening
in other little kingdoms just like ours?

In this semi-formal arena we belong to,
where people first gather,
and then plays emerge,
where a script might not exist,
a process may not be recorded,
it is difficult to be aware of
and, maybe, convenient to be ignorant of
what else is and has been created
by other practitioners,
just like us.

Lockdown had some benefits.

For me, a clear one was the reconnection with my childhood habit of avid reading. Being once again in communion with the vital energy of the thoughts and words of brilliant thinkers opened up paths ahead of me.

Within the precepts of *Ikigai*, these paths gained a defined place within the overall arrangement of my life. At a time of extended isolation and increasing disconnect from community, I understood that momentum to move forward can be absorbed from the courage of women and men who have taken us on a journey of truth and discovery, only to leave us on the threshold of astounding, unarticulated possibilities.

These vacuums—the unfinished stories, the unanswered questions—are the essential voids that exist on a macro scale. This is the common canon we inherit, the community we can claim beyond the idiosyncrasies of our lived, limited experiences. This, then, is how we connect to that ultimate path. We follow the footsteps of those who traveled before us, we understand the true shape of what has been left unsaid, and we then move in to fill these dynamic vacuums. In this manner, we, who are separated by time, death, geography, language, can move forward through the essential voids linking our collective human journey.

This little essay marks the beginning of a search for a shift in my practice—which has always been one of opening up creative spaces.

Whereas, by and large, I have been driven, inspired and reasonably satisfied with the work I have produced as a theatre practitioner, my exploration now is to understand if there would be a change in one's outlook and practice if one were to consistently apply the principles of Ikigai *to one's work and life.*

I stumbled upon Ikigai—*this new understanding of creative space and momentum—within the confines of lockdown and I chose to first reflect upon it in this brief 2000-word chapter. The limits of space and word count appear integral to this exploration, as the shift I am exploring hinges on nuances of shape and form.*

In my experience riding my bicycle, all that changed was that instead of me pushing myself forward, I found myself being pulled into being. However, with that shift, I found myself gliding into an effortless and integrated experience, where it was no longer me versus the bike, road, and wind, but me, the bike, road and energy around me working together as a complete unit. And within this unit, I was transported.

This experience of being carried forward, secured within a larger vital wholeness, a feeling that essential precision can be secured for each creative decision, could be a source of strength within the challenging and often lonely arena of applied theatre, where one frequently finds oneself in an unmarked playing field full of undefined spaces.

For now, within this word limit, this is all I can contemplate. But it has created, beyond, an essential void that I feel I have little choice but to explore.

And I will. When the time is right.

Notes

1   The year 2020, when the world came to a standstill on account of the Covid-19 pandemic.
2   Commercial capital of Sri Lanka.
3   By this time, I had about twenty years of experience working on devising plays with actors and non-actors.

Index

Printed in Great Britain
by Amazon

35865843R00165